THE PROFIT MOTIVE

What responsibility, if any, does a corporation have to society? How should corporations balance environmental, social, and governance factors? *The Profit Motive* addresses these questions of corporate purpose using historical, legal, and economic perspectives. Stephen M. Bainbridge enters the debate around corporate social responsibility to mount an unabashed defense of shareholder capitalism and maximizing shareholder value. The book offers context for the current questions about corporate purpose, and provides a reference going forward. Direct and corrective, *The Profit Motive* argues that shareholder value maximization is not only required by law, but what the law ought to require.

Stephen M. Bainbridge is the William D. Warren Distinguished Professor of Law at UCLA School of Law.

T0371086

The Profit Motive

DEFENDING SHAREHOLDER VALUE MAXIMIZATION

STEPHEN M. BAINBRIDGE
University of California, Los Angeles

CAMBRIDGE
UNIVERSITY PRESS

Shaftesbury Road, Cambridge CB2 8EA, United Kingdom

One Liberty Plaza, 20th Floor, New York, NY 10006, USA

477 Williamstown Road, Port Melbourne, VIC 3207, Australia

314–321, 3rd Floor, Plot 3, Splendor Forum, Jasola District Centre, New Delhi – 110025, India

103 Penang Road, #05–06/07, Visioncrest Commercial, Singapore 238467

Cambridge University Press is part of Cambridge University Press & Assessment, a department of the University of Cambridge.

We share the University's mission to contribute to society through the pursuit of education, learning and research at the highest international levels of excellence.

www.cambridge.org
Information on this title: www.cambridge.org/9781316515471

DOI: 10.1017/9781009025799

© Stephen M. Bainbridge 2023

This publication is in copyright. Subject to statutory exception and to the provisions of relevant collective licensing agreements, no reproduction of any part may take place without the written permission of Cambridge University Press & Assessment.

First published 2023

A catalogue record for this publication is available from the British Library.

Library of Congress Cataloging-in-Publication Data
NAMES: Bainbridge, Stephen M., author.
TITLE: The profit motive : defending shareholder value maximization /
Stephen M. Bainbridge, University of California, Los Angeles.
DESCRIPTION: Cambridge, United Kingdom ; New York, NY : Cambridge
University Press, 2023. | Includes bibliographical references and index.
IDENTIFIERS: LCCN 2022029374 | ISBN 9781316515471 (hardback) |
ISBN 9781009025799 (ebook)
SUBJECTS: LCSH: Corporation law – United States – Philosophy. | Stockholder
wealth – United States – Philosophy.
CLASSIFICATION: LCC KF1414 .B349 2023 | DDC 346.73/066–dc23/eng/20221201
LC record available at https://lccn.loc.gov/2022029374

ISBN 978-1-316-51547-1 Hardback
ISBN 978-1-009-01215-7 Paperback

Cambridge University Press & Assessment has no responsibility for the persistence or accuracy of URLs for external or third-party internet websites referred to in this publication and does not guarantee that any content on such websites is, or will remain, accurate or appropriate.

In memory of my friend and mentor Henry Manne.

Contents

Acknowledgments

My research assistants Brandon Zelner (UCLA Law Class of 2023), Connor Jordan (UCLA Law Class of 2021), and Ethan Salant (UCLA Law Class of 2021) are three of the finest young lawyers it has ever been my privilege to work with. Their contributions to this work were exemplary, reflecting their considerable research and drafting skills.

The UCLA School of Law Library reference librarians are one of the institution's crown jewels. I owe particular thanks to Library Director Kevin Gerson, Director of Reference & Research Services Jodi Kruger, and Head of Collection Development Jenny Lentz, all of whom went above and beyond the call of duty in rapidly tracking down obscure references.

Technology wizard Tal Greitzer (UCLA Law) rescued the document when the file corrupted, for which I am deeply grateful.

Finally, I thank Charles Elson and Marc Hodak for their very helpful comments on a draft and Helen Bainbridge for her outstanding edit.

Editorial Note

In citing references, I have followed the leading American system of legal citations, which is *The Bluebook: A Uniform System of Citation* (21st edition 2020). To avoid cluttering the page, citations appear in the endnotes at the back of the book, as does some minor explanatory text. In a few cases, I have used textual footnotes to convey what I regard as intermediately important information – that is, information too important to be relegated to an endnote that is unlikely to be read, but not important enough to justify inclusion in the main text. For the most part, these footnotes consist of sidenotes or explanations of technical aspects of the discussion that may be of interest to the reader although not so much as to justify interrupting the flow of the text. Recognizing that textual footnotes can be annoying and distracting, I have tried to keep them to the bare minimum.

Introduction

There are a lot of books on the market praising stakeholder capitalism. They proclaim a new age in which big corporations should embrace – and, in fact, are embracing – environmental, social, and governance (ESG) goals. Whether putatively objective academic tomes filled with statistics or mass market books filled with bullet points, the bottom line is the same; namely, that stakeholder capitalism is the right thing to do both morally and financially.

This is not one of those books.

I.1 DOES THE WORLD NEED ANOTHER BOOK ON STAKEHOLDER CAPITALISM?

We are concerned with the foundational question of corporate governance: What is the purpose of a corporation? Is it, as Nobel Economics laureate Milton Friedman famously claimed, "to increase its profits"?[1] Or is it, as the Business Roundtable recently claimed, "generating good jobs, a strong and sustainable economy, innovation, a healthy environment and economic opportunity for all."[2]

Although I try to be fair to competing perspectives, my goal is to put forward an unabashed defense of the proposition that the purpose of the corporation is to sustainably maximize shareholder value over the long term. The book defends that proposition as both descriptively accurate and normatively appealing, arguing that shareholder value maximization is both what the law requires and what the law ought to require. Admittedly, as we go along, we will need to introduce some nuances here and there but that basic claim makes an excellent starting point.

At the outset, it is appropriate to acknowledge that that claim has a long and controverted past. There is a very considerable body of scholarship on the corporate purpose and a corporation's social responsibility.[3] Academics in multiple disciplines beyond just law and business, not to mention corporate leaders, prominent lawyers, and politicians, spent much of the twentieth century arguing about the respective merits of profit maximization and social responsibility. In places, we thus will be traveling down a well-trodden path. So why go down that path yet again? Because things have changed or, at least, conventional wisdom so claims.

In the 1980s, it seemed like the debate had finally been settled in favor of what is variously known as shareholder value maximization or shareholder wealth maximization:

> [Economists] William Meckling and Michael Jensen ... argued that shareholder value maximization should be the primary metric for assessing the performance of a business. In 1990, Jensen co-authored another influential article in Harvard Business Review alongside Kevin Murphy which suggested CEOs were being paid like bureaucrats and therefore acting like bureaucrats rather than value-maximizing entrepreneurs. They recommended providing stronger incentives for CEOs to maximize the value of their companies, such as having CEOs become substantial owners of company stock and providing big financial rewards for superior performance. The following decades generated greater acceptance of these theories, and they had a profound impact on how businesses ran and operated, particularly in the United States.[4]

These and other similar developments led prominent corporate law professors Reinier Kraakman and Henry Hansmann to claim that we had reached, as the title of their 2001 article put it, *The End of History for Corporate Law*.[5] Their article's title was a play on the title of Francis Fukuyama's 1992 book, *The End of History and the Last Man*, which claimed that liberal democracy and democratic capitalism had triumphed over socialism and other competing ideologies.[6] Just as Fukuyama thought political science had reached the final phase of ideological evolution, Kraakman and Hansmann thought corporate governance had reached a final consensus. In their view, there was "no longer any serious competitor to the view that corporate law should principally strive to increase long-term shareholder value."[7]

Just as 9/11, the steady rise of state capitalist systems such as China, and many other factors called Fukuyama's thesis into question, so have similar developments called Hansmann and Kraakman's thesis into question. Indeed, it considerably understates the case to say shareholder value maximization is being called into question. Today, shareholder value maximization is under attack on multiple fronts.[*]

In the academic sphere, although stakeholder capitalism has long had substantial academic support, the weight of scholarly opinion has tilted even more greatly towards stakeholder capitalism in recent years.[8] My former colleague, the late law professor Lynn Stout, dismissed shareholder value maximization as a mere myth, albeit a powerful one she claimed "causes companies to indulge in reckless,

---

[*] Although we are focused herein on U.S. law and business, it is worth noting that Hansmann and Kraakman – like Fukuyama – claimed to have identified global convergence on their identified end of history. Indeed, at the turn of the millennium there was an emerging consensus that "the stakeholder ideal" was in retreat even in countries like Germany and Japan where it had traditionally prevailed. JOHN MICKLETHWAIT & ADRIAN WOOLDRIDGE, THE COMPANY: A SHORT HISTORY OF A REVOLUTIONARY IDEA 187 (2003). As with Fukuyama's thesis about political systems converging, however, claims that capitalism had settled on the shareholder rather than stakeholder version foundered on the success and spread of China's system of state capitalism. Tim Wu, *The Goals of the Corporation and the Limits of the Law*, THE CLS BLUE SKY BLOG (Sept. 3, 2019), https://clsbluesky .law.columbia.edu/2019/09/03/the-goals-of-the-corporation-and-the-limits-of-the-law/.

sociopathic, and socially irresponsible behaviors."[9] Canadian law professor Joel Bakan went even further by condemning the business corporation itself as a "pathological institution" whose relentless pursuit of profit has psychopathic attributes.[10] In making such arguments, they reflected a widely shared narrative that "corporations are powerful, evil, malevolent, bad-actors intent on profit-making at the expense of the health, safety, and well-being of individuals."[11]

In the investing world, there long have been so-called socially responsible investors, who structured their portfolios using various social justice filters that excluded companies believed to have negative social and environmental impacts. Although it was claimed that socially responsible investing was a profitable strategy, it was primarily justified by moral and ethical arguments. Today, however, as investor interest in ESG metrics has grown, there has been a distinct shift in recent years from moral and ethical justifications to financial justifications. Although many ESG investors likely are still motivated by traditional socially responsible investor concerns, ESG investing is explicitly premised on the belief that ESG oriented portfolios provide superior risk-adjusted returns to traditional portfolios lacking ESG or social responsibility filters. Hence, for example, the three largest institutional investors – asset managers BlackRock, State Street, and Vanguard – all claim to have embraced ESG because they believe that ESG factors are positively correlated with firm performance. They offer investment funds that supposedly invest exclusively in firms that score highly in ESG measures and that exercise their voting rights as shareholders to support ESG policies. ESG-focused investors thus are supposedly pushing both asset managers and portfolio companies to be more ESG friendly.[12] Whether that's true is an issue to which we will return in Chapters 8 and 10. *

Finally, stakeholder capitalism and politics are increasingly intertwined. In the 2020 US Presidential campaign, perhaps influenced by the Occupy Wall Street movement of a few years earlier, numerous Democratic politicians carved out strong positions in favor of stakeholder capitalism. Senator Elizabeth Warren (D-MA), for example, contended that a root cause of many of America's economic problems was the emphasis by businesses on maximizing shareholder wealth. Her proposed Accountable Capitalism Act would have required boards of public corporations with over $1 billion in revenues to consider the interests of stakeholders when making corporate decisions. Eventual Democratic 2020 nominee and now President Joe Biden called for an "end to the era of shareholder capitalism." Strikingly, however, one also finds skepticism about shareholder wealth maximization on the right end of the political spectrum. Senator Marco Rubio (R-FL), for example, argues that shareholder wealth maximization "provides a framework to reduce or ignore the longer-term, economy-and-society wide negative externalities that result [from business activity], by placing them outside the realm of business decisions."[13]

---

* It is estimated that by 2018 ESG funds managed about $22 trillion, which represented a quarter of the total assets under management of the global asset management industry. Stavros Gadinis & Amelia Miazad, *Corporate Law and Social Risk*, 73 Vand. L. Rev. 1401, 1451–52 (2020).

These political developments at least in part reflect the grass roots resurgence of populism on both the left and right, which share a distrust of big business and the pursuit of corporate profit.[14] The rise of the latter potentially is a particularly important development. Although there are older antecedents, such as the Southern Agrarians of the 1930s, right of center populist critiques of shareholder capitalism are properly traced to Pat Buchanan's 1996 campaign for the Republican presidential nomination. Unlike traditional pro-business conservative campaigns, Buchanan's campaign was marked by hostility to globalization, in general, and transnational corporations, in particular. His campaign solidified a view among the emergent populist movement that large corporations and crony capitalism were diluting America's exceptional culture and identity through globalization and impoverishing working-class Americans while enriching financial and technology oligarchs.

The Tea Party and the 2016 Trump campaign were of even greater import. They espoused a strong aversion to Wall Street, especially in their opposition to post-2008 financial crisis government bailouts of financial firms. Both movements share many attributes with the other major twenty-first century American populist movement – Occupy Wall Street – including an antagonism towards corporate power.[15]

The potential impact of these resurgent populist movements was noted by The Economist's Schumpeter column in the wake of Donald Trump's 2016 election:

> As they slid down the streets of Davos this week, many executives will have felt a question gnawing in their guts. Who matters most: shareholders or the people? Around the world a revolt seems under way. A growing cohort – perhaps a majority – of citizens want corporations to be cuddlier, invest more at home, pay higher taxes and wages and employ more people, and are voting for politicians who say they will make all that happen ….
>
> Should [corporate managers] fire staff, trim costs and expand abroad – and face the wrath of Donald Trump's Twitter feed, the disgust of their children and the risk that they'll be the first against the wall when the revolution comes? Or do they bend to popular opinion and allow profits to fall … ?[16]

Taken together, these developments inevitably impacted corporate C-suites. Leaders of the business community traditionally were somewhat ambivalent about shareholder value maximization. Today, some have actually switched sides and joined the stakeholder capitalism movement or, at least, claim to have done so. Consider, to cite but a few examples, recent high-profile disputes over public restrooms, travel and immigration, high capacity rifle magazines, and voting by mail. What these seemingly very disparate debates have in common was the active role played in each by US corporations aggressively supporting the progressive position.

In 2016, North Carolina adopted House Bill 2, which among other things required transgendered persons to use public restrooms assigned to their biological sex. In the uproar that followed, many corporations publicly opposed the new law. Over 200 major corporations signed an open letter calling for the law's repeal, arguing that it did not reflect their values. Some prominent firms put their money where their mouth was, by cancelling major investments in North Carolina.[17]

When former President Donald Trump took office in 2017 some observers expected – even hoped – that his would be a populist administration siding with workers rather than big business.[18] Although those expectations did not come to pass, neither did initial overtures between the Trump administration and business leaders. Trump's travel bans suspending the refugee program and barring entry by nationals of a number of predominately Muslim countries triggered a backlash from many major corporations, especially in the tech sector.[19] The subsequent suspension of the DACA program, which protected undocumented persons brought into the US as children from deportation, triggered a similar backlash.

The following year the 2018 mass shooting in Parkland, Florida, again brought a sweeping reaction from corporate America. Citigroup and Bank of America restricted loans to the gun industry. BlackRock rolled out new index funds excluding gun manufacturers and retailers. Numerous airlines and car rental companies cancelled discount programs offered to NRA members.[20]

Taken together, these developments gave an old legal term new life as a hot management buzzword: corporate purpose.[21] The surging interest in this issue is reflected in the substantial increase in the number of news articles dealing with it. In 2011, the Factiva data base listed 18,558 news articles containing the phrase "corporate social responsibility." By 2020 that number had risen to 24,253. In 2011, just 64 news articles contained the phrase "stakeholder theory." By 2020 that number had risen to 157.

The resurgent debate over corporate purpose hit a high point in August 2019, when the Business Roundtable rejected the view that the profit motive ought to drive decisions by corporate officers and directors. Instead, the Business Roundtable argued, corporate decision makers also should take into account the interests of various other constituencies, such as workers, customers, communities, and so on. The Business Roundtable matters because it is probably the most prominent and influential association of large corporation CEOs. Since its formation in 1972, the Roundtable has periodically issued policy statements on a wide range of economic, political, and social issues. Because the Roundtable's membership consists of approximately 200 CEOs whose companies collectively employ 20 million people, generate annual revenues of $9 trillion, and have a stock market capitalization of approximately $18 trillion, those policy statements have frequently proven quite influential.

Corporate purpose and governance long has been a core area of policy interest for the Business Roundtable. Since 1978, Business Roundtable has periodically issued statements on Principles of Corporate Governance, which purport to summarize law and best practice in this area. Since 1997, all versions of those statements embraced the view that corporations exist primarily to serve their shareholders. The original 1997 version, for example, stated:

In The Business Roundtable's view, the paramount duty of management and of boards of directors is to the corporation's stockholders; the interests of other stakeholders are relevant as a derivative of the duty to stockholders. The notion that the board must somehow balance the interests of stockholders against the interests of other stakeholders fundamentally misconstrues the role of directors. It is, moreover, an unworkable notion because it would leave the board with no criterion for resolving conflicts between interests of stockholders and of other stakeholders or among different groups of stakeholders.[22]

The Statement recognized that directors in appropriate cases could consider the effects of their decision on constituencies such as employees, but only when consistent with their duty to manage the corporation in the long-term interests of the shareholders.

In recent years, however, the rhetoric coming from America's C-suites increasingly took into account social "pressure for companies to articulate and justify their broader purpose, in terms of how they address society's unmet needs in an era of great social change, activism, and political uncertainty."[23] In response to that pressure, the Business Roundtable's 2019 statement adopted a much broader conception of corporate purpose, which posited that corporations should commit to a series of bullet points elevating shareholder theory over shareholder value maximization. According to the Business Roundtable's new conception, a corporation's purpose includes:

- *Delivering value to our customers* ....
- Investing in our employees. This starts with compensating them fairly and providing important benefits. It also includes supporting them through training and education that help develop new skills for a rapidly changing world. We foster diversity and inclusion, dignity and respect.
- Dealing fairly and ethically with our suppliers ....
- Supporting the communities in which we work. We respect the people in our communities and protect the environment by embracing sustainable practices across our businesses.
- Generating long-term value for shareholders, who provide the capital that allows companies to invest, grow and innovate. We are committed to transparency and effective engagement with shareholders.[24]

That statement – and the renewed debate it triggered – provided the primary motivation for this book. Accordingly, the Business Roundtable's statement is one of my principal foils throughout.

I.1.1 *What the Moment Requires*

In light of the developments we just traced, what the present moment requires is a defense of shareholder value maximization that takes those developments into account. Or, to paraphrase William F. Buckley, what the moment needs is for someone to stand athwart the tracks of corporate governance and yell "stop" as the stakeholder capitalism train pulls out of the station.

Accordingly, three major themes animate the project. First, any conception of corporate purpose that embraces goals other than creating value for shareholders is inconsistent with the mainstream of US corporate law. Second, directors do – and should – have wide and substantially unfettered discretion as to how they go about generating shareholder value. Although many commentators claim that those statements are inconsistent, in fact they both reflect fundamental normative principles deeply embedded in US corporate law. Third, a shareholder-centric conception of corporate purpose is preferable to stakeholder capitalism.

1.2 THE INTENDED AUDIENCE

I am an academic. The publisher is an academic press. But you do not need to be an academic to read this book. My goal in writing it is to be as clear as possible and even to entertain or amuse when appropriate. Toward those ends, I went so far as to make frequent of the first person singular, which is a mortal sin in purely academic prose.

Granted, the book is interdisciplinary in nature, drawing on law, history, and economics. It will be of interest to lawyers and legal academics, as it explains how current law evolved. Because the work will be written in a way that is accessible to the educated general reader, however, it should also appeal to businesspersons, management school academics, and other audiences interested in corporate governance. Accordingly, the book is intended to reach a large and varied audience; including anyone who is interested – for whatever reason – in how corporations work and how corporate governance can be improved.

1.3 WHY SHOULD WE CARE ABOUT CORPORATE PURPOSE?

Put simply, corporate purpose matters because corporations matter. Corporations are "far wealthier and far more able to negatively affect our individual lives than virtually any local government or even most Federal agencies."[25] Worse yet, like elephants crashing through a forest, corporations can trample individuals and communities underfoot without even meaning to do so. As such the corporation is "the perfect externalizing machine."[26] By incorporating a business, it becomes possible for the owners of the business – whether intentionally or not – to externalize substantial costs and risks onto corporate constituencies such as employees or creditors and society at large.

Limited liability is the attribute that makes this possible.[27] Put simply, limited liability means that shareholders of a corporation are not personally liable for debts incurred or torts committed by the firm. If the firm fails, a shareholder's losses thus are limited to the amount the shareholder has invested in the firm – that is, the amount the shareholder initially paid to purchase his or her stock. Creditors of the corporation may not seek compensation for unpaid debts or other obligations from the shareholders' personal assets.

Limited liability has been something of a mixed blessing. On the one hand, it is reasonable to say that the limited liability of corporations made our modern economy possible. Limited liability made it possible for entrepreneurs to raise the enormous amounts of investment capital necessary for large industrial corporations to arise and flourish by allowing many investors to invest small amounts of money in a business enterprise without risking their entire fortune. "One of the great advantages of the large corporate system is that it allows individuals to use small fractions of their savings for various purposes, without risking a disastrous loss if any corporation in which they have invested becomes insolvent."[28] As such, it is "an essential aspect of a large corporate system with widespread public participation."[29] President Nicholas Murray of Columbia University thus exaggerated only slightly when, in 1911, he opined that:

> I weigh my words when I say that in my judgment the limited liability corporation is the greatest single discovery of modern times …. Even steam and electricity are far less important than the limited liability corporation, and they would be reduced to comparative impotence without it.[30]

On the other hand, limited liability has a dark side. Specifically, as already noted, it allows shareholders to externalize part of the costs of their investment onto other corporate constituencies to society in general. A very simple example will suffice to illustrate the point.[31] Suppose a corporation borrowed $2,000 from a bank to invest. There are two available investments: A and B, each of which has three possible pay-offs: best case, worst case, and break even.

Investment A

	Probability	Nominal Value	Expected Value
Best-case	10%	$3,000	$300
Break-even	80%	$2,000	$1,600
Worst-case	10%	$1,000	$100
Expected Value			$2000

Investment B

	Probability	Nominal Value	Expected Value
Best-case	20%	$5,000	$1,000
Break-even	60%	$2,000	$1,200
Worst Case	20%	$0	$0
Expected Value			$2,200

Investment B is the more risky of the two options. Both default risk (the risk that the company won't be able to pay back its debt) and volatility risk (the likelihood of an outcome other than the break-even scenario) are much higher in Investment B.

In a world of zero transaction costs and unlimited liability – that is, one in which shareholders are personally liable for corporate debts – the bank would be indifferent as to which investment the company made. If the company fails, the bank can simply collect from the shareholder. Conversely, because the bank can collect any unpaid debt from the shareholder, the shareholder will fully internalize the risks associated with the choices.

In a world of limited liability – that is, one in which the shareholders have no liability for the corporation's contract debts – the bank will prefer Investment A. Even in the worst case scenario, the bank will get half its money back, plus there's a 90 percent probability the bank will be repaid in full. The bank will not be impressed that Investment B offers a higher expected return, because the bank has no claims on the residual. Anything over $2,000 goes to the shareholders, not the bank (ignoring interest). Conversely, shareholders will strongly prefer Investment B. Because creditors (like the bank) have a prior claim on the firm's assets and earnings, they get paid first; shareholders get the residual – whatever is left over. Shareholders thus prefer projects offering potentially high rate of returns, so there will be something left over after the creditors get paid.

The problem, of course, is that high return projects usually involve high levels of risk. The greater the risk, the more likely it becomes that the project will be unsuccessful. In that event, it becomes more likely that the firm's income will not suffice to pay the creditors, let alone leave anything over for the shareholders. Shareholders will not care about Investment B's greater risk, however, because the doctrine of limited liability means their personal assets are not at risk. Limited liability thus generates negative externalities by creating incentives for shareholders to cause the company to invest in higher risk projects than would the firm's creditors. Because shareholders do not put their personal assets at jeopardy, they effectively externalize some portion of the risk associated with such investments to creditors.

The externalities problem has been around since corporations were first vested with limited liability. As corporations grew ever larger in the wake of the industrial revolution, however, the scope of the problem likewise grew. In an industrial economy, limited liability is of particular concern because it may encourage overinvestment in hazardous activities. Because the shareholder can externalize some part of the risks associated with such activities, those activities could have a positive value for the investor even though they have negative net social costs.

Sometimes these externalities are the result of decisions by corporate management to transfer some of the costs of running their business onto the corporation's various constituencies or society at large. When I was young my family lived for a time at Fort Devens, Massachusetts, which is on the Nashua River. At that time, many textile and paper mills operated along the Nashua. Both industries generated enormous amounts of waste water and the mills simply dumped their effluent into the river. The river was incredibly noxious, with a reek that could be smelled at a considerable distance. As far back as 1877, a Massachusetts State Board of Health report opined that the river was "so polluted throughout its whole length that it would be unwise to use any part of it for a domestic water supply."[32] Instead of incurring costs to clean up their waste, the corporations whose plants abutted the river opted to externalize those costs onto those who lived downriver.

Other externalities, however, are the unintended consequence of what famed economist Joseph Schumpeter called "creative destruction." At the heart of the capitalist system is an engine of constant and dynamic change. New services and products arise, replacing old services and products and often displacing those who produced the older ones. Likewise, new ways of producing established goods are developed, potentially displacing those who were trained in the old ways.

At one level, the debate over corporate purpose thus is really a debate about how to deal with these corporate externalities. If we tell directors and officers to maximize corporate profits, will we simply encourage them to externalize even more costs? Conversely, is asking them to behave responsibly likely to induce them to internalize those costs?

Having said that, however, the corporate purpose debate goes beyond simply the negative externalities inevitably resulting from corporate activities. It also asks whether corporations should be managed so as to generate positive externalities. Should managers conduct the corporation's business so as to generate benefits to stakeholders and society in general? Advocates of stakeholder capitalism commonly contend that the profit motive discourages corporate directors and managers to ignore not just the social costs of corporate activities but also the potential for corporate activities to generate social benefits.

In many cases, however, corporate actions that benefit stakeholders – such as employees – help the firm become more profitable and thus redound to the benefit of shareholders. When the corporation faces a true zero-sum decision, however, one must make a choice between the competing interests of stakeholders and shareholders. In such cases, the law requires directors to prefer shareholder interests. This text will defend that claim as both a descriptive and normative matter.

I.4 DEFINING OUR TERMS

I.4.1 *The Corporation*

To say either that a corporation acted responsibly or irresponsibly is error. By making either statement, the speaker engages in reification; that is, treats an abstraction as a physical entity. While reification provides a necessary semantic shorthand, it creates a sort of false consciousness when taken to extremes.[33] The corporation is not a thing. The corporation is a legal fiction representing the unique vehicle by which large groups of individuals, each offering a different factor of production, order their relationships so as to collectively produce marketable goods or services. Accordingly, we must always keep in mind that when we talk about the corporation

we are talking about people. Analysis requires us to keep in mind the differing interests, incentives, knowledge, powers, and so on that those people possess.

The universe of corporations is highly diverse. In this book, as is typical of the
debate to which it contributes, we are concerned only with a fairly narrow segment
of that universe. Specifically, we are concerned solely with for-profit business corporations. Among that subset of corporations, we are also concerned with publicly held
rather than closely held corporations. Close corporations tend to be small, but their
key defining characteristic is that their shares are not listed for trading on a public
secondary market such as the New York Stock Exchange (NYSE) or NASDAQ.
As a result, they tend to have a small number of shareholders, most of whom are
actively engaged in the management of the company. Such companies tend to be
managed so as to maximize the value of the owners' equity. In some cases, where
the shareholders are in agreement, however, other values may influence management's decisions.

Arts and craft store chain Hobby Lobby, to cite but one prominent example, is a
for-profit corporation owned by David and Barbara Green and their three children.
The company has adopted a statement of purpose, signed by each shareholder,
committing the company to "[h]onoring the Lord in all [they] do by operating the
company in a manner consistent with Biblical principles," even where that might
reduce corporate profits.[34] Whether that purpose and the religious beliefs underlying it entitled Hobby Lobby to an exemption from the Patient Protection and
Affordable Care Act of 2010's mandate that employers provide health insurance
plans including coverage for various contraceptive methods was at issue in the US
Supreme Court's well known *Burwell v. Hobby Lobby Stores, Inc.*, decision. While
the Supreme Court's decision that Hobby Lobby was entitled to such an exemption
was and remains highly controversial, many scholars accept that Hobby Lobby's
shareholders were entitled to run their corporation in ways that depart from the
shareholder wealth maximization norm.[35]*

---

* Whether shareholder value maximization ought to be a default rule out of which the company's
shareholders should be allowed to opt or a mandatory rule they must be bound by is an interesting
normative question, which has been the subject of some debate. Likewise, there has been some
debate over the positive question of whether the law does allow them to opt out of shareholder value
maximization. *See, e.g.*, Joan MacLeod Heminway, *Shareholder Wealth Maximization as a Function
of Statutes, Decisional Law, and Organic Documents*, 74 WASH. & LEE L. REV. 939, 957 (2017) (arguing that "a charter provision that is inconsistent with the shareholder wealth maximization norm
should be valid"); Stefan J. Padfield, *The Role of Corporate Personality Theory in Opting Out of
Shareholder Wealth Maximization*, 19 TRANSACTIONS: TENN. J. BUS. L. 415, 439 (2017) (suggesting
that "Chancellor Chandler's comments in the *eBay* decision suggest that" efforts to opt out of shareholder value maximization may be unavailing). My own view at one time was that "state law arguably
does not permit corporate organic documents to redefine the directors' fiduciary duties." Stephen
M. Bainbridge, *Interpreting Nonshareholder Constituency Statutes*, 19 PEPP. L. REV. 971, 985 (1992).
Today, however, my view is that it is a question that has been essentially mooted by the availability of
the benefit corporation option (see Chapter 6).

Although we are thus focused on public corporations, not all public corporations fall within the scope of our inquiry. A substantial number of public corporations have a controlling shareholder. Such a shareholder will often be concerned with maximizing their own total utility, rather than the wealth of all shareholders. By definition, moreover, such a shareholder will have considerable influence – at the very least – over the board of directors and thus may often be able to act at the expense of minority shareholders. The body of law governing such conduct is separate from the law of corporate purpose.[36]

Instead, we are concerned here primarily with the duties owed by directors and managers of publicly held corporations to their shareholders.[37] Although public corporations constitute a small fraction of the total universe of business corporations, they are a hugely important fraction. They are the economy's largest employers and produce the biggest share of private sector economic output. They wield substantial political influence. Perhaps most importantly for our purposes, they are the entities most likely to generate huge externalities to be borne by their stakeholders and society at large.

I.4.2 *Corporate Purpose*

The term corporate purpose is used in two distinct ways. One speaks to the type of business the corporation was formed to conduct. The other speaks to the reason for the corporation's existence. At one time, they were closely related. Today, however, they are essentially separate. Herein, we are concerned solely with the latter. Some commentators define corporate purpose as incorporating opposition to the profit motive.[38] Harvard Business School professors Rebecca Henderson and George Serafeim, for example, "define corporate purpose as 'a concrete goal or objective for the firm that reaches beyond profit maximization' and define such a purpose as authentic if the firm routinely makes costly investments in it at the expense of immediate profitability."[39] In this text, by way of contrast, corporate purpose is used neutrally.

As for the former meaning of corporate purpose, it is rooted in the early history of corporate law. In England, corporate charters were granted by the King. After the American Revolution, state legislatures took over that function. Every newly formed corporation required a unique statute granting the company its own individual charter. In theory, the legislature assessed "each entity's proposed business purpose and the societal or communal need for the entity's specific contribution to the state's economy (e.g., building roads or bridges)."[40] Antebellum corporation codes thus typically required that the articles of incorporation set forth with specificity the purposes for which the corporation was organized and the powers it would utilize in pursuit of those purposes. If the corporate entity entered into a transaction for an unauthorized purpose or that required it to make use of an unauthorized power, the transaction was *ultra vires* and would be declared void.[41]

Over time, however, the *ultra vires* doctrine eroded and eventually became essentially toothless. In practice, the regime under which corporate charters were individually granted by state legislatures led to a good deal of corruption, as persuading the legislature to pass the necessary statute frequently required under the table payments. The old system thus gradually gave way to one in which general corporation laws allowed businesses to be formed without legislative involvement. Today, one forms a corporation simply by filing articles of incorporation with the appropriate state office and paying the requisite franchise tax.

The Delaware General Corporation Law now allows a corporation to pursue "any lawful business."[42] Likewise, although the Delaware code requires that the articles of incorporation include a statement of corporate purpose, it suffices for the articles to state that the corporation's purpose "is to engage in any lawful act or activity."[43] Many states lack even that minimal requirement.[*]

As we will see below, at one time issues of corporate social responsibility were litigated under the *ultra vires* doctrine. Today, however, with the erosion of the *ultra vires* doctrine, questions of corporate purpose doctrine are litigated not under that doctrine but under that of fiduciary obligation.[44]

I.4.3 *Shareholder Value Maximization*

Shareholder value maximization is often confused with shareholder primacy. In fact, however, shareholder primacy should be understood as making two distinct claims: "(1) that shareholders are the principals on whose behalf corporate governance is organized and (2) that shareholders do (and should) exercise ultimate control of the corporate enterprise."[45] We are concerned here only with the former aspect of shareholder primacy, which we shall refer to as shareholder value maximization, which stands for the normative proposition that directors are obliged to make a decision based solely on the basis of long-term shareholder gain.

---

[*] In US corporate law, the critical question is where Delaware law comes down on an issue. Delaware is the state of incorporation for over half of US public corporations and is also the leading choice of companies that choose to incorporate in a state other than the one in which they are headquartered. Because of a conflict of laws rule known as the internal affairs doctrine, which provides that corporate law questions are governed by the law of the state of incorporation, matters of internal corporate governance for companies incorporated in Delaware are governed by Delaware's corporate statutory and case law. *See* Shaffer v. Heitner, 433 U.S. 186, 215 n.44 (1977) ("In general, the law of the State of incorporation is held to govern the liabilities of officers or directors to the corporation and its stockholders.").

Delaware's dominance is magnified because courts in many states will follow Delaware law when their own state's law is silent on an issue. *See* Jens Dammann & Henry Hansmann, *Globalizing Commercial Litigation*, 94 CORNELL L. REV. 1, 19 (2008) (stating that "courts from other U.S. states often follow the lead of Delaware's judiciary when faced with issues of corporate law"). As a result, there has been an effective "convergence on the Delaware General Corporation Law as a de facto national corporate law." Ronald J. Gilson, *Globalizing Corporate Governance: Convergence of Form or Function*, 49 AM. J. COMP. L. 329, 350 (2001).

I use the term shareholder value maximization rather than common alternatives such as shareholder wealth maximization or profit maximization so as to distinguish our focus from caricatures often deployed by proponents of stakeholder capitalism. Probably the most famous defense of shareholder value maximization remains Milton Friedman's 1970 essay "The Social Responsibility of Business Is to Increase Its Profits."[46] Many stakeholder theorists claim Friedman promulgated a doctrine of short-term profit maximization, but such claims are either uninformed or disingenuous. Friedman postulated that a business should pursue profit maximization while conforming to "the basic rules of the society, both those embodied in law and those embodied in ethical custom."[47] Shareholder value maximization is thus fully consistent with – indeed requires – playing fair within the rules of the game, engaging in open and free competition rather than pursuing monopoly status, eschewing deception and fraud, and obeying the law.

Accordingly, as retired Chief Justice of the Delaware Supreme Court Leo Strine has observed,* shareholder value maximization "does not mean that corporate managers cannot think long-term and must pursue the action that will generate the most short-term profit, if that would impair the corporation's ultimate ability to generate the highest returns for stockholders."[48] Likewise, as Strine also observed, shareholder value maximization "does not mean that corporate managers cannot consider other constituencies and interests affected by the corporation's conduct – such as employees, customers, communities in which it operates, and society generally – but it does mean that they can only do so when that is instrumental to profit generation."[49] To the contrary, it will often be the case that it will be in the shareholder's interests for management to treat stakeholders well.[50] In sum, to again quote Chief Justice Strine, shareholder value maximization simply contemplates

---

* I shall refer frequently herein to Chief Justice Strine's voluminous writing on corporate purpose. In part, this is due to the importance of Delaware law. In larger part, however, it is due to Strine's personal standing in the field. Strine served on Delaware's dedicated corporate law court, the Court of Chancery, as a Vice Chancellor and then as its Chancellor, and then served as Chief Justice of Delaware's Supreme Court. While I have acknowledged that even mighty Homer nods occasionally, I have also observed that:

> When any Chief Justice of the Delaware Supreme Court speaks on a corporate law topic, lawyers and academics who toil in that doctrinal vineyard listen. When that Chief Justice is Leo Strine, they listen especially closely. The "well-respected" Chief Justice after all is the "[w]underkind of U.S. corporate law" and has been "recognized among academics, practitioners, and other judges" as an "intellectual leader" of the Delaware judiciary.

Stephen M. Bainbridge, *Corporate Social Responsibility in the Night-Watchman State*, 115 COLUM. L. REV. SIDEBAR 39 (2015). Readers of a certain age will recognize the cultural reference to the E. F. Hutton television commercial tag line "'When E. F. Hutton talks, people listen' (which usually involved a young professional remarking at a dinner party that his broker was E. F. Hutton, which caused the moderately loud party to stop all conversation to listen to him)." *E. F. Hutton & Co.*, Wikipedia, http://en.wikipedia.org/wiki/E._F._Hutton_%26_Co.

that directors and officers must "pursue a good faith strategy to maximize profits for the stockholders," while giving them "substantial discretion, outside the context of a change of control, to decide how best to achieve that goal and the appropriate time frame for delivering those returns."[51]

I.4.4 *Stakeholders (a.k.a. Non-shareholder Constituencies)*

The term "stakeholders" reportedly originated in a 1963 Stanford Research Institute memorandum as a descriptive term for "those groups without whose support the organization would cease to exist."[52] Obviously, this definition is too vague to be particularly useful. As an alternative, prominent stakeholder theorist Edward Freeman defined the term to include "any group or individual who can affect or is affected by the achievement of the organization's purpose."[53] Obviously, that definition is not an improvement. Worse yet, it is so broad as to be essentially meaningless. Indeed, Freeman garnered considerable opprobrium in some circles by suggesting that, under his definition, "some corporations must count 'terrorist groups' as stakeholders."[54]

A narrower and thus more useful definition encompasses those non-shareholders whose business relationship with the company gives rise to implicit claims of good faith and fair dealing. Examples include "car buyers having an implicit claim to continued service, software companies offering routine upgrades, suppliers making key parts available, and employees being treated fairly when seeking promotion."[55]

Yet, even that narrower definition is contested. Nobel laureate economist Eugene Fama, for example, would exclude suppliers from the list of a corporation's stakeholders on grounds that they can protect themselves.[56] The logic of Fama's argument would also seem to exclude any other constituency that can effectively bargain with the firm for contractual protections, such as creditors. In any case, Fama would also exclude customers because in a competitive market firms that fail to keep customers satisfied will not survive for long. Again, however, that argument is problematic because it would seem to apply to any other constituency that could cripple the firm by withdrawing its services. Fama's narrow focus on internal constituencies, moreover, excludes broader societal concerns such as climate change.

Even if one sets aside Fama's objections, defining who constitutes a stakeholder remains problematic. Consider, for example, a corporate decision to close an antiquated factory located in a Rust Belt state and open a new highly automated factory in a right to work state. Do we include within the definition of stakeholders not just the employees at the plant to be closed and the communities in which they live but also the prospective employees to be hired at the new plant and the communities in which they live? As that example suggests, there is also a time element with which we must deal.[57] Do only current stakeholders count or do former and/or future stakeholders also count? Who decides and who balances the chosen interests?

I.4.5 *Stakeholder Capitalism*

Stakeholder capitalism – also sometimes referred to as stakeholder theory – posits that when making decisions a corporation's directors and officers should consider the interests of all the corporation's stakeholders, not just its shareholders. In appropriate cases, many stakeholder theorists argue, directors and officers may balance the interests of shareholders and stakeholders or even subordinate the former's interests to those of the latter.[58] Some go even further to argue that the law should require directors and officers to do so.

So defined, stakeholder capitalism addresses only one of the two basic questions of corporate law. Those questions are: (1) who makes decisions for the corporation?; and (2) what is the decision-making norm that should guide the chosen decision makers? Reformers who wish to use corporate law and governance to change the way corporations interact with society thus have only two options. They can try to change the decision makers or they can try to change the decision-making principle.[59] Some countries have pursued the former option, most notably Germany through its system of codetermination in which the corporation's board of directors has both shareholder and employee representatives. Although some academic commentators have proposed moving the US system toward codetermination, American labor law remains basically adversarial and American corporate law retains its system of a unitary board elected solely by shareholders.[60] Efforts to change the way US corporations make decisions thus have historically focused on changing the norm by which corporate decisions are made from shareholder capitalism to stakeholder capitalism.

Stakeholder capitalism obviously overlaps to a considerable degree with corporate social responsibility and ESG. Some commentators in fact use them interchangeably. Given our definition of stakeholder capitalism, however, corporate social responsibility and ESG are broader conceptions that embrace entities and causes beyond our definition of stakeholders. Specifically, corporate social responsibility and ESG speak to how the corporation relates to society as a whole, the environment, inequalities of wealth, and a host of other social ills, as well as the interests of true stakeholders.[61]

Advocates of corporate social responsibility today place strong emphasis on environmental issues, for example, especially climate change. But the environment is hard to fit into stakeholder theory. There is no single constituency representing the environment. After all, who speaks for the planet? One would need to adopt a very broad understanding of stakeholder theory, in which governments, nongovernmental organizations, and civil society at large are deemed stakeholders to fit the environment into stakeholder theory, which would stretch the theory beyond the point of usefulness.

The climate issue also comes up in a common progressive critique of stakeholder theory, which is that stakeholder theory can be too narrowly focused on internal stakeholders. Climate activists use the term Scope 1 emissions to refer to those greenhouse gas emissions emitted by sources owned or directly controlled by the company in question. Scope 2 emissions are those generated by the providers from which the company purchases energy in the form of electricity or fuel. Finally, Scope 3 emissions are those generated by the company's upstream supply chain and its downstream customers. Some climate activists assert that a company should be focused on all three categories but worry that stakeholder theory's focus on internals would lead companies to pay little attention to Scope 3 emissions, even though for many companies Scope 3 emissions probably account for a majority of the greenhouse gas emissions attributable to the company's business operations.

Put more generally, progressive critics of stakeholder theory contend it fails to account for the broader range of ways in which companies affect society. Consider for example the case of Starbucks, which makes much of its commitment to engagement with its stakeholders. Certain British critics of Starbucks acknowledge Starbuck's commitment to its stakeholders, but criticize it for using potent tax avoidance strategies to minimize the amount of taxes it pays in the UK. Although Starbucks did not break any tax laws, it had offended British social norms against tax avoidance. Minimizing its taxes doubtlessly benefited Starbucks' shareholders and may even have benefited some of its stakeholders, such as creditors who had a greater prospect of being paid in full or employees who might have had greater job security, but there was a perception that Starbucks was freeloading off British society.[62]

I.4.6 *Corporate Social Responsibility*

Many definitions of corporate social responsibility are on offer.[63] The first definition worthy of exploration is the triple bottom line. It claims that corporations should care about three Ps; that is, profits, people, and the planet. It thus posits that companies should be aware not only of their financial results, but also their impact on society and the environment. An important variant of the triple bottom line approach to corporate social responsibility asserts that while being socially responsible may be costly in the short run, it produces superior financial performance in the long run. As we shall see, this definition closely overlaps with the ESG approach to corporate purpose.

A version of this understanding of corporate social responsibility was ably articulated by London School of Business professor Alex Edmans in his 2020 book *Grow the Pie*. Edmans asserts that business is not a zero-sum game in which shareholders and stakeholders compete to divide a static pie. Instead, working together collaboratively, they can grow the pie, creating "shared value in a way that enlarges the slices of everyone – shareholders, workers, customers, suppliers, the environment, communities and taxpayers."[64] Providing a just slice of the enhanced pie to stakeholders is critical to this effort, so as to incentivize them to be more productive. Indeed, Edmans puts the case even more strongly, arguing that the road to profits necessarily leads through the land of social responsibility. Some commentators nevertheless distinguish Edman's approach from stakeholder theory by adopting a narrow definition of the latter, "which suggests that a company cannot adequately serve stakeholders' best interests if it is trying to maximize profit in its business strategy and operations."[65]

There are multiple difficulties with this account of corporate social responsibility. First, while it may be true that a firm can do well by doing good, it may also be true that only firms that are doing well can afford to do good. In other words, "for profit" corporate social responsibility is costly and, as a result, only top performers can afford to engage in it. This criticism suggests that one should be skeptical of empirical projects claiming to find a positive correlation between corporate social responsibility and firm performance, because there may be a selection bias problem in that a sample of firms engaged in socially responsible activities may be disproportionately weighted towards strong financial performers. We return to this issue in Chapters 8 and 9.

Second, while it is true that a rising tide often lifts all boats, it is not always true. Put another way, not all business decisions involve win-win decisions in which is it possible to simultaneously make shareholders and stakeholders better off even when measured in the long run. Sometimes business faces true zero sum choices. As we shall see, neither corporate social responsibility nor stakeholder theory provide useful guides for making decisions in those situations.

Third, the empirical evidence does not support the claim that social responsibility necessarily redounds to improved firm performance. At least in zero sum cases, corporate social responsibility necessarily contemplates transferring wealth from shareholders to stakeholders. As we shall see, such transfers not only injure shareholders but society as a whole.

Finally, a firm's embrace of corporate social responsibility may be purely cosmetic rather than being motivated by pro-social considerations. Firms may publicize their purported commitment to pro-social conduct not so much to benefit society but rather to attract consumers whose view of socially responsible goods and services is sufficiently positive to induce them to pay more for such goods and services. Critics contend that corporate social responsibility of this sort may assuage the social conscience of wealthy consumers but does little to benefit the workers who produced the goods or services. Critics of fair trade certified coffee, for example, contend that the certification is concerned more with pleasing consumers than with benefitting small coffee producers. This type of corporate social responsibility also tends to be associated with monopolists and oligopolists, as margins in competitive markets are often too thin to justify diverting revenues into what amounts to a marketing scheme. It also tends to be associated with luxury items, as wealthier consumers have more disposable income to expend on paying premium prices for goods such as fair trade coffee.

A second way of defining corporate social responsibility argues that concern for stakeholders is motivated not by profits or shareholder value maximization but communitarian concerns about distributive justice. The effort to impart communitarian values to the large for-profit corporation, however, is simply unpersuasive. The idea that global investors, shop floor employees at many locations scattered around the world, Wall Street bankers and Main Street creditors, and so on all belong to a single, mutually interdependent community is risible at best. Even a prominent stakeholder theorist such as law professor David Millon concedes that the communitarian argument as applied to such firms strains credulity past the breaking point.[66]

A third definition of corporate social responsibility might be called "elite charity." The directors and managers who make corporate decisions commonly reside in the highest income and social classes and often use their power to direct corporate resources in support of causes popular in their set. This may include benevolence towards the "little people," but it often means that corporate efforts focus on high end philanthropy. Concert halls, orchestras, museums, and other cultural institutions often survive on corporate largesse.[67]

This understanding of corporate social responsibility is typically expressed through corporate philanthropy, which consists of devoting some portion of corporate earnings to charitable organizations or causes. It can focus narrowly on charitable activities that benefit the company's own stakeholders or more broadly on those that benefit communities or society as a whole. If one embraces the narrow definition of corporate social responsibility set out below, corporate philanthropy arguably is not an example of socially responsible conduct. It often generates good will and tax benefits that contribute to the corporation's bottom line. Conversely, corporate philanthropy is often used as a conduit for directing corporate earnings to a director or executive's personal philanthropic preferences.

The difficulties of this conception of corporate social responsibility are twofold. First, it is not directed at the purportedly core social problem of ameliorating the externalities the corporation imposes on its stakeholders. Second, there is no obvious link between such activities and corporate performance even in the long run. To the contrary, corporate philanthropy is an example of the principal–agent problem that lies at the heart of corporate governance.*

---

* As we'll discuss in more detail in Chapter 10, the principal–agent problem arises because agents of a firm will not internalize all of the costs of shirking. By shirking, I do not mean merely laziness. Instead, in principal–agent economics, shirking is defined to include any action by a member of a production team that diverges from the interests of the team as a whole. As such, shirking includes not only goofing off, but also culpable cheating, negligence, oversight, incapacity, risk aversion, and even honest mistakes. *See generally* Roy Radner, *Hierarchy: The Economics of Managing*, 30 J. ECON. LIT. 1382, 1405–07 (1992) (identifying the incentives of rational agents to shirk). The principal reaps the gains created by the agent's work, less the compensation paid the agent and other expenses, but bears the full cost of shirking by the agent. To the extent that shirking produces gain, such as the pleasure derived from leisure, the agent receives all of that value. This results in an incongruence between the principal's and the agent's preferences. Even granting that agents have multiple motivations beyond naked self-interest, there remains a substantial risk that, in the absence of appropriate *ex ante* and *ex post* accountability structures, the agent will choose different options for expending time and effort than the principal would prefer. The resulting necessity for accountability mechanisms is why the principal incurs agency costs, which are defined as the sum of the monitoring and bonding costs, plus any residual loss, incurred to prevent shirking by agents. *See* Eugene F. Fama & Michael C. Jensen, *Separation of Ownership and Control*, 26 J. L. & ECON. 301, 304 (1983); Michael C. Jensen & William H. Meckling, *Theory of the Firm: Managerial Behavior, Agency Costs, and Ownership Structure*, 3 J. FIN. ECON. 305, 308 (1976).

A fourth definition narrowly limits corporate social responsibility so as to limit it to cases of true altruism. My friend, the late law and economics scholar Henry Manne, for example, argued that the only truly socially responsible corporate action is "one for which the marginal returns to the corporation are less than the returns available from some alternative expenditure," is purely voluntary, and is an actual corporate expenditure rather than a conduit for individual largess.[68] So defined, corporate social responsibility is neither simply doing what the law requires nor affirmatively embracing enlightened self-interest or long-run profit maximization.[69] Instead, according to Manne, meaningful corporate social responsibility entails economic losses to shareholders and corresponding gains to some other corporate stakeholders or society at large.

Finally, business ethics scholar Archie Carroll, a very prominent advocate of corporate social responsibility in the second half of the twentieth century, defined it as "the economic, legal, ethical, and philanthropic expectations placed on organizations by society at a given point in time."[70] His definition thereby combines "economic expectations to generate a profit … with legal expectations to obey the law, ethical expectations to do what is right and fair, and philanthropic expectations to be a good corporate citizen."[71] In other words, Carroll's definition includes aspects of each of the foregoing definitions.

Carroll illustrated his approach using a pyramid to express the hierarchy of values it espoused. At the base is the need to generate sustainable profits to ensure the long-term health of the enterprise. A company that does not ensure its survival is not fulfilling its most basic responsibility. Next is the company's legal obligations. Next is the company's ethical obligations, reflecting societal expectations that companies do the right thing even when not required by law. At the top of the hierarchy is the discretionary level, which reflects being a good citizen.

Note that business ethics – doing the right thing even when not legally obliged to do so – overlaps with corporate social responsibility. Ethics is concerned more with the moral decisions of individual actors, however, while corporate social responsibility is concerned more with the obligations of incorporated entities. One thus can imagine directors acting ethically even while operating within an organization committed to shareholder value maximization.

I.4.7 *Environmental, Social, and Governance*

ESG currently is one of the hottest buzzwords in both management and investing. A rather considerable industry has grown up around ESG. There are asset managers and investment advisers who specialize in advising clients about making ESG-friendly investments. There are mutual funds and exchange traded funds that use ESG ratings in selecting portfolio companies in which to invest. There are ratings firms that provide the necessary ratings to guide such decisions. There are companies that produce ESG-weighted indices for passively managed index funds to track.

ESG has been defined as including "environmentally sustainable investments, social investments or good governance investments."[72] Others define it as a set of metrics for measuring a company's performance on environmental, social, and corporate governance dimensions. Still others define it "to refer not only to sustainability measures or to environmental, social, or governance practices specifically, but to all nonfinancial fundamentals that can impact firms' financial performance, such as corporate governance, labor and employment standards, human resource management, and environmental practices."[73]

Using any of those definitions, corporate social responsibility and ESG overlap to a considerable extent. Indeed, some observers treat ESG as essentially synonymous with corporate social responsibility, defining ESG as a mechanism for raising the consciousness of both managers and investors so that they do the right thing regardless of economic impact.[74] According to this view, ESG's goal is achieving a more equitable balance between shareholder and stakeholder interests.

An important alternative views ESG primarily in an economic sense. In this view, which is closely akin to the for profit variant of corporate social responsibility, shareholder value maximization leads to an undesirable focus on short-term profit maximization at the expense of long-term profitability. Proponents of this version of ESG argue that, for example, investing in employee welfare generates higher employee satisfaction and, as a result, productivity gains.[75] Improved corporate governance will discourage managers from actions that benefit themselves at the expense of shareholders and/or stakeholders. Likewise, investing in environmental enhancements will reduce long-term costs from climate change, and so on.[76] As with the for profit definition of corporate social responsibility, we shall see there are substantial reasons to doubt these claims.

Other commentators explain the relationship between corporate social responsibility and ESG by treating the former as a theoretical framework and the latter as a mechanism for operationalizing that framework. In other words, while corporate social responsibility is concerned with advocating for corporations to take social concerns into account when making decisions, ESG proponents assert that it is concerned with providing specific metrics to assess the extent to which firms do so.[77]

> ESG takes on [corporate social responsibility] and builds on it in a manner that takes it out of the realms of pure philanthropy, to a concrete set of numbers which can be used by investors and consumers alike in understanding a company's philanthropic, social and internal governance practices.
>
> ESG provides quantifiable indicators (including sustainable, ethical and corporate governance issues such as managing the company's carbon footprint and making sure there are systems in place) to measure accountability. It applies numerical figures as to how companies treat their staff, manage supply chains, respond to climate change, increase diversity and inclusion, and build community links.[78]

An increasing number of asset managers use these ESG metrics to supplement financial metrics in making investment decisions. In turn, there are growing pressures on managers to manage not just to the quarterly earnings numbers but also to ESG results. As we shall see in Chapters 8 and 9, however, there are good reasons to doubt whether using ESG as a management tool benefits either shareholder or stakeholders.

1.5 PLAN OF THE WORK

My focus is on US law and practice. As observed by a prominent European scholar of corporate social responsibility, Jeremy Moon of the Copenhagen Business School, the US is generally acknowledged to be the home of corporate social responsibility.[79] The idea that corporations owed responsibilities to society above and beyond the legal obligations imposed by that society originated in US academic and management circles. Edward Freeman, arguably the father of stakeholder theory, was an American professor of business administration. Conversely, corporate social responsibility's most famous critic, Milton Friedman, was an American professor of economics.

Professor Edward Rock contends that recent corporate purpose scholarship tends to conflate four issues that ought to be kept distinct from one another: "(1) the legal debate on what is the best theory of the corporation, (2) the corporate finance debate about conceptualizing the corporation in theoretical models and empirical research, (3) the management debate about successful management strategies for building valuable firms, and (4) the political debate about the social responsibility of large listed companies."[80] I take his point, but I come at the question from a different perspective. Because this book was motivated in large part by the Business Roundtable's 2019 statement on corporate purpose, I focus on two questions. First, does the law either require or, at least, allow public corporation directors and managers to adopt the version of stakeholder capitalism embraced in the Business Roundtable statement? Second, why did the Business Roundtable CEOs change the organization's longstanding position on corporate purpose? In answering those questions, I am not engaging the extensive ethical, philosophical, and theological literature on stakeholder capitalism, but rather the legal and policy issues it presents.[81]

Part I thus focuses on whether corporate law embraces shareholder value maximization or stakeholder capitalism. The general reader might think that a question better for an academic legal journal than a book intended for a wider audience than just lawyers. In fact, however, stakeholder capitalism's proponents commonly conflate the legal and policy arguments. They claim that the law already permits directors to make tradeoffs between shareholder and stakeholder interests. In other words, they claim the law allows directors to transfer wealth from shareholders to stakeholders. They presumably make this claim so as to avoid the need for persuading legislatures and courts to change the law so as to empower directors to make such tradeoffs. As Leo Strine observed:

In current corporate law scholarship, there is a tendency among those who believe that corporations should be more socially responsible to avoid the more difficult and important task of advocating for externality regulation of corporations in a globalizing economy and encouraging institutional investors to exercise their power as stockholders responsibly. Instead, these advocates for corporate social responsibility pretend that directors do not have to make stockholder welfare the sole end of corporate governance, within the limits of their legal discretion, under the law of the most important American jurisdiction—Delaware.[82]

Note that caustic word "pretend." As Strine suggested, despite the claims of various academics, shareholder value maximization is the core principle of corporate director and officer's fiduciary duties under the law.

Some pro-stakeholder capitalism commentators have tried to skirt that rule by arguing that the directors' fiduciary duty to the corporate entity encompasses a duty on directors to consider stakeholder interests when making corporate decision or, at least, allows them to do so.[83] Delaware law clearly rejects that position, as well. *North American Catholic Educational Programming Foundation, Inc. v. Gheewalla*, for example, held that "directors of Delaware corporations have 'the legal responsibility to manage the business of a corporation for the benefit of its shareholders owners [sic].' Accordingly, fiduciary duties are imposed upon the directors to regulate their conduct when they perform *that* function."[84]

Directors thus owe no fiduciary duties either directly or indirectly to employees,[85] communities, or most other stakeholders.[86] A very narrow exception is recognized by some courts, which have held that when the corporation is insolvent directors' fiduciary duties shift from shareholders to creditors.[87] Alternatively, some courts hold that creditors of an insolvent corporation may bring derivative suits on behalf of the corporate entity against directors or officers who breach fiduciary duties to the entity.[88]

Part I focuses on elaborating that summary of directors' fiduciary duties, which – as Strine's comments suggest – remains surprisingly controversial in some circles. As we shall see, however, there are also a host of other legal rules that require or, at least, incentivize corporate directors and managers to put shareholder interests first. Indeed, it's fair to say that you'd have to change almost all of corporate law in order to swap out shareholder value maximization in favor of stakeholder capitalism.

Part II turns to the question of why the Business Roundtable changed position. As we will see, there are good arguments and bad arguments for shareholder value maximization, just as there are good arguments and bad arguments for stakeholder capitalism.[89] As one engages those arguments, the words of Qoheleth inevitably come to mind; that is, there is "nothing is new under the sun. Even the thing of which we say, 'See, this is new!' has already existed in the ages that preceded us."[90] Indeed, it seems as though every generation of scholars feels obliged to contribute to the debate, even though many are simply reiterating points that go back to the Berle–Dodd debate in the 1930s.[91] Although our analysis inevitably must allude to that history, I do not propose to burden the reader with a blow-by-blow description of 100 years of arguments by legal scholars, business ethicists, corporate leaders, and the others who have been engaged in the debate.[92] Instead, although that history is far from irrelevant, I focus mainly on the set of recent developments that occasioned the need for this book. All of which leads to a final question; namely, whether the Business Roundtable CEOs really meant what they said or whether the statement was just talk?

The analysis proceeds in three stages. First is the question of whether there is a justification for the Business Roundtable's change of position. Chapter 7 tackles the main policy arguments in favor of stakeholder capitalism. Chapter 8 asks whether the empirical evidence makes a business case for stakeholder capitalism. Both chapters conclude that the affirmative case for stakeholder capitalism is seriously flawed. If theory and evidence do not support the Business Roundtable's change of position, why did the signatory CEOs approve it? Chapter 9 speculates as to their possible motivations. Finally, Chapter 10 argues that the Business Roundtable CEOs should have stuck with their prior positions.

1.6 A NOTE

In the corporate purpose literature, terms such as social justice, socially responsible, or social responsibility typically connote support for progressive positions on a wide range of social and political issues. To say that a corporation is socially responsible is thus typically understood to mean that the corporation embraces progressive positions on issues such as climate change. In contrast, companies that embrace right-of-center positions on such issues will be deemed socially irresponsible. Herein I use the terms in their conventional sense without necessarily intending to convey approval of certain policies as responsible or irresponsible.

PART I

The Law

1

The Battle of River Rouge

The Ford Motor Company (FMC) was incorporated in 1903. It was hugely success-ful almost from the outset. By the time the 1916 fiscal year ended, FMC was earning almost $60 million on annual sales of $207 million. In just thirteen years, it had accumulated a surplus of $112 million, even while paying out $41 million in special dividends on top of regular quarterly dividends "equal to 5 per cent monthly on the capital stock of $2,000,000."[1]

FMC's financial success came despite – or, as some have argued, because of – pursuing policies that today might well be regarded as socially responsible. In 1914, FMC raised its shop floor employees' minimum pay to $5 per day, which was twice the going rate for industrial workers.[2] FMC claimed that the new pay rate was intended to give employees a stake in the business. Indeed, it characterized half of the new pay packet not as wages but as a share of company profits. In addition to the increased daily pay, FMC cut the working day from nine to eight hours. These new policies infuriated the business community, while drawing praise from some surprised social reformers.

As far as customers were concerned, FMC benefited that critical constituency by consistently lowering prices. In 1910, for example, it cut the Model T's price from $950 to $780. Further cuts followed annually, with the price dropping to $360 per car by 1916.[3] Not surprisingly, customers flocked to FMC. It was working at full capacity and selling cars as fast as it could make them.

The driving force behind all of these dramatic developments was Henry Ford, who was FMC's largest shareholder (owning 59 percent of the stock), a director, and president of the company. The other shareholders included the Dodge brothers – John and Horace – who each owned 5 percent of FMC's stock. In addition to being investors, the Dodge brothers were also suppliers, as FMC outsourced the making of its cars' engines to the Dodge's machinery company. In 1913, the Dodge brothers also became competitors, as they founded their eponymous automobile manufac-turing company, using the massive dividends they received on their FMC shares to help get Dodge Motor off the ground.[4]

In October 1915, FMC stopped paying the special dividends. Instead, FMC plowed the bulk of its earnings back into the business. As a result, by the end of the 1916 fiscal year, FMC had accumulated over $52 million in cash (out of total assets of $132 million). Ford announced that the accumulating cash would be used to further reduce the price of the company's cars and to construct a new plant at River Rouge, Michigan, which would be the world's largest auto factory.

In response, the Dodge brothers sued. They sought an injunction forbidding FMC from undertaking the River Rouge expansion and compelling FMC to issue a special dividend out of its accumulated earnings. The trial court granted both requests, ordering FMC to pay half of its cash assets out as a dividend. Ford and the other defendants appealed.

1.1 THE HISTORICAL CONTEXT

Although there were a few recognizably modern business corporations in Colonial America, they remained rare until the late 1700s. Into the early 1800s, moreover, most business corporations in the US were actually quasi-public works such as canals and turnpikes.[5] Almost all early corporations thus served public interests beyond making a profit for their shareholders.

The public-regarding nature of these early corporations was reinforced by the moral climate and social structures within which they operated. The owners of these businesses often were leaders of the local communities their businesses served. Many of these owners believed that noblesse oblige was the order of the day.[6]

Early American society was not prepared to trust the goodwill of corporate share-holders and directors, however. At that time, forming a corporation required obtaining a charter from the state legislature. This requirement likely reflected the 'cloud of disfavor under which corporations labored' in the early years of this Nation,[7] which was driven by fear of "the evils attendant upon the free and unrestricted use of the corporate mechanism."[8]

Supreme Court Justice Louis Brandeis claimed that, as a consequence of this fear, state legislatures granted charters only when "necessary in order to procure for the community some specific benefit otherwise unattainable."[9] If Brandeis intended to suggest that an explicit commitment to social welfare was legally required in order to obtain a legislative charter, there is no evidence of such a requirement.[10] If all Brandeis meant was there was an expectation that corporations have a public-regarding purpose, however, there is some evidence of such an expectation at least up until the 1830s. In the famed *Dartmouth College* case, for example, Chief Justice John Marshall observed that states created corporations to accomplish such "objects … as the government wishes to promote."[11] The "advantages to the public" that followed from granting a charter constituted the sole consideration to which the state was entitled.[12]

In any case, after New York in 1811 adopted the first modern enabling corpora-tion statute – pursuant to which one may form a corporation simply by filing the appropriate paperwork with the requisite state agency – special legislative chartering quickly fell by the wayside. The considerably greater ease of incorporating a business provided by the new enabling statutes facilitated a vast increase in the number of corporations in the US during the nineteenth century. More importantly, the nature of corporations drastically changed. Instead of being quasi-public enterprises, the vast majority of corporations were now recognizably modern business corporations devoted primarily to the private pursuit of profit. Corporations were mainly engaged in manufacturing or finance rather than the turnpikes, canals, and so on of late eighteenth- and early nineteenth-century corporations. Many rivaled today's large business corporations in size and influence:

> Before the 1880s, even the largest factories employed no more than a few hundred workers, and even these larger enterprises were still predominately family-owned. By contrast, the business corporation of the latter half of the nineteenth century grew in size and complexity. Each of the large railroads employed more than 100,000 workers by 1890 and the common stock of many of the largest corporations was publicly traded. The single-plant, one-function enterprise was replaced by a multifaceted and vertically integrated operation spread over several locations, often in different states.... Corporations were becoming "large-scale, hierarchical business enterprises."[3]

These developments fundamentally changed the relationship between society and incorporated businesses. Indeed, by the middle part of the nineteenth century, the law recognized that the rationale of existence for business corporations was private profit rather than public benefit.[14] The issue posed by *Dodge* was how to operationalize that recognition. Did the fiduciary duties of corporate directors and officers make the pursuit of private profit mandatory or merely permissive?

1.2 WAS THERE A BUSINESS CASE FOR FORD'S PLANS AND POLICIES?

What is rather curious about *Dodge* is the way in which Ford eschewed what likely would have been a winning argument. Consider, for example, Ford's policy of steady reductions in the Model T's price. FMC's profit per car fell, but dramatically increased sales volume more than made up the difference. As Ford himself observed, every time he cut the price by a dollar, he gained "a thousand new buyers."[15] FMC's share of the new car market in fact rose from 9.7 percent in 1909 to 42.4 percent in 1917, before eventually peaking at 55.7 percent in 1921.[16] As a result, FMC achieved nearly monopoly status in the inexpensive car market sector.[17] Granted, customers might have wanted more variety, such as the ability to buy a car in a color other than black – the provision of which eventually allowed General Motors to catch FMC – but Ford had turned the automobile from an expensive hobby for the rich into everyday transportation for the masses.

As for employees, there was likewise a business case to made for FMC's treatment of its workers. Ford was one of the early adopters of so-called scientific management.

As popularized by management theorist Frederick W. Taylor, scientific management had three core principles: (1) distilling of craft knowledge into work rules
taught to employees; (2) advance planning of worker schedules by management;
and (3) eliminating of the need for thinking by workers.[18] These principles were
implemented by industrial engineers and management experts, who broke down
a given production process into a large number of small steps, each allocated to
a single worker who was closely supervised. Thus was born the idea behind the
mass production assembly line. Ford's genius was turning that academic theory into
industrial practice.

As anyone who has ever worked on an assembly line knows, the work is repetitive,
often boring, and sometimes dangerous. The upshot was that FMC faced massive
problems with absenteeism and turnover. In 1914, for example, absenteeism was
such a problem that FMC had to maintain a workforce of 20,000 to ensure that the
necessary 10,000 workers would show up on any given day.[19] Both the higher pay
and its structure were intended to discourage absenteeism and turnover. In addition
to providing pay so high that workers who lost their job would not be able to replace
their lost income, the profit-sharing aspect of the pay structure gave workers a feel-
ing of ownership in the enterprise that further incentivized them. Not surprisingly,
the policies proved highly successful in reducing absenteeism, increasing employee
retention, and attracting new workers. Upon introduction, for example, the wage
plan slashed employee turnover from an annual rate of over 400 percent to 50 percent and, after just one year, to a mere 15 percent.[20]

Although some of Ford's fellow industrialists virulently objected to his new policies, fearing that it would lead the public to regard those who did not match his
new policies as greedy robber barons and promote worker unrest, his paternalistic
attitude toward his workers and customers was not wholly atypical of the era's corporate giants. Indeed, the phenomenon of industrial paternalism was an important
antecedent to the development of modern corporate social responsibility concepts.
In 1912, for example, US Steel provided a range of health insurance and pension
benefits to its employees.[21] Other corporations went even further by providing such
amenities as housing, recreational facilities, hospitals, and educational programs.
But while some leading industrialists thus "were keen on demonstrating their concern for their workers, and their commitment to improving their conditions," they
were not necessarily acting from altruistic motives but instead were often seeking
to stave off unionization and government regulation – a pattern we see recurring
frequently even up to today.[22]

Ford's policies with respect both to his customers and his employees, as well as his
plans for the River Rouge plant expansion, were no different. As Harvard corporate
law professor Mark Roe explains, the "$5/day wage, the company's pricing strategy
for its automobiles, and the River Rouge construction should be reinterpreted as
an uneasy labor-owner coalition that was splitting a monopoly profit and aiming to
keep that monopoly, both for Ford Motor's owners and its employees."[23] Smaller

competitors could not match FMC's new pay scale, which limited their ability to compete with Ford. The proposed plant expansion would give FMC significant economies of scale, which its smaller competitors could not achieve, further enhancing Ford's competitive position. Cutting the dividend would put less money in the Dodge brothers' pockets, thereby undermining one potentially important competitor. As Roe points out, however, "Ford could not have built and kept that monopoly unless he had sufficient labor peace, with the $5/day wage being his main way to achieve it."[24] Lastly, in addition to maximizing FMC's market dominance, the plan helped stave off efforts to unionize FMC's workforce.[25] The Industrial Workers of the World was trying to unionize the automotive industry, including both manufacturers like FMC and their suppliers. Ford was notoriously antiunion and FMC developed a reputation for going to extreme lengths to fend off unions. The labor peace bought by Ford's policies thus was intended not only to reduce absenteeism and turnover, but also to discourage workers from unionizing.

1.2.1 *If Ford Had Made the Business Case, What Would the Court Have Said?*

If Ford had chosen to lay out the business case for his plans and policies, the court likely would have approved. Indeed, there was well-established case law at the time permitting employer concern with employee welfare. As the 1909 New York decision in *Metropolitan Life Insurance Co. v. Hotchkiss* explained,[26] however, the law did not permit unfettered business altruism. Corporate expenditures for the benefit of employees could be challenged if they were "shown to be wasteful of the company's money and unproductive of beneficial results."[27] As such, expenditures for the benefit of employees were "not to be defended upon the ground of gratuity or charity, but [because they] were a part of the inducement for the employee to enter the employment and serve faithfully for the wage agreed upon."[28] If Ford had framed his defense on these lines, "he undoubtedly would have won."[29] As we have seen, the pay raise and other benefits were all intended to attract and retain high quality employees.

1.2.2 *Ford Declines to Make the Business Case*

In testifying at trial in *Dodge*, Ford did not make the business case for his plans and policies. Instead, he defiantly expressed "the attitude towards [FMC's] shareholders of one who has dispensed and distributed to them large gains and that they should be content to take what he chooses to give."[30] His stated ambition was not to increase profits, which he supposedly thought were already excessive and therefore should be shared "with the public," but rather "to employ still more men, to spread the benefits of this industrial system to the greatest possible number, to help them build up their lives and their homes."[31] In sum, his stated goal was to do "as much good as we can, everywhere, for everybody concerned … [a]nd incidentally to make money."[32] Whether his testimony was sincere or was part of a disingenuous effort to persuade his workers and customers that FMC was a socially responsible business rather than a union-busting quasi-monopoly remains the subject of debate.

1.3 THE OPINION

Much of the Michigan Supreme Court's opinion is devoted to a rather long and somewhat tedious recitation of the facts of the dispute, most of which were relevant mainly to the dispute about payment of dividends. As to the dividend issue, one of the Dodge brothers' arguments relied on a provision in the Michigan corporation statute limiting the total authorized capital stock of the corporation to $50 million. According to the Dodge brothers, although the authorized capital stock in FMC's articles of incorporation was $2 million, Ford's policy of retaining and accumulating earnings had increased FMC's "capital" to over $60 million.

As the Michigan Supreme Court recognized, the term "capital stock" as used in the statutory provision on which the Dodge brothers relied meant the total value of the money, property, or other assets the shareholders had agreed to contribute to the company in return for their shares. Unlike most other states, Michigan law at the time limited the amount shareholders could contribute to the company as start-up capital. As the court interpreted the statute, however, the cap did not apply to "the value of assets – capital – which may be" accumulated as a result of profitable earnings. FMC's accumulation of net assets exceeding $60 million thus did not violate the statutory limitation.[33]

This may seem like a minor point of legal capital arcana, which deals with an esoteric legal limitation that was rare at the time and was repealed a century ago.[34] It is relevant for our purposes, however, because the court's conclusion that the statute did not apply to post-incorporation retained earnings rested on an assumption that while "the Legislature looked with disfavor upon an initial aggregation of capital exceeding a certain amount," the Legislature did not look "with disfavor upon a profitable corporate existence."[35] This assumption rested on the court's belief that the purpose of a corporation is making profits, which may be retained and used to grow the business. The discussion thus foreshadowed the critical holding to follow.

The Michigan Supreme Court then disposed of a number of makeweight arguments advanced by the Dodge brothers. It concluded, for example, that vertical integration of the business was not *ultra vires*. FMC may have been organized to manufacture automobiles, but that did not limit FMC to assembling parts made by others or even to making and assembling its own parts. Instead, manufacturing might include not just processing raw materials into parts but also owning and operating the sources of the raw materials.[36] The ruling could not have surprised anyone, since the Dodge brothers had not seriously pressed the point on appeal, but it was significant because it preserved the possibility that Ford's expansion plans would survive judicial review.

Finally, after fourteen pages of preliminary throat clearing, the Michigan Supreme Court came to the meat of the case. The court began with the question whether the trial court had erred in ordering FMC to reinstate the former dividend policy. As the court acknowledged, the decision whether to pay a dividend was vested in the board of directors. If the directors chose to retain earnings and reinvest them in growing the business, the shareholders generally had no legal recourse. A court will only intervene to compel payment of a dividend if the complaining shareholders can prove that the directors' refusal to pay one amounted to an abuse of discretion.[37]

Noting that Ford was "the dominant force" in FMC's business, the Michigan Supreme Court pointed to multiple statements by Ford conveying an impression that he had an "attitude towards shareholders of one who has dispensed and distributed to them large gains and that they should be content to take what he chooses to give."[38] The Michigan Supreme Court further surmised from Ford's statements "that he thinks the Ford Motor Company has made too much money, has had too large profits, and that, although large profits might be still earned, a sharing of them with the public, by reducing the price of the output of the company, ought to be undertaken."[39]

Although there is some reason to think Ford's embrace of social responsibility was disingenuous,[40] the Michigan Supreme Court took him at his word:

> A business corporation is organized and carried on primarily for the profit of the stockholders. The powers of the directors are to be employed for that end. The discretion of directors is to be exercised in the choice of means to attain that end, and does not extend to a change in the end itself, to the reduction of profits, or to the nondistribution of profits among stockholders in order to devote them to other purposes.[41]

Consequently, the court explained, "it is not within the lawful powers of a board of directors to shape and conduct the affairs of a corporation for the merely incidental benefit of shareholders and for the primary purpose of benefiting others, and no one will contend that, if the avowed purpose of the defendant directors was to sacrifice the interests of shareholders, it would not be the duty of the courts to interfere."[42] As we will see in Chapter 4, while this was not the birth of the shareholder value maximization norm, it was a clarion call that echoed down through the decades that followed.

Dodge should not be read as requiring corporate directors to behave like Scrooges focused exclusively on short-term profits. The Michigan Supreme Court acknowledged that directors should be free to plan for the long term, recognizing "that plans must often be made for a long future, for expected competition, for a continuing as well as an immediately profitable venture."[43] Likewise, the Michigan Supreme Court further acknowledged that directors had discretion to set the "details of business, including the wages which shall be paid to employees, the number of hours they shall work, the conditions under which labor shall be carried on, and the price for which products shall be offered to the public."[44] Accordingly, the Michigan Supreme Court drew what it called an "obvious" distinction between "an incidental humanitarian expenditure of corporate funds for the benefit of the employees, like the building of a hospital for their use and the employment of agencies for the betterment of their condition," which would be permissible, "and a general purpose and plan to benefit mankind at the expense of others...."[45] Ford lost because he claimed to have embraced the latter.

Turning to the Dodge brothers' requested relief, the Michigan Supreme Court agreed with the trial court that the dividends should be resumed. As we just saw, it was a well-established principle that the decision whether to pay a dividend or not was one for the board of directors to make, as to which the board was "at liberty to exercise a very liberal discretion."[46] As long as the board made its decision in good faith, its decision was "final, and not subject to judicial revision," even if the decision proved to be "injudicious."[47] Courts therefore would not compel an unwilling board to pay a dividend unless the board's failure to do so was an abuse of discretion amounting to "an arbitrary refusal to do what the circumstances required to be done."[48] On the facts before it, given FMC's substantial profits and rapidly growing reserves, coupled with Ford's alleged effort to turn FMC into what the Dodge brothers called a "semi-eleemosynary institution," the Michigan Supreme Court affirmed the trial court's order that FMC resume paying special dividends.

On the other hand, however, the Michigan Supreme Court reversed the trial court's injunction against FMC's expansion plans. The Michigan Supreme Court explained its reticence by observing that "judges are not business experts."[49] In contrast, as the court further observed, FMC's successes were evidence of "capable management of its affairs."[50] The court's ruling thus operationalized its observation that, so long as the directors are exercising their discretion so as to maximize shareholder value, courts will defer to the board rather than evaluating the merits of the board's decision. Directors have wide discretion to make business plans, develop long-term strategies, set prices, and determine employee working conditions, pay, and benefits, as long as they claim to be doing so in the name of shareholder value rather than stakeholder capitalism.

Although the Michigan Supreme Court did not use the phrase, its analysis strongly suggests that it was invoking the business judgment rule.[51] The business judgment rule was at least a century old when *Dodge* was decided.[52] Under it, as an 1847 Alabama decision explained, directors could not be held liable for errors of judgment, "unless the error be of the grossest kind."[53] Accordingly, courts would defer to the judgment of the directors unless a complaining shareholder could show something beyond mere negligence, such as fraud or self-dealing on the directors' part.[54] Subsequent courts fleshed out the rule, explaining that "directors' decisions will be respected by courts unless" the plaintiff can show that "the directors are interested or lack independence relative to the decision, do not act in good faith, act in a manner that cannot be attributed to a rational business purpose or reach their decision by a grossly negligent process that includes the failure to consider all material facts reasonably available."[55] In the specific context of disputes over corporate purpose, Chancellor William Chandler of the Delaware Chancery Court explained that:

> When director decisions are reviewed under the business judgment rule, this Court will not question rational judgments about how promoting non-stockholder interests – be it through making a charitable contribution, paying employees higher salaries and benefits, or more general norms like promoting a particular corporate culture – ultimately promote stockholder value. In adopting a business judgment rule-based approach to reviewing board decisions, *Dodge* thus set a critical precedent that continues to define the extent to which directors who depart from shareholder value maximization face personal liability to shareholders or the entity.[56]

1.4 THE AFTERMATH

Ford complied with the court's dividend ruling, causing FMC to pay out $19 million in dividends. But the Michigan Supreme Court's refusal to issue the injunction against the River Rouge plant expansion basically put the kibosh on the Dodge brothers' effort to stymie Ford's plans to dramatically increase FMC's market share by cutting car prices while greatly boosting output. Although Ford probably had not intended at the outset to squeeze out the Dodge brothers, the litigation and prospect of competition from the brothers left Ford fed up with dealing with them and the other minority shareholders. Using a combination of threats and various complex legal machinations, Ford persuaded first the Dodge brothers and then the other shareholders to sell their shares to a Ford-controlled entity at a price quite favorable to Ford.[57]

Having fended off the Dodge brother's efforts to block his construction plans, Ford was able to go forward with building the River Rouge plant. Construction had begun in 1917 and, with the litigation resolved and the objecting shareholders bought out, the plant was finally finished in 1928. When completed it was – and, by some accounts, still is – the largest manufacturing facility in the world. The plant had both rail and water transportation links, its own power plant and steel mill, and thus was one of the most thoroughly vertically integrated manufacturing facilities ever built. At its peak, it employed 100,000 workers and made 4,000 cars a day.[58]

During the Second World War River Rouge was one of the most important armament factories on the Allied side, churning out jeeps, trucks, aircraft engines and components, and armor plate among other essential items. The core Dearborn Assembly plant that had begun producing Model A cars in 1927 was closed in 2004 when it was producing Mustangs. Although that assembly plant was torn down in 2008, the larger River Rouge facility has been transformed into a FMC-dominated industrial park with 6 factories producing F-150 trucks.

On the other hand, the River Rouge project failed to perpetuate FMC's dominant market share. Distributing the court-mandated dividend, buying out the Dodge brothers, paying above-market wages to his employees, and building the River

Rouge plant collectively generated serious cash flow problems for FMC, which were compounded by a business downturn in the early 1920s. Meanwhile, FMC's competitors – especially General Motors – adopted a strategy of offering consumers a choice of models at various price points and coming in more colors than FMC's proverbial black. By 1929, General Motors had overtaken Ford as the largest automobile manufacturer.

2

Fireplug Funding for Princeton

World War II worked dramatic changes in American business. The surge in economic output generated by the need to meet wartime production requirements restored business confidence and profits, which had suffered so severely during the Depression. Patriotism and social solidarity in the face of existential threats "loosened company pursestrings and quickened corporate consciences."[1]

In the aftermath of the war, as returning veterans began rising through the corporate ranks, business was booming and, yet, fearful. On the domestic front, the Truman administration's "Fair Deal" policies continued and even extended Franklin Roosevelt's New Deal regulatory restrictions on private enterprise. Surprisingly little in the way of regulatory relief was forthcoming when the Eisenhower administration took office. To the contrary, Eisenhower largely accepted and solidified the New Deal settlement.[2]

Turning to the global scene, communism appeared to pose an existential threat to democratic capitalism. As a result, business was at least as vulnerable to the Red Scare of the 1950s than any other segment of society. Inevitably, business responded by expanding its social horizons and accepting the need for engagement with society, in hopes doing so would build support for democracy and capitalism.

Taken together, these developments caused many business leaders to reevaluate "the nature and extent of corporate interest in community problems" that "previously had received only casual attention."[3] Education was an early beneficiary of this new engagement. As business became a specialist occupation, higher education became an essential part of the preparation of new generations of business leaders. But business was also dependent on science and engineering education and research, which made supporting efforts in those areas appear highly desirable if not essential. Conversely, the post-war surge in college and university enrollment forced institutions of higher education to seek out substantial new funding sources. The result was a "new alliance" between the presidents of corporations and universities.[4]

The alliance included such prominent executives as Frank Abrams of Standard Oil (New Jersey), Irving Olds of U.S. Steel, and Alfred Sloan of General Motors. Their stamp of approval gave emergent corporate social responsibility concerns a

37

legitimacy they might otherwise have lacked. Among other things, it gave cover for business associations like the National Association of Manufacturers (NAM) to embrace the new concern for supporting education.[5]

There was a fly in the ointment, however. Although individual philanthropy by wealthy business owners such as Ford had existed for decades, if not even longer, what the business community now wanted was corporate philanthropy. The question thus arose as to whether business executives could justify to themselves and their shareholders using corporate resources to make "gifts to institutions which, at first glance, seemed remote from the direct interests of profit-making concerns."[6] Was corporate philanthropy lawful?

2.1 THE HISTORICAL CONTEXT

Although questions about corporate philanthropy and corporate social responsibility more broadly seemed particularly pressing to the business community of the 1950s, they were not new questions. Big business suffered from periodic attacks in the late nineteenth and early twentieth centuries from populists of both the right and left, as well as members of the early twentieth century Progressive movement. By the 1920s, corporate executives were beginning to embrace so-called managerial capitalism, which included evaluating the relationship between businesses and the communities in which they functioned.[7] Inevitably, the 1929 stock market crash and the Depression that followed generated a social and intellectual ferment in which the emergent question of corporate purpose came to a head.

2.1.1 *The Berle–Dodd Debate*

A key moment in the debate over corporate social responsibility was the famous exchange between law professors Adolf Berle and E. Merrick Dodd in the early 1930s.[8] Both Berle and Dodd thought that corporate managers should be viewed as akin to trustees, with the question that divided them being for whose benefit the managers should use their powers.[9] Although his policy views evolved over time, Berle throughout his career was concerned that too much power was being concentrated in the hands of those who ran large corporations.[10] Accordingly, constraining managerial power was a consistent theme of his thinking, even as his views as to how that could best be accomplished changed with changing circumstances. In his 1930s debate with Dodd, which is the period of Berle's career with which we are most concerned, he focused on constraining management power by imposing a fiduciary duty on managers to run the corporation in the best interests of the shareholders.[11]

Dodd concurred with Berle's view that managers' power – especially their power to engage in self-dealing – needed to be constrained. But Dodd rejected "the view that business corporations exist for the sole purpose of making profits for their stockholders."[12] Dodd advanced several lines of argument in support of that claim. First, he contended that "managers ... may easily come to feel as strong a community of interest with their fellow workers as with a group of investors whose only connection with the enterprise is that they or their predecessors in title invested money in it, perhaps in the rather remote past."[13] As the reference to the potential antiquity of a company's equity capital suggests, Dodd's argument rested in large part on his belief that equity capital had diminished importance in the economy of his day. He asserted that "[s]ome of our most successful industrial corporations have for years obtained all the additional capital which they needed out of surplus profits without any further issue of securities."[14] Managers could thus downplay the interests of shareholders both because they had no need to raise equity capital and because the antiquity of equity capital's claims diluted the strength of their claim on the corporation's current earnings.

Second, Dodd believed that the very survival of capitalism itself depended on corporate managers assuming social responsibilities, especially with respect to the welfare of their workers. Recall the historical context of the debate. In 1932, communism had ruled the Soviet Union for almost fifteen years, Mussolini's fascists had been in power for a decade, and Hitler had forced Paul von Hindenburg into a runoff in the German presidential election and the Nazis had become the largest party in the Reichstag. At home in the United States, the Depression was in its third year, unemployment reached 24 percent, and the Bonus Army had marched on Washington. As with the subsequent Red Scare of the 1950s, there was a widely shared sense that capitalism was under siege by increasingly powerful forces. Against that background, it is hardly surprising that Dodd saw corporate social responsibility as necessary to preserve capitalism. Specifically, Dodd approvingly quoted from a speech by the then Dean of the Harvard business school in which the latter posited that defending capitalism required corporate leaders to accept corporate social responsibility and thereby meet "the sound needs of the great majority of our people. Such leadership will seek to form constructive plans framed not in the interest of capital or capitalism but in the interest of the American people as a whole."[15]

As Dodd observed, many business leaders of the period were prepared to show just such leadership:

> The view that those who manage our business corporations should concern themselves with the interests of employees, consumers, and the general public, as well as of the stockholders, is thus advanced today by persons whose position in the business world is such as to give them great power of influencing both business opinion and public opinion generally.[16]

Dodd expressly quoted pro-corporate social responsibility statements by such prominent figures as RCA chairman Owen D. Young and General Electric president Gerard Swope. The former in fact sounds a lot like our present day Business Roundtable CEOs: "One no longer feels the obligation to take from labor for the benefit of capital, nor to take from the public for the benefit of both, but rather to administer wisely and fairly in the interest of all."[17]

Ultimately, the corporate social responsibility debate was not resolved in the 1930s, as the New Dealers chose to focus their response to the Crash and the Depression on securities regulation rather than corporate governance. As we've seen, however, the debate came back into prominence in the postwar period. Many business leaders of the 1950s were prepared to pick up where Young and Swope had left off.

2.2 CONCOCTING A TEST CASE

What the 1950s business community wanted was a test case and NAM set out to provide one. Along with a key aide to Standard Oil's Abrams, NAM executives arranged for the A.P. Smith Manufacturing Company of New Jersey – a manufacturer "of valves, fire hydrants and special equipment, mainly for water and gas industries"[18] – to make a $1,500 gift to Princeton University's 1951 Annual Giving campaign. The Smith Company then sought a declaratory judgment against certain of its shareholders who purportedly argued that the contribution was a misappropriation of corporate funds and an *ultra vires* act. The Ford Foundation and Standard Oil financed the case's expenses.[19] As law professor Geoffrey Miller aptly concludes, "this was a collusive lawsuit brought and funded for the twin purposes of authorizing companies to make charitable gifts and encouraging them to make such gifts going forward."[20]

The putative defendants advanced two legal arguments against the donation. First, they claimed that under the common law corporations had no implied power to make charitable donations. Second, New Jersey statutes authorizing corporate philanthropy could not validly be applied to a corporation that had been incorporated before the statutes came into force. We'll take up those arguments in reverse order.

2.3 CORPORATE PHILANTHROPY STATUTES AND THE RESERVE CLAUSE

A 1930 New Jersey statute had expressly authorized corporations to make such charitable contributions "as the directors 'deem expedient and as in their judgment will contribute to the protection of the corporate interests.'"[21] Shareholders were entitled to notice of contributions in excess of 1 percent of the company's capital and shareholder approval would be required if the holders of 25 percent or more of the company's shares submitted written objections. In 1949, the statute was amended to raise the threshold at which shareholder notice was required to one percent of capital and surplus.

In 1950, a new statute was passed, which declared it to be the public policy of New Jersey that "encouragement be given to the creation and maintenance of institutions engaged in community fund, hospital, charitable, philanthropic, educational, scientific or benevolent activities or patriotic or civic activities conducive to the betterment of social and economic conditions ...."[22] The statute expressly empowered corporations acting "to contribute reasonable sums to such institutions, provided, however, that the contribution ... shall not exceed 1% of capital and surplus unless the excess is authorized by the stockholders at a regular or special meeting."[23]

These statutes alleviated concerns that corporate philanthropy was *ultra vires*. As we have seen, until relatively recently, corporate statutes imposed restrictions on the purposes for which corporations could be organized and the powers corporations were authorized to exercise. In addition, these statutes required that the articles of incorporation specify which of the permissible purposes the corporation was organized to achieve and which of the statutory powers it would exercise.[24] If a corporation exceeded the powers and purposes set forth in the statutes or the firm's articles, it was said to be acting *ultra vires*. An *ultra vires* act was illegal and, accordingly, null and void.[25] The responsible directors and officers could be held personally liable for any losses resulting from the action.[26]

It long was "the general rule that a gift of its property by a corporation not created for charitable purposes is in violation of the rights of its stockholders and is ultra vires, however worthy of encouragement or aid the object of the gift may be."[27] Statutes such as those adopted by New Jersey were intended to reverse that rule by expressly empowering corporations to make charitable contributions. As the *Smith Manufacturing* defendants' argument suggests, however, there long had been a debate as to whether new statutes applied retroactively to previously incorporated companies.

The question arose out of U.S. Chief Justice John Marshall's opinion in *Trustees of Dartmouth College v. Woodward*.[28] Marshall held that a corporation's charter was a contract between the state of incorporation and the company. As such, a subsequently adopted statute that would have imposed new requirements on the company violated the provision of the U.S. Constitution banning states from impairing contracts. In his concurrence, however, Justice Joseph Story had suggested states could end-run that limitation by including a reserve clause in articles of incorporation authorizing ex post statutes to apply retroactively.

As its sister states had done, New Jersey picked up on Justice Story's hint. In 1846, the state legislature adopted a statute providing that every corporate charter granted thereafter could be amended or altered at will by the legislature. A similar reserve power subsequently was incorporated into the state constitution. As a result, New Jersey courts "repeatedly recognized that where justified by the advancement of the public interest the reserved power may be invoked to sustain later charter alterations even though they affect contractual rights between the corporation and its stockholders and between stockholders Inter se."[29]

The *Smith Manufacturing* court had no difficulty concluding that the reserve power allowed the corporate philanthropy statutes to apply retroactively. In its view, New Jersey had "not only joined with other states in advancing the national interest but [had] also specially furthered the interests of its own people who must bear the burdens of taxation resulting from increased state and federal aid upon default in voluntary giving."[30] Because the court believed the philanthropy statutes thus advanced the public interest, they validated the donation at issue.

Today, like New Jersey, virtually all states have adopted statutes specifically granting corporations the power to make charitable donations, which eliminates the *ultra vires* issue.[31] Unlike the New Jersey statutes at issue in *Smith Manufacturing*, however, these statutes typically contain no express limit on the size of permissible gifts. But courts interpreting the statutes commonly require corporate charitable donations to be reasonable both as to the amount and the purpose for which they are given.[32] The federal corporate income tax code's limits on the deductibility of corporate charitable giving are often used by analogy by courts seeking guidance on whether a gift was reasonable in amount.

Harvard law professor Einer Elhauge contends that these statutes are evidence that state corporate law (importantly, including that of Delaware) suggest that directors have power to consider ESG factors in pursuit of stakeholder capitalism.[33] As Leo Strine observed, however, "the reality is that case law interpreting the [Delaware] statute further proves the [shareholder value maximization] rule: when approving contested charitable gifts, Delaware courts have emphasized that the stockholders would ultimately benefit from the gift in the long run."[34]

2.4 THE COMMON LAW AND A JUDICIAL CIVIC LESSON

Having determined that the contested donation was within the bounds imposed by the statutes and that those statutes validly applied to Smith Manufacturing, the New Jersey Supreme Court could have – and perhaps should have – stopped there. Anything it might have said about the common law would have been mere dicta.[35] Perhaps because this would have obviated the need for the court to provide a civics lesson on the importance of corporate social responsibility, the court went out of its way to suggest that the New Jersey statutes "simply constitute helpful and confirmatory declarations" of directors' common law powers.[36]

The court began its analysis with a brief recounting of the history we traced in the Introduction. When the US was young and corporations were small, most companies had an at least quasi-public purpose. Over time, however, "the end of private profit became generally accepted as the controlling one in all businesses other than those classed broadly as public utilities."[37] With that understanding of the corporate purpose well established, the common law adopted the rule that corporate philanthropy was permissible only where the contribution demonstrably benefited the corporation.

In the court's opinion, the growth of corporations and changed social circumstances required revisiting the common law rule. The public increasingly supported corporate philanthropy. Various captains of industry, law, and the academy had testified at trial that society expected corporations to support charitable entities and that institutions of higher education were especially deserving of support because they trained future generations of business leaders. The court embraced those views, concluding that corporations should "assume the modern obligations of good citizenship in the same manner as humans do."[38]

In addition, as my colleague Adam Winkler explained, the court invoked the Red Scare in hyperbolic terms to justify its holding.[39] The court posited that, despite the nation's victories in two world wars, "we are faced with other, though nonetheless vicious, threats from abroad which must be withstood without impairing the vigor of our democratic institutions at home and that otherwise victory will be pyrrhic indeed."[40] Accordingly, the court concluded that "our democracy and the system of free enterprise" would be endangered if corporations were unable to support Princeton and its ilk.[41] After all, as the President of Princeton testified, "democratic society will not long endure if it does not nourish within itself strong centers of non-governmental fountains of knowledge ...."[42]

2.5 DID *SMITH MANUFACTURING* REJECT *DODGE*?

Some commentators have gone so far as to describe *Smith Manufacturing* as a "watershed case" that actually requires "corporate directors to consider more than the interests of shareholders when making decisions."[43] Even commentators who did not go that far regarded the decision as clearing the way for corporate social concern.[44] No less a commentator than Adolf Berle – who had filed an amicus brief in *Smith Manufacturing* supporting the defendants – conceded in 1954 that *Smith Manufacturing* had settled his 1930s debate with E. Merrick Dodd "(at least for the time being) squarely in favor of Professor Dodd's contention."[*]

---

[*] ADOLF A. BERLE, THE 20ᵀᴴ CENTURY CAPITALIST REVOLUTION 169 (1954). Berle later qualified that statement by explaining that he had only intended to concede the descriptive question of "how social fact and judicial decisions turned out." Adolf A. Berle, Jr., *Foreword, in* THE CORPORATION IN MODERN SOCIETY xii (E. Mason ed. 1959). As far as the normative question of whether corporate powers should be regarded as being held in trust for stakeholders, however, Berle asserted that he continued to disagree with Dodd. *Id.*

Despite Berle's 1954 statements, Professors Bratton and Wachter point out that the final chapter of Berle's 1932 book, *The Modern Corporation and Private Property*, argued that "since the shareholders had given up responsibility for corporate property, other constituents should join them as corporate beneficiaries ...." *See* William W. Bratton & Michael L. Wachter, *Tracking Berle's Footsteps: The Trail of the Modern Corporation's Last Chapter*, 33 SEATTLE U.L. REV. 849, 850 (2010). Professors Bratton and Wachter argue that the apparent conflict in Berle's views should be understood as reflecting the evolution of his political views from the pre-Great Crash 1920s to his involvement in the New Deal of the early 1930s. *Id.* at 850. By the 1930s, they contend, Berle had embraced a corporatist view of politics and the economy in which government developed policy in consultation with business, unions, and other major social groups. Once a consensus as to the public good was reached, business was expected to adapt to it. In this model, managers were technocrats operating the corporation so as to maximize social policies rather than shareholder profit. Berle's views continued to evolve during the 1930s and 1940s. Even so, however, he continued to view managers as

It is certainly true that *Smith Manufacturing* embraced Dodd's contributions to that debate. The court, for example, cited Dodd for the proposition that "corporations may properly support charities which are important to the welfare of the communities where they do business …."[45] The court also cited Dodd for the proposition that "the end of private profit became generally accepted as the controlling one in all businesses other than those classed broadly as public utilities."[46]

In reality, however, *Smith Manufacturing* decided very little. First, the corporate social responsibility discourse is entirely dicta. The real issue in the case was whether the reserve clause validly allowed the relevant statutes to be applied retroactively. The court's affirmative answer to that question resolved any lingering doubts about the validity of corporate philanthropy, but it hardly stands for the broader proposition that *Dodge* was no longer the law:

> An exception on the fringe of a rule, such as the ability of a board of directors to engage in minor acts of social philanthropy with corporate assets, does not vitiate the rule. Just as a board that donates a small amount of corporate profits to, say, a local school, can do so without fear of claims it has breached its duties, a board that managed the corporation in a way that favored giving to local schools over producing returns for shareholders would most certainly run afoul of the applicable corporate law statute of its jurisdiction of incorporation.[47]

Second, one can readily reconcile the result in *Smith Manufacturing* with that of the *Dodge* court's resolution of the plant expansion aspect of the latter case. Most commentators concede that charitable philanthropy generates public good will toward the corporation, which in the long-term benefits shareholders in the form of increased profits.[48] Indeed, "corporate managers and fundraisers agree that corporate transfers to charity represent a calculated purchase of advertising services or goodwill."[49] No less a figure than Smith Manufacturing's President Hubert F. O'Brien embraced that view, arguing that the company's donation to Princeton generated good will in the community. As to the specific donation in question, O'Brien further opined that well-funded institutions of higher learning were necessary to ensure a continuous flow of capable and well-educated managerial employees. Accordingly, the legality "of charitable giving may [simply] indicate a broadening of acceptable means used to earn profits or an elongation of the time frame in which a court evaluates corporate activity, all with the ultimate goal of earning profits for shareholders."[50] The decision to engage in corporate philanthropy is thus a business decision differing little from any other decision entrusted to the board of directors and, accordingly, is just as entitled to the protections of the business judgment rule as any other business decision.[51]

---

a sort of quasi-civil servant. *Id.* at 862. They therefore claim that Berle assumed that corporations would continue to function within a highly regulated state that would demand corporations serve the public interest. Although their analysis is of considerable historical interest, for our purposes whether Berle changed his mind or not affects only whether we can rely on his views to make what rhetoricians call an argument from authority.

A final objection to *Smith Manufacturing*'s status as a watershed validation of corporate social responsibility arises out of its origin as a test case. As Professor Miller observes:

> In the name of combating threats to American political institutions, the New Jersey courts participated in a subversion of one of the most important of such institutions, the adversarial lawsuit. Fearing Stalin's disrespect for truth and suppression of dissent, they conducted a show trial worthy of the most cynical of apparatchiks. Witnesses with obvious conflicts of interest and questionable credentials were enlisted to support dubious assertions about social policy and historical change. Overall, the opinion can be seen as a sorry spectacle.[52]

To be sure, as Miller further observes, some might find such chicanery justified because it "arguably contributed to beneficial results – not the defeat of communism, but the freeing up of corporations to make gifts to worthy institutions in the spirit of public service."[53] Extending *Smith Manufacturing* to corporate social responsibility, however, stretches the proposition that ends justify the means beyond any reasonable limits.

3

Why Didn't the Cubs Have to Play Night Baseball?

Dodge is the leading example of what have been called confessional cases, in which the dominant manager "admits that he is treating an interest other than stockholder wealth as an end in itself, rather than as an instrument to stockholder wealth."[1] In the more recent *eBay* case, for example, the defendant controlling shareholders lost because they admitted "that they personally believe craigslist should not be about the business of stockholder wealth maximization, now or in the future."[2] These are easy cases because if a fiduciary admits that he is treating an interest other than stockholder wealth as an end in itself, rather than an instrument to stockholder wealth, he is committing a breach of fiduciary duty.[3] But what happens when there is no such confession?

3.1 SHLENSKY'S FACTS

Baseball history – oddly enough – provides the answer. The Cincinnati Reds installed lights at Crosley Field in 1935 and are credited with beating the Philadelphia Phillies 2–1 on May 24, 1935 in Major League Baseball's first night game.[4] Night baseball radically changed baseball's economics, by making the game available to a much larger pool of potential spectators than those whose job or school situation allowed them to attend day games.[5] Although major league baseball nevertheless was surprisingly slow to transition to night baseball, by 1948 all but one major league team had installed lights in their home fields. The sole exception was the Chicago Cubs.

   Team owner Phillip K. Wrigley had declared in 1945 that the Cubs would be the "last outpost of 100 percent daytime baseball," arguing that "baseball is a daytime sport to be played in the sunshine."[6] Some twenty years later, in *Shlensky v. Wrigley*,[7] a plaintiff finally challenged Wrigley's refusal to install lights in Wrigley Field. William Shlensky was a minority shareholder in the corporation that owned the Chicago Cubs and operated Wrigley Field. Wrigley was the majority stockholder (owning 80 percent of the stock) and president of the company. In the relevant period, 1961–1965, the Cubs consistently lost money. Shlensky alleged that the losses were attributable to their poor home attendance. In turn, Shlensky alleged that the low attendance was attributable to Wrigley's refusal to permit installation of lights and night baseball. Shlensky contended Wrigley refused to institute night baseball because the latter believed that baseball was a day-time sport and that night baseball might have a negative impact on the neighborhood surrounding Wrigley Field. The other defendant directors allegedly were so dominated by Wrigley that they acquiesced in his policy of day-only baseball, which allegedly violated their duty of care.

Law professor Geoffrey Miller aptly compares the court's version of *Shlensky's* facts of to a 1991 Danny DeVito movie:

> The narrative in *Shlensky v. Wrigley* resonates with dramas such as *Other People's Money*, in which the proprietor of an old and established company resists the depredations of a cynical opportunist interested only in maximizing profits. In place of Jorgy Jorgenson, the crusty proprietor of New England Wire and Cable, we can substitute Philip K. Wrigley, son of the ball club's founder and dominating figure in the Cubs organization since 1932. Like Jorgenson, Wrigley seeks to protect values such as tradition and concern for neighbors, even at the expense of short-term profit. In place of Larry the Liquidator, the ruthless corporate raider, the narrative casts William Shlensky, the named plaintiff—a man who, like his movie counterpart, thinks in terms of profit and the bottom line, and who ignores the costs his actions might impose on others.[8]

To which Shlensky might have responded that it is one thing for a sole proprietor to decide that agapic love for his neighbors should be his guiding star in making business decisions. When such a proprietor chooses a less profitable course of conduct for altruistic reasons, he is in effect spending his own money. In contrast, when a corporate director or manager does so, he is spending someone else's money and therein lies a critical difference.

In any case, Miller acknowledges – although possibly with his tongue firmly wedged in his cheek – that "it would be rash to say that courts in Chicago decide cases on political grounds."[9] Having said that, however, Miller goes on to note that Shlensky was a young lawyer who owned only two shares of Cubs stock and was a political nobody. In contrast, P. K. Wrigley was a prominent, respected, and powerful figure on the Chicago scene. His decision against night baseball was very popular with the neighborhood. The politics of the case thus cut sharply in Wrigley's favor.

3.2 THE OPINION

Unlike *Dodge* where both plaintiffs and defendants were disingenuous about their motives or *Smith Manufacturing* where both sides colluded to create a test case, *Shlensky* was a real dispute. The defendants moved to dismiss for failure to state a claim, arguing "that the courts will not step in and interfere with honest business judgment of the directors unless there is a showing of fraud, illegality or conflict of interest."[10] The court agreed, citing cases from a number of states. In *Wheeler v.*

Pullman Iron & Steel Co., for example, the Illinois Supreme Court held that "courts of equity will not undertake to control the policy or business methods of a corporation, although it may be seen that a wiser policy might be adopted, and the business be more successful if other methods were pursued."[11] Likewise, the court cited a Delaware decision, *Davis v. Louisville Gas & Electric Co.*, for the proposition that it is not part of the judicial function to resolve disputes between controlling directors and shareholders over "questions of policy and business management. The directors are chosen to pass upon such questions and their judgment unless shown to be tainted with fraud is accepted as final."[12] Accordingly, "the authority of the directors in the conduct of the business of the corporation must be regarded as absolute when they act within the law, and the court is without authority to substitute its judgment for that of the directors."[13]

Like the Michigan Supreme Court's decision in *Dodge*, the Illinois court's opinion in *Shlensky* did not expressly use the term "business judgment rule." As with *Dodge*, however, it is widely accepted that the decision rests on that rule.[14] As explained by the *Shlensky* court, absent a showing of fraud, illegality, or conflict of interest, the court must abstain from reviewing the directors' decision.[15] Because Shlensky's complaint contained no particularized allegations of any such misconduct, the court granted the defendants' motion to dismiss, which is precisely what the business judgment rule requires.

The *Shlensky* court thus could have – and, perhaps, should have – dismissed plaintiff's claim without touching on the substantive merits of the defendants' decision or the motivation behind that decision. Curiously, however, the court took some pains to posit legitimate business reasons for that decision. In fact, there was a plausible argument for Wrigley's position. Unlike most modern stadiums, Wrigley Field is not located in some suburban site surrounded by acres of parking lots. Instead, it is an urban stadium that is well integrated into its surroundings. Wrigleyville was (and is) a walkable mix of shops, bars, and residences. Because Wrigley Field was built before cars became the dominant mode of transportation, there is very limited parking in the vicinity. Cubs fans who drive to a game thus end up parking on residential streets and alleys. Cub games thus impact the park's neighborhood in an almost uniquely major way. Fans who spent three hours at a baseball game imbibing refreshing adult beverages, possibly preceded or followed by hours in the bars surrounding the park, easily could be viewed as a serious blight on the neighborhood. The risk of hooliganism and vandalism presumably would be greater at night than in daylight. Indeed, when the Cubs finally installed lights in 1988, neighborhood concern about that risk generated sufficient opposition that forced the Cubs to agree to schedule just seven night games for that season and to stop alcohol sales at 9:20 PM.

Recall that the corporation owned not just the Cubs team but also Wrigley Field. In those days, when the reserve clause limited player salaries, the value of the real estate likely made up a considerable portion of the Cub's value. Preserving the quality of the neighborhood might well have been viewed as essential to maintaining the value of the corporation. Avoiding night games thus might have had a negative impact on the Cub's income statement while preserving its balance sheet shareholder equity.

The court likely was aware of such concerns, since it opined that "the effect on the surrounding neighborhood might well be considered by a director."[16] Likewise, the court asserted that "the long run interest" of the firm "might demand" consideration of the effect night baseball would have on the neighborhood.[17] Does this mean that courts will examine the substantive merits of a board decision? No. The court did not require defendants to show either that such considerations motivated their decisions or that the decision in fact benefited the corporation. To the contrary, the court acknowledged that its speculations in this regard were irrelevant dicta:

> By these thoughts we do not mean to say that we have decided that the decision of the directors was a correct one. That is beyond our jurisdiction and ability. We are merely saying that the decision is one properly before directors and the motives alleged in the amended complaint showed no fraud, illegality or conflict of interest in their making of that decision.[18]

Shlensky thus differs sharply from *Smith Manufacturing*. The Illinois court nowhere expresses an opinion about the impact of Wrigley's decision on the local community or other stakeholders. The focus is exclusively on judicial deference to director decisions so long as those decisions are not tainted by fraud, illegality, or self-dealing.

Instead, *Shlensky* offers a more developed version of the *Dodge* court's refusal to enjoin the River Rouge plant expansion. Recall that the *Dodge* court recognized that, while their end goal must be profit, a corporation's directors have "discretion [as to] the choice of means to attain that end ...."[19] *Shlensky* simply elaborates on that proposition by ensuring "that directors, when acting deliberately, in an informed way, and in the good faith pursuit of corporate interests, may follow a course designed to achieve long-term value even at the cost of immediate value maximization."[20]

4

Defending *Dodge*

Dodge v. Ford Motor Co. and "its statement of shareholder primacy have taken on lives of their own in law school casebooks, in the academic literature, and in the minds and hearts of American businesspeople."[1] Despite being over 100 years old, it remains the case, as law professor Adam Winkler observes, that "today nearly every law student reads the [*Dodge*] case and learns that, by law, a corporation exists to further the interests of stockholders, not the interests of employees, customers, or the larger community."[2] *Dodge* was not the genesis of that rule but it was the moment the rule took on its modern form.

At least in the recent academic legal literature, however, *Dodge*'s fame comes mainly from the vituperation with which progressive legal academics have damned it. The late legal scholar Lynn Stout took the academic critiques to their logical extreme in a book chapter arguing that corporate law teachers should simply stop teaching *Dodge*.[3] She subsequently expanded that article into a book, entitled *The Shareholder Value Myth*, which claimed the shareholder value maximization norm harms investors, stakeholders, and the public.[4] Stout's work has been described as "novel and provocative"[5] and offering "a compelling critique of the shareholder-centric view,"[6] which makes her work an invaluable foil for the analysis that follows.

Stout's critique of *Dodge* ranged widely across a number of arguments. Indeed, so much so that she was criticized for "conflating prospective policy arguments for replacing shareholder primacy with stakeholder theory with claims that stakeholder theory is, in fact, already the guiding principle."[7] In this Chapter, we take up her doctrinal arguments.[8] In the next Part, we will take up her normative arguments (as well as those of many other scholars).

4.1 IS *DODGE* MERE DICTA?

Stout contended that *Dodge*'s famous statement of shareholder value maximization was merely "an offhand remark" that can be dismissed as dicta.[9] Granted, Stout's position is not an outlier; to the contrary, many other critics have made the same argument.[10] But, as Yale law professor Jonathan Macey has explained, a close examination of the decision demonstrates "the shareholder maximization ideal actually drives the holding and is not mere dicta."[11] In addition to the structure and text of the opinion itself, efforts to dismiss *Dodge* as mere dicta flounder on the fact that the decision was a logical extension of legal trends of the time and was accepted almost immediately by both judges and scholars as a correct statement of the law of corporate purpose.

As we've seen, Henry Ford likely would have won the case if he had been willing to embrace profit maximization as the motivation for his decisions. As Professor Macey observes, the court expressly confirmed "that the issues in the case, including (but presumably not limited to) employee wages, working hours and conditions, and product pricing are at the discretion of the directors."[12] Accordingly, Macey argues, "what mattered in this case was not what Mr. Ford did, but what he said he was doing."[13] Ford therefore lost precisely because he repeatedly testified that he would not exercise that discretion "in the choice of means to" carry on the corporation's business affairs "primarily for the benefit of the stockholders."[14] The necessary holding of the case thus was that "it is not within the lawful powers of a board of directors to shape and conduct the affairs of a corporation for the merely incidental benefit of shareholders and for the primary purpose of benefiting others."[15]

Put another way, in order to compel FMC to pay the special dividend demanded by the Dodge Brothers, the Michigan Supreme Court had to hold that Ford and FMC's board abused their discretion by refusing to pay a dividend. In turn, to hold that the board had abused its discretion, the board had to conclude that the board was conducting FMC's business "for the merely incidental benefit of shareholders and for the primary purpose of benefitting others ...."[16] The conclusion that Ford had abandoned shareholder value maximization was thus essential to the result, which makes the court's statement of corporate purpose holding rather than dicta.[*]

4.1.1 Dodge's *Judicial Antecedents*

Turning to *Dodge*'s antecedents, although the case law from the 19th and early 20th Centuries is sparse, it is fair to say that *Dodge* did not spring fully formed and utterly original from the mind of the Michigan Supreme Court as Athena did from the mind of Zeus. Instead, it rested on principles that had been developing for some time. As even Merrick Dodd admitted in 1932, *Dodge* represented the orthodox understanding at that time of the law governing directors duties.[17]

---

[*] *Dodge*'s discussion of corporate purpose is thus distinguishable from *Smith Manufacturing*'s lecture on corporate social responsibility and the common law. As we saw in the preceding Chapter, the latter was demonstrably dicta. The legislature had expressly validated gifts of the sort Smith Manufacturing gave Princeton. The reserve power made the statute retroactively applicable to Smith Manufacturing. As such, adoption of the statute vitiated the need to address the common law, which made the court's musings on corporate social responsibility dicta. Having said that, however, we will see below that the holding/dicta dichotomy is less important than Professor Stout apparently believed.

As we saw in the Introduction, early enabling corporation codes typically required that the articles of incorporation set forth with specificity the purposes for which the corporation was organized and the powers it would utilize in pursuit of those purposes. If the corporate entity entered into a transaction for an unauthorized purpose or that required it to make use of an unauthorized power, the transaction was *ultra vires* and would be declared void. In a number of pre-*Dodge* cases, acts that today would be regarded as socially responsible were challenged as being *ultra vires*. In *Steinway v. Steinway & Sons*, for example, a late nineteenth century New York court held "that the acts of the trustees of Steinway & Sons in providing … for the physical, intellectual, and spiritual wants of their employés, under the circumstances of the case, were not *ultra vires*."[18] Although the court thus framed its analysis in terms of corporate powers and purposes, rather than fiduciary duties, it anticipated *Dodge's* view that while incidental expenditures to benefit employees were not impermissible the purpose of the corporation remains the benefit of the shareholders:[19]

> The corporation is and has been doing all that the court could require it to do in transmuting [expenditures for the benefit of employees] into money. The expenditures to which I have referred were advantageous to the property, such as at some time at least would have to be made, and tended to render the property salable.[20]

In 1922, a federal district court cited *Steinway* as supporting the court's view that corporate charitable donations to the University of Buffalo and Canisius College were not ultra vires but rather were within the corporation's power because the contributions tended to benefit the corporation. The court opined that the donations "would in all probability inure to the future advantage of the company to be able to secure employees trained and skilled in corporate business and industrial affairs," since both colleges had active business education programs.[21] In addition, the court recognized that public donations of this sort amounted to advertising that would generate considerable goodwill for the corporation. The latter was of particular concern in this instance because several of the corporation's competitors had made similar donations. Failing to match those contributions, the court explained, might result in the company losing prestige in the community.[*]

Conversely, however, an Illinois court of the same time period expressly held that corporate charitable contributions were *ultra vires*. The court found that the financial contribution by the First National Bank of Charleston to a local manufacturer for the alleged retention of further services within their city was not within the bank's incidental powers. To the contrary, the court held that the law presumed that

---

[*] An interesting wrinkle to the case is the court's observation that the board of directors and senior officers made their decision only "after full discussion as to the possible benefits to be derived by the corporation from their action." Armstrong Cork Co. v. H.A. Meldrum Co., 285 F. 58, 58 (W.D.N.Y. 1922). The court further noted that, in doing so, they "exercised their best judgment." *Id.* at 59. Such findings were not necessary to the court's decision, which turned solely on the *ultra vires* issue, but today would be highly relevant. Today, as we shall see, the case doubtless would be decided under the business judgment rule and, accordingly, whether the directors made an informed decision would be a critical issue.

such "donations are injurious to a bank and unwarrantable."[22] The court conceded that the retention of the manufacturer might generally benefit the city and therefore benefit the bank indirectly; however, the court reiterated that the funds could still only be used for the "strict furtherance of the business objects and financial prosperity" of the bank and that the bank's own "pecuniary interest will be advanced and directly forwarded cannot be assumed" in such cases of charitable contributions.[23]

As we also saw in the Introduction, the legal regime governing corporate purpose eventually segued from *ultra vires* to fiduciary duties of directors and officers. In *Raynolds v. Diamond Mills Paper Co.*,[24] a case involving facts quite similar to *Dodge*, a New Jersey court declined to compel payment of a dividend where the directors (and majority shareholders) were retaining earnings to finance a program of expansion. The minority shareholder alleged the directors' repeated decision to exclusively expand the business year after year without declaring a dividend left the shareholder without any claim to the increased value of the company. Although the court sympathized with the difficulty the minority shareholder faced with being unable to sell his shares to a publicly traded market given the nature of a closely held corporation, the court nonetheless stated it was a matter of common knowledge that to "enable the business to be prosecuted advantageously and with profit" it must expand.[25] Despite this knowledge, the court still limited the directors' ability to expand indefinitely without consideration to the stockholders. The court reminded the directors it could only retain profits and expand so long as it did the not lead to the "practical starvation of the stockholders."[26]

Accordingly, as with *Dodge*, the *Raynolds* court essentially invoked – albeit without naming it – the business judgment rule.[27] Having done so, however, the court emphasized that directors need "to bear in mind that the only sure benefit to stockholders to be derived from the successful prosecution of the corporate business must come from the distribution of dividends in cash ...."[28] The court's emphasis on shareholder value maximization was further reflected in its observation that "[t]he success of a great business or manufacturing corporation is measured by what the stockholders get, and not by mere accumulation of assets."[29]

Whether they relied on the *ultra vires* doctrine or fiduciary duty concepts, the net effect of such precedents was that as early as the 1850s legal treatise writers concluded that "[b]oth the property and the sole object of every such corporation are essentially private, and from them the individuals composing the company corporate are to derive profit."[30] *Dodge* was the logical culmination of these developments. "The purpose of the corporation was increasingly understood to be private and pecuniary, until in 1919, ... the Michigan Supreme Court famously declared, as if it had always been true, that '[a] business corporation is organized and carried on primarily for the profit of the stockholders.'"[31]

4.1.2 *A Digression on Anglo-American Law*

Although we are concerned herein with the development of the law in the United States, it is interesting to note that *Dodge* was consistent with the general trend of Anglo-American law. In *Hutton v. West Cork Ry. Co.*,[32] a case from the United Kingdom, for example, a railway corporation was preparing for dissolution and decided to pay – without legal obligation to do so – remuneration to its exiting directors. The court rejected this attempt at remuneration because the directors' decision did not pass its test of being "done within the ordinary scope of the company's business, and [being] reasonably incidental to the carrying on of the company's business for the company's benefit."[33] The court further explained, regardless of whether the remuneration attempt was laudable, that the "law doesn't say there are to be no cakes and ale, but that there are to be no cakes and ale except such as are required for the benefit of the company."[34] As law professor Robert Miller observes:

> *Hutton* even anticipates the more famous [Delaware Supreme Court] holding in *Revlon* that, once the board has decided to sell the company for cash, ... consideration of the interests of other corporate constituencies becomes impermissible, and the board must focus exclusively on maximizing value for shareholders. That is, in *Hutton*, because the company was winding up its affairs and was no longer a going concern, "the company was gone as a company carrying on business for the purpose of making profit," and so amounts not legally required to be paid to employees "could not be looked upon as an inducement to them to exert themselves in future, or as an act done reasonably for the purpose of getting the greatest profit from the business of the company," with the result that corporation could not make such payments.[35]

Professor Miller also notes two additional nineteenth century U.K. cases applying the rule that short-term deviations from profit maximization are permissible where they would redound to the shareholders' benefit via larger gains in the future.

A 1912 case from The High Court of Australia, *Miles v Sydney-Meat Preserving Co. Ltd*,[36] echoed this sentiment. In *Miles*, a shareholder sued the company for failure to declare a dividend and not acting in the interest of the shareholders given the company's policy of retaining profits to create a purchase price subsidy for their cattle suppliers. The court dismissed the claim on the grounds that the directors' considerations of the economic interests of their suppliers was actually advantageous to the shareholder and to the company's benefit and that "[t]his subsidy, then, has really enabled the company to do the things of which the plaintiff complains."[37]

4.1.3 *Contemporaneous Scholarly Comment on* Dodge

In addition to these judicial antecedents, the efforts of Professor Stout and her allies to dismiss *Dodge* as an outlier are undermined by contemporaneous commentary on *Dodge*, which immediately recognized it as an accepted rule of law. A 1919 American Law Reports annotation, for example, described *Dodge* as bringing "into clear relief the principle, which earlier decisions had previously

recognized, that the fundamental purpose of a business corporation is to earn as
large a profit as trade conditions and the business sagacity of its management will
permit ...."[38] A 1920 Chicago legal newspaper described *Dodge* as confirming that
"the fundamental purpose of a business corporation is to earn as large a profit as
possible," although incidental expenditures for the benefit of employees are permissible so long as doing so redounds to the corporation's long-term benefit.[39] An
essay in the 1922–23 volume of the Yale Law Journal by Donald Richberg, who at
that time was a prominent union lawyer and progressive politician, cited *Dodge*
for the proposition that "the primary objective of industry is the enrichment of
the owner of the property or tools utilized in the industry; and that the objectives
of the public and of the workers are secondary" and that that principle had "been
little affected by ideas of social responsibility or of the interdependence of man
upon man in modern life."[40] Taken together, the contemporaneous commentary
thus tends to confirm that *Dodge* was seen as restating an established principle of
law as to the purpose of a corporation rather than making new law.[41]

4.1.4 *Assume for the Sake of Argument that* Dodge *was Dicta: Would it Matter?*

For the sake of argument, let us assume that Professor Stout and her allies are correct about *Dodge* being dicta. The distinction between dicta and holding is both less
evident and less important than implied by Stout's critique. Contrary to her apparent assumption that identifying a passage as dicta is dispositive, the holding/dicta
distinction is both difficult to make and, more importantly, not very interesting.

In 2008, Professor Josh Blackman undertook a survey of over 400 opinions examining the holding/dicta distinction. He identified five major tests courts have used
to draw that distinction, each of which have multiple variations. Courts are not
consistent as to which test they use and typically fail to articulate why a particular
test was used in one case and not another. He concluded that the distinction is a
"standardless standard."[42]

Another empirical study by David Klein and Neal Devins identified "1649 cases
from the US courts of appeals, 8809 cases from US district courts, and 3365 cases
from state trial and intermediate appellate courts" referencing the holding-dicta distinction.[43] They then selected a random sample of each category for review. From
that sample of 1106 cases they identified "213 cases in which a lower court identified
a statement from a higher court as dictum."[44] Further processing of the data leads
them to the conclusion that "the distinction between dictum and holding plays an
important role in lower court decision making in fewer than 1 in every 2000 federal
district court cases (140 out of 327,524) and in fewer than 1 in every 4000 state court
(60 out of 295,452) or federal circuit court (20 out of 80,421) cases."[45]

In sum, labelling a particular passage as dicta is essentially meaningless. The
process by which that label comes to be applied is arbitrary and standardless. As
federal judge Patricia Wald observed, "line drawing between holding and dicta can

be blurry; as we have seen, the same language of a prior opinion is often classified differently by future judges dependent on whether they like what it says or not."[46] In any case, even when a court slaps the label dicta on a particular statement in an earlier opinion, the court often will still look to that statement for guidance.

4.2 IS *DODGE* TOO OLD TO MATTER?

Professor Stout also asked "[w]hy rely on a case that is nearly one hundred years old if there is more modern authority available?"[47] Note how her question actually conflates two distinct issues. One is an implied claim that there is modern authority that contradicts *Dodge*. As we shall see, however, modern authority supports *Dodge*. The other implied claim is that old cases have minimal precedential weight.

As to the latter component of her argument, Stout is demonstrably wrong. A federal judge emphatically explained that "State supreme court decisions do not lose precedential value as they age."[48] To the contrary, the court noted, the proposition "that cases lose their precedential value as they age" is "completely erroneous."[49] The Supreme Court of New Hampshire likewise declined a defendant's "invitation to discount [an 1864 decision's] precedential value on account of its age."[50]

In fact, one can go further. Stout's argument got it backwards. US Supreme Court Justice Antonin Scalia observed, albeit in dissent, that "the respect accorded prior decisions increases, rather than decreases, with their antiquity, as the society adjusts itself to their existence, and the surrounding law becomes premised upon their validity."[51] He explained that "[t]he freshness of error not only deprives it of the respect to which long-established practice is entitled, but also counsels that the opportunity of correction be seized at once, before state and federal laws and practices have been adjusted to embody it."[52]

4.3 DOES MODERN CASE LAW REJECT *DODGE*?

As discussed in the preceding section, Stout claimed that "shareholder wealth maximization is not a modern legal principle" in part because it is not supported by modern corporate case law.[53] That is, even if *Dodge*'s statement that "a business corporation is organized and carried on primarily for the profit of stockholders"[54] was binding precedent at some time in the past, it is no longer binding precedent.[55]

While it is admittedly true that there have been relatively modern few cases on point, the relative precedents uniformly confirm that *Dodge* remains a well-accepted holding. The Westlaw database of judicial opinions identifies only two cases as negatively referencing *Dodge*: *Churella v. Pioneer State Mut. Ins. Co.*[56] and *Hill v. State Farm Mutual Automobile Ins. Co.*[57] Neither really poses any threat to *Dodge*. Indeed, to the contrary, both actually confirm *Dodge*'s holding. Both involved not business corporations but rather mutual insurance companies. As the Michigan appellate court explained in *Churella*, the distinction between business corporations and mutual insurance companies is critical because while "the purpose of a business corporation is to provide profit to its share-holders … this is not the purpose of a mutual insurance company. The purpose of a mutual insurance company is to provide affordable insurance coverage to its members."[58]

Michigan cases dealing with business corporations confirm the state's continuing commitment to *Dodge*. Michigan Supreme Court decisions in 1931 and 1934 cited *Dodge* with approval,[59] for example, as did a 2006 Michigan Court of Appeals deci-sion.[60] A 2020 Michigan federal court determined that it was still "well established under Michigan law that the primary purpose of a business corporation is to benefit and profit the stockholders."[61] Most recently, an April 2022 decision of the Michigan Supreme Court reaffirmed that because "a corporation is carried on primarily for the profit of its shareholders, … the 'essence' of directors' fiduciary duties is to 'pro-duce to each stockholder the best possible return for his [or her] investment.'"[62]

Outside of Michigan, a 1933 West Virginia Supreme Court cited *Dodge* with approval.[63] A 1964 Missouri Court of Appeals decision stated that the court had "no quarrel with" the proposition that *Dodge* (among other decisions) governed the deci-sions of a board of directors.[64] A 1973 federal district court decision described *Dodge* as finding "that the [FMC] directors were running the corporation for the benefit of persons other than the stockholders," while explaining that the case at bar presented no such facts.[65] A dissenting opinion in a 1983 US Supreme Court decision stated that "Henry Ford's philanthropic motives did not permit him to set Ford Motor Company dividend policies to benefit public at expense of shareholders."[66] And, a concurring opinion in a 1986 federal Ninth Circuit decision cited *Dodge* for the proposition that a corporation's "management have the duty to maximize the value of the corporation's assets for the benefit of the corporation's residual claimants."[67] In sum, contrary to Stout's claim, "*Dodge* remains good law and the shareholder wealth maximization theory has been widely upheld and accepted by courts."[68]

4.4 WHAT DOES DELAWARE SAY?

Along with many scholars, Stout claimed that Delaware law does not embrace share-holder value maximization as articulated by *Dodge*.[69] In fact, however, Delaware courts arguably have embraced an even stronger version of shareholder value maxi-mization than did *Dodge*. Recall that the latter held that business corporations are "organized and carried on *primarily* for the profit of the stockholders."[70] According to some commentators, the qualifier "primarily" "suggests that other things may be considered in the operation of the corporation."[71] Whether or not that claim is cor-rect, the relevant Delaware cases contain no such limitation.[72]

In *Katz v. Oak Industries Inc.*, for example, the late Delaware Chancellor William Allen stated that directors have obligation "to attempt, within the law, to maximize the long-run interests of the corporation's stockholders."[73] In the early 1980s, Oak Industries fell into serious financial difficulties. It suffered several consecutive years of losses. Oak's balance sheet tipped deeply into the red, such that the shareholder equity account showed a $62 million deficit. In the balance sheet meaning of the term, Oak was thus insolvent. Its stock price plummeted from over $30 to less than $2. Its debt securities were trading at substantial discounts.

Oak's board of directors undertook a massive restructuring involving the sale of certain assets and an exchange offer that swapped some of Oak's outstanding debenture for a package of notes, stock, and warrants. The initial restructuring helped but did not solve Oak's long-term problems. Accordingly, the board entered into negotiations with Allied-Signal. Oak and Allied-Signal eventually entered into two agreements. The key one for our purposes was the Stock Purchase Agreement, pursuant to which Allied-Signal agreed to inject new equity capital into Oak by buying 10 million Oak common shares for $15 million. The agreement conditioned Allied-Signal's obligation to effect the purchase on the holders of at least 85 percent of Oak's outstanding debt securities accepting an exchange offer in which the debt would take a haircut. Bondholders who accepted the offer would receive a payment certificate for between $655 to $918 in cash for each $1,000 face value bond they surrendered, with the amount depending on which class of bonds the holders surrendered.

The indentures for all of six classes of Oak's debt contained restrictive covenants that precluded the company from effecting the exchange offer. Accordingly, bondholders who wanted to accept the offer were required to vote in favor of amending the indentures to remove those covenants. If the requisite number of bonds voted for the amendments, holders of any remaining unexchanged bonds would be left holding illiquid securities that had been stripped of key contractual protections. The plaintiff bondholder sued, claiming that the exchange offer was intended by the board "to benefit Oak's common stockholders at the expense of the Holders of its debt securities ...."[74]

Chancellor Allen had little difficulty rejecting plaintiff's arguments. As noted, he stated that the directors have a fiduciary duty to try to maximize long-term shareholder value. Critically, he went even further, explaining that directors "may sometimes do so 'at the expense' of" other corporate constituencies.[75] Accordingly, just as the Illinois appellate court refused to allow Shlensky to come to bat, Allen stated the *Oak Industries* plaintiff's argument "does not itself appear to allege a cognizable legal wrong."[76]

Given that no one seriously argues that directors should break the law in pursuit of shareholder value maximization, *Oak Industries* stands as an unqualified statement of shareholder value maximization by one of the most prominent corporate law jurists of the twentieth century.[77] As such, it poses a serious problem for those commentators who claim Delaware law does not embrace shareholder value maximization. Professor Stout tried to avoid that problem by focusing on the supposed "qualifying phrases 'attempt' and 'long-run,'" claiming they allow courts to make tradeoffs favoring stakeholders at the expense of shareholders,[78] but that claim is obviously specious. Surely no one thinks directors must succeed in maximizing shareholder value in order to avoid liability. Instead, they merely must attempt to do so. Trying to succeed is what the law requires, not actual success. Otherwise, every director of every company that suffers a loss would have breached their fiduciary duty. Turning to the supposedly qualifying phrase "the long run," recall that not even Milton Friedman thought directors should maximize short-term profits.[*]

In any case, Stout's dismissal of *Oak Industries* ignores other statements of Delaware law lacking such qualifiers. In *TW Services, Inc. v. SWT Acquisition Corp.*, for example, Chancellor Allen held that directors "owe a duty to shareholders as a class to manage the corporation within the law, with due care and in a way intended to maximize the long run interests of shareholders."[79] Similarly, in *Malone v. Brincat*, the Delaware Supreme Court explained held that directors have a "legal responsibility to manage the business of a corporation for the benefit of its shareholder owners."[80] More recently, albeit after Stout's book was published, in *In re Trados, Inc. S'holder Litigation*, Vice Chancellor Travis Laster held that "the standard of conduct for directors requires that they strive in good faith and on an informed basis to maximize the value of the corporation for the benefit of its residual claimants, the ultimate beneficiaries of the firm's value, not for the benefit of its contractual claimants."[†]

A critical refinement of Delaware law on this issue came in the mid-1980s in response to the emergence of hostile corporate takeovers and target company defenses against them. In *Unocal Corp. v. Mesa Petroleum Co.*, Delaware Supreme Court held that a target company board of directors deciding how to respond to an unsolicited takeover proposal could consider the impact of that proposal on numerous concerns, including "the impact on 'constituencies' other than shareholders (i.e., creditors, customers, employees, and perhaps even the community generally) ...."[81] Oddly, the court cited no statute or judicial precedent in support of that claim. As law professor

---

[*] Stout's argument was inapt, moreover, because it conflated the issue of whether *Oak Industries* embraces shareholder value maximization with the role of the business judgment rule in litigating shareholder value maximization cases.

[†] In re Trados, Inc. S'holder Litig., 73 A.3d 17, 40–41 (Del. Ch. 2013). Recall from Chapter 1 that there has been a longstanding normative debate about whether shareholder value maximization should be a mandatory rule or a default rule out of which parties may contract. Citing Vice Chancellor Laster's *Trados* decision, Robert Miller argues that, as a descriptive matter, Delaware law is mandatory:

> [T]he language typically used in describing the board's consideration of other constituencies under the shareholder-wealth maximization model—the board may consider the interests of other constituencies, subject to the fundamental limitation about increasing value for shareholders—is unjustifiably permissive. It is not that the board may consider such constituencies; if the relevant condition is satisfied, that is, if conferring a benefit on the other constituency results in a net benefit for the shareholders, then the board not only may act to benefit the other constituency but must act to do so under Delaware's applicable standard of conduct (at least if there is not some other use for the available funds that would produce an even greater benefit for the shareholders) .... The duty does not become optional when the best available means of maximizing value for the shareholders involves payments to non-shareholder constituencies. In other words, the commonly used language is permissive (the board may consider other constituencies, if the relevant condition applies) but the actual standard of conduct is mandatory (the board shall consider other constituencies, if the relevant condition applies).

Robert T. Miller, *How Would Directors Make Business Decisions Under a Stakeholder Model?*, 77 Bus. Law. 773, 786 n.31 (2022).

David Yosifon notes, that is a remarkable omission.[82] In any event, the Delaware Supreme Court reversed course almost immediately.

In *Revlon, Inc. v. MacAndrews & Forbes Holdings, Inc.*,[83] the Delaware Supreme Court reviewed a number of takeover defenses adopted by Revlon in response to an unsolicited tender offer by Pantry Pride. For present purposes, the critical stage of the takeover fight came at the end when Revlon's board authorized management to negotiate with other prospective bidders. That process culminated with an agreement between Revlon and private equity fund Forstmann Little & Co., pursuant to which Forstmann would acquire Revlon through a leveraged buyout. The deal included three provisions intended to ensure that Forstmann would prevail over Pantry Pride. First, Forstmann was given an option to buy two Revlon business divisions at a below market price in the event that some other party – including Pantry Pride – acquired 40 percent or more of Revlon's stock. Such options are known as asset lockups, because they are intended to end or prevent competitive bidding for the target – i.e., to lockup the deal. Accordingly, the subject of the option is usually either the assets most desired by a competing bidder or those essential to the target's operation. Second, Revlon agreed to a no shop clause, pursuant to which it agreed not to negotiate with any other potential buyers (including Pantry Pride). Finally, the deal required Revlon to pay Forstmann a cancellation fee of $25 million in the event the Forstmann acquisition failed to take place. All of these are examples of what today are called "deal protection devices"; i.e., contractual terms intended to ensure that the favored bidder prevails in the event that one or more competitors offers an alternative acquisition proposal.

The Delaware Supreme Court held that deal protection devices are not illegal *per* se, but that the specific devices adopted by *Revlon* were invalid given the facts at bar:

> The *Revlon* board's authorization permitting management to negotiate a merger or buyout with a third party was a recognition that the company was for sale. The duty of the board had thus changed from the preservation of Revlon as a corporate entity to the maximization of the company's value at a sale for the stockholders' benefit.... The directors' role changed from defenders of the corporate bastion to auctioneers charged with getting the best price for the stockholders at a sale of the company.[84]

The situations in which directors are obliged to act as auctioneers rather than corporate defenders are collectively known as *Revlon*-land.[85]

In the course of the opinion, the Delaware Supreme Court imposed two important limitations on its earlier *Unocal* holding. First, once the board enters *Revlon*-land, any "concern for non-stockholder interests is inappropriate."[86] In other words, getting the best possible deal for the shareholders – regardless of the potential impact on other corporate constituencies – must be the board's sole focus. Second, even when the board is not in *Revlon*-land, it can consider the interests of non-shareholder constituencies only if "there are rationally related benefits accruing to the stockholders."[87]

In other words, shareholder value must remain the board's focus, although the board is allowed to consider whether concern for stakeholders would redound to the benefit of the shareholders.

As with *Oak Industries*, *Revlon* poses a serious problem for those who claim Delaware does not embrace shareholder value maximization. Not surprisingly, Professor Stout therefore attempted to explain it away. In her article advising law professors to stop teaching *Dodge*, she dismissed it as "a dead letter" that "for practical purposes" "is largely irrelevant to modern corporate law and practice."[88] Put bluntly, this is simply false. In fact, *Revlon* governs "the majority of friendly deals affecting a Delaware public company."[89] As such, *Revlon* is "the basis of the Delaware law governing negotiated transactions,"[90] which hardly sounds like a dead letter.

In her book, *The Shareholder Value Myth*, Stout elaborated on her critique of *Revlon*, arguing that it is the "exception that proves the rule."[91] She explained that, in her view, *Revlon* carves out a very narrow and largely trivial requirement pursuant to which directors must "embrace shareholder wealth as their only goal" "only when a public corporation is about to stop being a public corporation."[92] In fact, however, *Revlon* applies to a much broader range of situations in which there is a change of control of the company or certain other fundamental transformations.[93]

More important, as David Yosifon explains, Stout's analysis "committed the fallacy of 'denying the antecedent'":

> For the logical statement, "if A, then B" it is a fallacy to conclude "not A, therefore not B." In *Revlon*, the Delaware Supreme Court held that if [A] the firm is for sale, then [B] directors must maximize profits. Stout concludes from this that if the firm is not for sale, directors do not have to maximize profits. But this does not follow as a matter of logic, and it is not *Revlon*'s teaching.[94]

Yosifon therefore rhetorically asked: "If Delaware really blankets workers, consumers, and communities with the warmth of directorial attention in the days, weeks, and years before a sale of the firm is in the works, … then why would it yank it off and leave these groups cold at the very moment where they are most vulnerable to the (market) elements?"[95] In fact, contrary to Stout and her allies, Delaware only allows directors to pay attention to "workers, consumers, and communities … in the days, weeks, and years before a sale of the firm is in the works" if there is a nexus between the stakeholder interests and profit.[96] Professor Yosifon's view are particularly worthy of consideration because he expressly acknowledges having a "normative agenda" of replacing shareholder value maximization with stakeholder capitalism but also strongly argues "that shareholder primacy *is* the law …."[97]

This brings us to the third problem with Stout's analysis of *Revlon*. A few pages before her book's analysis of *Revlon*, Stout wrote:

> [S]ome cases explicitly state that directors can look beyond shareholder wealth in deciding what is best for the corporation. For example, in the 1985 opinion *Unocal Corp. v. Mesa Petroleum Co.*, the Delaware Supreme Court stated that in weighing

the merits of a business transaction, directors can consider "the impact on 'constituencies' other than shareholders (i.e., creditors, customers, employees, and perhaps
even the community generally)."[98]

Apparently Stout wanted readers to believe that *Unocal* thereby stated the general
rule to which *Revlon* is a limited exception, but that is simply not true. First, Stout's
earlier essay had cited *Unocal* as an example of "modern cases ... contain[ing] contrary *dicta* indicating that directors owe duties beyond those owed to shareholders."[99] Second, in neither her book nor her essay, does Stout acknowledge the
Delaware Supreme Court's statement in *Revlon* that that was the case in which
the Court was "address[ing] *for the first time* the extent to which a corporation may
consider the impact of a takeover threat on constituencies other than shareholders,"[100] which implies that the earlier discussion in *Unocal* was not binding. Third,
Stout nowhere acknowledges the limitation *Revlon* puts on consideration of non-
shareholder interests in cases falling outside *Revlon*-land. In particular, "she never
quotes the Delaware Supreme Court's crucial statement in *Revlon* that there must
be 'rationally related benefits accruing to the stockholders' before the considerations
noted in *Unocal* would be permissible."[101]

Stout is not the only commentator to have misread *Revlon*. Professor Elhauge per-
petuated Stout's error in the portion of his article discussing the content of Delaware
law. At that point in the article, he cited *Unocal* as a statement of Delaware law without
acknowledging the limitations *Revlon* imposes on *Unocal*.[102] Almost 100 pages later,
he noted the limiting language from *Revlon* but dismissed it essentially out of hand.[103]

Finally, we come to a case that Professor Stout simply ignored; i.e., Delaware
Chancellor William Chandler's opinion in *eBay Domestic Holdings, Inc. v.
Newmark*.[104] In *eBay*, Chandler faced a case whose key facts were oddly reminiscent
of *Dodge*. eBay was a minority shareholder of the corporation that owned internet
online classified ad website craigslist.com. Craig Newmark ("Craig") and James
Buckmaster ("Jim") were the company's controlling shareholders and dominated
the board of directors, just as Henry Ford was the dominant shareholder of FMC.
Craig and Jim explicitly rejected shareholder value maximization, proclaiming that
craigslist.com was – and in the future would remain – concerned with aiding local,
national, and global communities rather than profit for the shareholders.

Chancellor Chandler expressed his personal admiration of Craig and Jim's
altruism, but made clear that the law does not allow them to put other interests
ahead of those of the shareholders:

> The corporate form in which craigslist operates ... is not an appropriate vehicle for
> purely philanthropic ends, at least not when there are other stockholders interested
> in realizing a return on their investment. Jim and Craig opted to form craigslist,
> Inc. as a for-profit Delaware corporation and voluntarily accepted millions of
> dollars from eBay as part of a transaction whereby eBay became a stockholder.
> Having chosen a for-profit corporate form, the craigslist directors are bound by the
> fiduciary duties and standards that accompany that form. Those standards include

acting to promote the value of the corporation for the benefit of its stockholders. The "Inc." after the company name has to mean at least that.[105]

Although Stout's essay critiquing *Dodge* predated *eBay*, the subsequent book that grew out of that essay was published two years after *eBay* was decided but the book failed to address it. As Professor Yosifon aptly observed, that "omission is particularly troubling given that Stout's book is aimed not just at scholars and corporate insiders, but also 'informed laypersons,' who would have no reason to note or decide for themselves about the significance of omitting a case so obviously relevant to the discussion."[106]

Turning to those commentators who have addressed *eBay*, some forthrightly acknowledge that *eBay* is a clear statement of Delaware law embracing shareholder value maximization.[107] On the other hand, some commentators contend that the opinion leaves directors with wiggle room to pursue purposes other than shareholder wealth maximization, at least so long as there is some benefit to the shareholders.[108] As usual, others dismiss Chandler's statement as mere dicta.[109]

Former Delaware Supreme Court Chief Justice Leo Strine came down firmly in the former camp in a 2015 law review article:

> As with Chancellor Allen's reading of *Dodge v. Ford*, scholars have taken issue with Chancellor Chandler's holding, indicating that he did not need to rule for the reasons he said he did, or did not in fact premise his ruling on the reasons he stated. I understand that there are forms of legal thought tied to deconstructionist linguistics and philosophy, such as critical legal studies, and that are premised on the idea that authors themselves can never understand what they intend to say or are in fact saying. For those of us who are more traditional, we tend to credit accomplished jurists such as Chancellor Chandler, Chancellor Allen, and Justice Moore with understanding most of what they write, especially when it is in a high-profile context and when they underscore their understanding of the importance of the subject matter they are addressing.[110]

In that same article, Strine more broadly addressed claims by numerous progressive corporate law scholars "that directors may subordinate what they believe is best for stockholder welfare to other interests, such as those of the company's workers or society generally."[111] In assessing that claim, the Chief Justice minced no words; to the contrary, he hurled multiple verbal grenades into the debate:

- "These well-meaning commentators, of course, ignore certain structural features of corporation law ...."[112]
- "Indeed, these commentators essentially argue that Delaware judges do not understand the very law they are applying, and the Delaware General Assembly does not understand the law it has created."[113]
- "It is not only hollow but also injurious to social welfare to declare that directors can and should do the right thing by promoting interests other than stockholder interests."[114]

Perhaps most damningly, however, Strine essentially accused the commentators –
whom he called out by name in lengthy string cites[115] – of misrepresenting the law,
arguing that they "*pretend* that directors do not have to make stockholder welfare the
sole end of corporate governance, within the limits of their legal discretion, under the
law of the most important American jurisdiction – Delaware."[116] Professor Yosifon
more gently described these arguments as reflecting "some sloppiness."

Chief Justice Strine's pronouncements in scholarly settings are, at the very least,
strong evidence of what the law is and, arguably, themselves should be treated as
law. An analogy to international law may be helpful. Article 38 of the Statute of the
International Court of Justice codifies the principle that "the teachings of the most
highly qualified publicists of the various nations" may be looked to "as subsidiary
means for the determination of rules of law."[117] The US Supreme Court has likewise explained that, when presented with questions of international law as to which
"there is no treaty and no controlling executive or legislative act or judicial decision,
resort must be had to the customs and usages of civilized nations, and, as evidence
of these, to the works of jurists and commentators who by years of labor, research,
and experience have made themselves peculiarly well acquainted with the subjects
of which they treat."[118] The Court further explained that informed scholarship represents not just "the speculations of their authors concerning what the law ought to
be," but in fact are "trustworthy evidence of what the law really is."[119]

To be sure, both the ICJ statute and the Supreme Court's decision in *Paquete
Habana* deal with determining the content of international law rather than domestic corporate law. Yet, the principle of *opinio juris* seems equally apt to the latter
context. As eminent constitutional scholar Edward S. Corwin reportedly observed,
"[i]f judges make law," "then so do commentators." As such, while it is true that
"legislators and judges create new law," one can argue that "law is also created by
commentators writing in law reviews."[120]

By expressly referring to the "most highly qualified publicists," however, the ICJ
statute clearly suggests "that not all writings are of comparable value."[121] Who could
be more "highly qualified" (ICJ) and "peculiarly well acquainted" (*Paquete Habana*)
with Delaware corporate law than Leo Strine, who has been a Vice Chancellor,
the Chancellor, and the Chief Justice of that state? Surely the opinions of such a
jurist are entitled to greater weight than those of virtually any other commentator.
So when Strine says shareholder value maximization is the law of Delaware, I am
prepared to take that as given.

4.5 IS *DODGE* LIMITED TO CONTROLLERS
OF CLOSE CORPORATIONS?

In a thoughtful analysis, Gordon Smith advanced the provocative argument that
Dodge is properly understood as a case about the duties controlling shareholders of
close corporations owe to minority shareholders.[122] Lynn Stout likewise claimed that

Dodge sets out not the law of corporate purpose but rather the law governing efforts by a controlling shareholder to oppress minority shareholders.[123] Einer Elhauge similarly argues that the case is really one about the conflict of interest between controlling and minority shareholders.[124]

It is certainly true that Henry Ford was FMC's dominant shareholder.[125] It is also true that some contemporaneous scholarship treated *Dodge* as being about minority shareholders, right to dividends.[126] Yet, as Professor Amir Licht observes, this reading of *Dodge* ultimately proves unpersuasive. "If *Dodge* had been merely a case of majority-minority relationships in the corporation it would not have gained the pride of place it has among the seminal authorities on US corporate law."[127] The bulk of contemporary scholarship treated *Dodge* as stating a rule applicable to corporations generally rather than as one announcing a rule confined to close corporations.[128]

Turning to the modern cases discussed above, the leading *eBay* decision admittedly was also a case involving a dispute between the controlling and minority shareholders of a close corporation. But nothing in Chancellor Chandler's opinion suggests that he was limiting his decision to close corporations. To the contrary, Chandler stated that "[f]iduciary duties apply regardless of whether a corporation is 'registered and publicly traded, dark and delisted, or closely held.'"[129] In any case, *Revlon* and *Oak Industries* both involved public corporations neither of which had a controlling shareholder. Accordingly, even if *Dodge* originally was intended as a statement about the duties of controllers, the evolutionary processes of the common law have led to *Dodge* being interpreted as establishing a basic rule for all boards of directors; namely, that the board has a duty to maximize shareholder wealth

4.6 OPTING IN/OPTING OUT

Professor Stout made much of the fact that corporate articles of incorporation almost never explicitly opt into shareholder value maximization. She correctly observed that state corporation codes generally oblige the articles of incorporation to include a statement of corporate powers and the purposes for which those powers will be exercised. Yet, she noted, although it would be easy enough to include shareholder value maximization as one of those stated purposes, it is almost unheard of for articles to include such a statement.[130]

This argument should be given no weight in the analysis. Under the Model Business Corporation Act, a purpose provision is purely optional.[131] The Delaware business corporation statute still requires a statement of the purposes for which the business was formed, but provides that a statement that the corporation was formed to conduct any lawful business will suffice.[132] Most corporations use that broad formulation rather than offering a more specific statement.[133]

Contrary to Stout's argument, the fact that most articles of incorporation are silent on the issue actually suggests that shareholder value maximization is the law. If shareholder value maximization is the default rule of corporate law, it would be

surprising to see firms expressly embracing shareholder value maximization. After
all, the whole point of a default rule is to reduce transaction costs by eliminating
the need for contracts or other standard form documents to address the issue. The
silence of corporate articles is thus evidence that shareholder value maximization
is the law.

The silence of corporate articles is also evidence that most corporations prefer
shareholder capitalism to stakeholder capitalism. As Leo Strine observed, "one does
not find many, if any, public companies that say that they exist to pursue any lawful
business for the purpose of protecting the environment, curing disease, or alleviat-
ing hunger."[134] The absence of efforts to opt out of the default rule suggests that most
firms are content with the default rule.[135]

4.7 DOESN'T THE BUSINESS JUDGMENT RULE MAKE ALL OF THIS MOOT?

Suppose Netflix signed a contract with a top Hollywood star to appear in a planned
film. At the last minute, the star backed out, causing the project to collapse and cost-
ing Netflix an enormous amount of money. The star is in clear breach of contract. If
Netflix sued, the case would be the proverbial slam dunk. Yet, Netflix's board opted
not to authorize bringing suit. This might very well be a smart business decision.
After all, preserving goodwill with the star and the broader talent community easily
could pay off in the future. Yet, if a Netflix shareholder sued to challenge that decision, the judge – as with the appellate court in *Shlensky* – likely would not inquire
into the board's motives. Instead, the court would simply invoke the business judgment rule and dismiss the case long before trial.[136]

Or suppose that the board of directors of a cigarette manufacturer voluntarily adopted
a complete ban on advertising its products. The board does so despite being fully aware
that the company will sell fewer cigarettes as a result. Again, the business judgment rule
doubtless would insulate the board's decision from judicial review, just as it insulated
Henry Ford's decision to pay the $5 per day wage and to build the Rouge River plant.[137]

Many scholars have argued that the business judgment rule thus makes *Dodge* irrelevant. Professor Stout, for example, contended that when board decisions are "challenged on the grounds that the directors failed to look after shareholder interests, courts
shield directors from liability under the business judgment rule so long as any plausible connection can be made between the directors' decision and some possible future
benefit, however intangible and unlikely, to shareholders."[138] Professor Jeffrey Lipshaw
asserted that the business judgment rule, not shareholder value maximization, "is the
prevailing rule of decision when the dispute arises from management's ordinary and
routine mediation of various constituency interests."[139] Law professor David Millon
likewise observed that, where the business judgment rule applies, "courts will not
second-guess decisions – including decisions that appear to benefit nonshareholders
at the expense of shareholders – as long as management can assert some plausible

connection with the corporation's long-run best interests."[140] Harvard law professor Einer Elhauge similarly contended that, the business judgment rule makes plain that the duty of care cannot be enforced in a way that would bar managers from exercising discretion to sacrifice corporate profits in the public interest.[141] Constant repetition of the argument by multiple academics, however, doesn't make it true.[142]

In the first place, of course, the business judgment rule does not always insulate board decisions from judicial review in all cases. The business judgment rule did not preclude judicial review in *eBay*, *Oak Industries*, or *Revlon*. As we have seen, while *eBay* was a somewhat unique case, there are many recapitalization transactions governed by *Oak Industries* and even more mergers governed by *Revlon*, with annual values in the billions of dollars.

In the second place, the business judgment rule is neither a rule of decision, a standard of liability, nor a standard of review.[143] Instead, the business judgment rule is properly understood as an abstention doctrine.[144] A decision to abstain is not a decision on the merits of a case.[145] To the contrary, when a court abstains, it is expressly refusing to decide the case on the merits.[146] In other words, in abstention cases, there is an underlying rule of law that the court for prudential or other reasons has decided not to apply to the facts of the case before it.

When I teach the business judgment rule in class, I use a homely analogy to make the point. I show a PowerPoint slide with a picture of a Tootsie Pop. The reader will recall that the Tootsie Pop is a lollipop with a hard candy shell filled with a chocolate-flavored chewy candy. As long as the hard candy shell remains intact, it protects the center chewy candy from being eaten. Yet, even though the shell insulates the center, no one would deny that there really is a center.

Just so, even though an abstention doctrine (the hard candy shell) prevents the court (the eater) from invoking the underlying substantive doctrine, no one would dispute that there is still a substantive doctrine at the core of the case. This is precisely what the business judgment does. In the typical business judgment rule case, the underlying doctrine is the duty of care.[147] The fact that the business judgment rule applies to such cases does not mean that there is no underlying duty of care.[148] Likewise, the fact that the business judgment rule typically precludes a court from deciding whether directors breached the shareholder wealth maximization norm does not mean that the norm is not the underlying doctrine. The *Dodge/eBay* rule thus remains the chewy center even when the hard candy shell of the business judgment rule protects it from judicial review.

Put another way, the fact that the business judgment rule sometimes will preclude judicial review of decisions in which directors departed from shareholder value maximization is not the intended purpose of the rule but rather an unintended consequence of the board centric nature of corporate law. Recall that the two basic questions of corporate governance are (1) who makes decisions for the corporation?: and (2) what decision-making norm should guide the chosen decision makers? In a series of articles that culminated in my book, *The New Corporate Governance in*

Theory and Practice, I offered a theory called director primacy to answer those questions.[149] This book expands on my thinking as to the latter question. As to the former, director primacy argues that corporate decision-making powers are vested in the board of directors and that those powers are original and undelegated. Shareholders have an extremely constrained role in corporate governance, the only truly important element of which is their ability to elect the board.

The director primacy model begins with the proposition that all organizations must have some mechanism for aggregating the preferences of the organization's constituencies and converting them into collective decisions. As Kenneth Arrow explained, such mechanisms fall out on a spectrum between "consensus" and "authority."[150] Consensus-based structures are designed to allow all of a firm's stakeholders to participate in decision making. Authority-based decision-making structures are characterized by the existence of a central decision maker to whom all firm employees ultimately report and which is empowered to make decisions unilaterally without approval of other firm constituencies. Such structures are best suited for firms whose constituencies face information asymmetries and have differing interests. It is because the corporation demonstrably satisfies those conditions that vesting the power of fiat in a central decision maker – i.e., the board of directors – is the essential characteristic of its governance.

As for the differing interest condition, shareholders have widely divergent interests and distinctly different access to information. To be sure, most shareholders invest in a corporation expecting financial gains, but once uncertainty is introduced shareholder opinions on which course will maximize share value are likely to vary widely. In addition, shareholder investment time horizons vary from short-term speculation to long-term buy-and-hold strategies, which in turn is likely to result in disagreements about corporate strategy. Likewise, shareholders in different tax brackets are likely to disagree about such matters as dividend policy, as are shareholders who disagree about the merits of allowing management to invest the firm's free cash flow in new projects.

As to Arrow's information condition, shareholders lack incentives to gather the information necessary to actively participate in decision making. A rational shareholder will expend the effort necessary to make informed decisions only if the expected benefits outweigh the costs of doing so. Given the length and complexity of corporate disclosure documents, the opportunity cost entailed in making informed decisions is both high and apparent. In contrast, the expected benefits of becoming informed are quite low, as most shareholders' holdings are too small to have significant effect on the vote's outcome. Accordingly, corporate shareholders are rationally apathetic.

In sum, it would be surprising if the modern public corporation's governance arrangements attempted to make use of consensus-based decision making anywhere except perhaps within the central decision-making body at the apex of a branching hierarchy. Given the collective action problems inherent with such a large number of potential decision makers, the differing interests of shareholders, and their varying levels of knowledge about the firm, it is "cheaper and more efficient to transmit all the pieces of information to a central place" and to have the central office "make the collective choice and transmit it rather than retransmit all the information on which the decision is based."[151] Shareholders therefore will prefer to irrevocably delegate decision-making authority to some smaller group.

Corporate statutes accommodate that preference by providing that the business of the company will be managed or overseen by neither the shareholders nor the managers but by the board of directors.[152] The separation of ownership and control thus established obviously raises accountability concerns. There is a serious risk that directors will use their power to pursue their own selfish interests at the expense of the shareholders' interests (or that of some other corporate constituency, for that matter). The trouble is that ensuring power is used accountably is ultimately inconsistent with respecting the decision-making authority corporate law has wisely delegated to boards. As Arrow explained:

> [Accountability mechanisms] must be capable of correcting errors but should not be such as to destroy the genuine values of authority. Clearly, a sufficiently strict and continuous organ of [accountability] can easily amount to a denial of authority. If every decision of A is to be reviewed by B, then all we have really is a shift in the locus of authority from A to B and hence no solution to the original problem.[153]

This remains true even if only major decisions of A are reviewed by B.

The business judgment rule's purpose is preventing such a shift in the locus of decision-making authority from boards to judges. It does so by establishing a limited system for case-by-case oversight in which judicial review of the substantive merits of those decisions is avoided. The court begins with a presumption against review. It then reviews the facts to determine not the quality of the decision, but rather whether the decision-making process was tainted by self-dealing and the like.[154] The questions asked are objective and straightforward: Did the board commit fraud? Did the board commit an illegal act? Did the board self-deal? Whether or not the board exercised reasonable care is irrelevant, as well it should be.[155]

In contrast, the questions courts would have to ask to determine whether the board intentionally deviated from shareholder value maximization are much less straightforward:

> When a company fails (or simply has deeply disappointed shareholders), it will inevitably appear that managers were not acting in the shareholders' interests, even if they were. In fact, because shareholders are residual claimants who may hold fully diversified portfolios of securities, maximizing profit for shareholders often requires significant risk-taking. Thus, ironically, companies that are engaged in shareholder wealth-maximizing, risk-taking activities may wind up in financial distress. On the other hand, companies that are pursuing strategies that primarily serve the interests of workers, such as expanding only to increase market share or acquiring other companies in unrelated fields to reduce risk, may never become insolvent.[156]

Accordingly, as Professor Macey explains, "it simply is not possible or practical for courts to discern ex post when a company is maximizing value for shareholders and when the officers and directors are only pretending to do so."[157]

The business judgment rule thus builds a prophylactic barrier by which courts pre-commit to resisting the temptation to review the merits of the board's decision. Declining to review cases in which directors may have made decisions seemingly inconsistent with shareholder value maximization, as the court did in *Shlensky*, is a necessary cost of building that barrier. But it does not mean that the underlying rule is anything other than shareholder value maximization. As Professor Yosifon notes, "just because shareholder primacy cannot be easily enforced through lawsuits does not alter the fact that it is the prevailing law of corporate governance in Delaware" and, one might add, elsewhere.[158]

4.8 BUT WHAT ABOUT CONSTITUENCY STATUTES?

Thirty states have adopted constituency statutes (a.k.a. non-shareholder constituency statutes or stakeholder statutes). Although the details vary somewhat, Massachusetts' statute is typical:

> (a) A director shall discharge his duties as a director, including his duties as a member of a committee: … (3) in a manner the director reasonably believes to be in the best interests of the corporation. In determining what the director reasonably believes to be in the best interests of the corporation, a director may consider the interests of the corporation's employees, suppliers, creditors and customers, the economy of the state, the region and the nation, community and societal considerations, and the long-term and short-term interests of the corporation and its shareholders, including the possibility that these interests may be best served by the continued independence of the corporation.[159]

Although these statutes seem to contradict *Dodge*, it is easy to make too much of them.

First, understanding the statutes requires that they be contextualized. The statutes were not adopted in response to some burgeoning demand for corporate social responsibility or ESG. Instead, they were almost uniformly adopted as part of a package of state anti-takeover laws passed in response to the wave of hostile takeovers in the 1980s and early 1990s.[160] Their intended beneficiaries were not corporate stakeholders but rather corporate managers faced with a hostile takeover bid likely to result in significant job losses at the management level.[161] The principal legislative goal was to prevent courts of the adopting states from following *Revlon* and thereby allow directors to invoke purported concerns about the effect of a takeover on non-shareholder constituencies in justifying takeover defenses.[162]

Second, notice that the statute is permissive not mandatory. This is universally the case; none of the statutes mandate that directors consider any interests other than shareholders.[163] At one point, Connecticut was a lonely outlier, mandating that directors consider such interests, but it has since amended its statute to make such consideration optional on the part of the board.[164] Because the statutes are permissive they create no duties on the part of directors that are enforceable by stakeholders. Several courts have interpreted the Ohio constituency statute, for example, as making "consideration of creditors' interests permissive" and, accordingly, as imposing no fiduciary duty on directors to consider creditor interests when making decisions.[165] As such, the statutes fall considerably short of the stakeholder theorists' ideal.[166]

Third, while constituency statutes allow directors to consider interests of non-shareholder constituencies, the statutes do not expressly authorize directors to harm shareholder interests in order to benefit stakeholders.[167] A North Carolina court discussing the context in which the constituency statutes arose explained that:

> Illinois, for example, adopted a statute that specifically authorized directors to consider the interests of corporate constituents other than shareholders when responding to a hostile takeover. In doing so, Illinois statutorily adjusted the balance of power between shareholders and other corporate constituents by giving additional power to directors that *Revlon* had arguably taken away. It did so not to advance the power of directors, but to permit directors to assert the interests of other corporate constituents in the heat of the takeover battle. It did not eliminate shareholder rights; it arguably put a little more tension in the elasticity on the side of the directors so that they could consider "corporate value" as including values important to society.[168]

Accordingly, as the American Bar Association's Committee on Corporate Laws explained, the constituency statutes could plausibly be interpreted as preserving a requirement that director actions taken after considering stakeholder interests must still be rationally related to shareholder interests.[169] Or, as Macey put it, the most pro-stakeholder capitalism spin one can put on the statutes is that they "are mere tie-breakers, allowing managers to take the interests of non-shareholder constituencies into account when doing so does not harm shareholders in any demonstrable way."[170]

Fourth, cases in which the statutes have been invoked are extremely rare. Cases in which the statutes have been dispositive of the result are essentially non-existent. As of 2020, courts in only fifteen states had even cited one of these statutes. The total number of decisions in which the statutes have been cited barely exceeds thirty, which is surprising given that some of these statutes have been on the books since as long ago as 1984 and all but two were in force by 2000.[171] Most of the claims were brought by creditors rather than the other classes of stakeholders – such as employees and communities – with which corporate social responsibility advocates are mainly concerned.[172] Courts have generally seemed reluctant "to deviate from the longstanding principle of shareholder primacy."[173] All of which tends to confirm that the statutes have had little impact on the development of the law. Accordingly, it seems fair to conclude that "constituency statutes currently function only to the extent that they do not conflict with shareholder primacy."[174]

In any case, a number of important states declined to adopt a constituency statute. *Dodge*'s home state – Michigan – has not adopted a constituency statute but rather, as we have seen, continues to endorse *Dodge*. The drafters of the Model Business Corporation Act declined to include a constituency provision in their statute,[175] although a substantial number of Model Act states nevertheless deviated from the model statute by adopting constituency provisions. Most importantly, Delaware has no such statute. As David Yosifon notes, the Delaware legislature's failure to adopt a constituency statute plausibly can be "read to express legislative acquiescence in shareholder primacy," since the legislature and Delaware bar are alert to important developments and has been willing to reverse judicial decisions of which it disapproves.[176]

It is thus difficult to disagree with Professor Julian Velasco's conclusion that the constituency statutes have proven "ultimately insignificant as a practical matter":[177]

> Cases involving constituency statutes have been few and far between, and they rarely, if ever, hinge upon such provisions. More importantly, there is no evidence that constituency statutes have had any effect on director behavior. In light of the foregoing, it would be specious to argue that constituency statutes have effected a fundamental change in corporate law.[178]

4.9 SUMMING UP

Lynn Stout wanted us to believe that *Dodge* tells a "charming and easily understood fable of shareholder wealth maximization."[179] In fact, however, it is her interpretation of the law that is a fable. As Professor Marc Greendorfer correctly notes, "the position that board actions that ignore shareholder wealth maximization in favor of the promotion of third-party stakeholder interests are a proper corporate goal is a fringe, aspirational position, rather than a reflection of what the law and weight of scholarship articulate."[180]

5

To Make Stakeholder Capitalism the Rule, You Would Have to Change Most of Corporate Law

Imagine a world in which *Smith Manufacturing*'s was the general rule rather than mere dicta buttressing a narrow exception for corporate philanthropy. Would that world be a utopia in which corporations were socially responsible actors that treat the environment gently and help solve a multiple of social ills? Or would that world look a lot like our own world, in which CEOs give lip service to ESG and generally put shareholder interests ahead of those of stakeholders (see Chapter 9 for a defense of that description of today's business environment)?

To answer those questions we need to understand that corporate law is an extensive body of law broadly regulating the rights, powers, and duties of a corporation's shareholders, directors, managers, and, to a lesser extent, creditors. Almost all of those rules are founded on an assumption that directors and managers are solely accountable to shareholders. Taken together, many provisions of corporate law require or incentivize corporate directors to put shareholder interests ahead of those of stakeholders.[1] Making the law amendable to stakeholder capitalism would therefore require changing not just *Dodge* but a host of other rules.

A few examples may suffice.

5.1 ONLY SHAREHOLDERS ELECT DIRECTORS

Edmund Burke famously opined that a representative owes the electorate "not his industry only, but his judgment," which the representative should not sacrifice to the electorate's opinion. In theory, corporate law embraces that idea. As Chancellor Allen once observed, the mere fact that "shareholders would prefer the board to do otherwise than it has done does not … afford a basis to interfere with the effectuation of the board's business judgment."[2]

Suppose, however, that you are a director of a corporation whose board is presented with an opportunity that, if taken, would increase profits significantly but would result in losses to employees. Let's assume that the business judgment rule would preclude judicial review of the decision, regardless of whether the board opted to take or reject the opportunity. Although you may not worry about your

73

liability exposure, you would like to keep your job as a director. Assuming the board's nominating committee nominates you to serve another term, it will be up to the shareholders to decide whether or not you will be reelected.

Whether the question is electing directors, amending the articles of incorporation or the bylaws, approving a merger, or some other fundamental matter, only share-holders get to vote. Obviously, any and all of those decisions will impact a variety of stakeholders, but none of them get a vote. All might be well from the stakeholder perspective if shareholders exercise their voting rights to encourage directors to con-sider ESG factors, but we'll see reasons in Chapter 10 to be skeptical that they will do so. In any case, the key point is the voting rules will tend to align director incen-tives with shareholder interests.[*]

5.2 ENFORCEMENT OF DIRECTORS' AND OFFICERS' FIDUCIARY DUTIES TO THE CORPORATION AND ITS SHAREHOLDERS

Corporate directors and officers owe fiduciary duties to both the shareholders and the corporate entity.[3] The former set of duties is enforced through direct lawsuits, typically brought as a class action representing all affected sharehold-ers.[4] The latter set is enforced through derivative lawsuits, which are brought on behalf of the company for redress of an injury done to the company. Only share-holders have standing to bring a derivative proceeding. Employees and other stakeholders lack standing to sue derivatively, except for the limited case of an insolvent corporation, in which cases creditors – but only creditors – may bring a derivative proceeding.

> Directors are supposed to act in the best interests of the corporation and the corporation consists of more than just the sum of its shareholders. However, ... only shareholders have standing to derivatively sue directors for breaches of duty to the corporation. Logically, shareholders are unlikely to bring a derivative action for the protection of 'corporate' interests unless their own interests are sufficiently affected. Consequently, ... nonshareholder constituents of the corporation have no effective method for holding directors accountable....[5]

In turn, it seems unlikely that directors would consistently prefer the interests of those with no ability to hold them accountable to those with the sole ability to hold them accountable.

---

[*] *See* Stephen M. Bainbridge, *The Board of Directors as Nexus of Contracts*, 88 Iowa L. Rev. 1, 8 (2002) ("Because only shareholders are entitled to elect directors, for example, boards of public corpora-tions are insulated from pressure by nonshareholder corporate constituencies, such as employees or creditors.") I have elsewhere argued that corporate law correctly gives only shareholders voting rights but also correctly limits the scope of issues on which shareholders are entitled to vote so as to pre-serve the board-centric nature of corporate governance. Stephen M. Bainbridge, *The Case for Limited Shareholder Voting Rights*, 53 UCLA L. Rev. 601 (2006).

5.3 WHO PAYS THE PIPER CALLS THE TUNE

As adopted in 1993, Internal Revenue Code § 162(m) capped the deductibility of compensation paid to a public corporation's CEO and specified other highly compensated employees at one million dollars per year. Various forms of performance-based pay, however, were exempt from the cap. The availability of those exemptions accelerated a pre-existing trend toward basing compensation on the company's performance. In particular, there was a dramatic rise in the percentage of a CEO's pay that came in the form of stock options, restricted stock, and other stock price-linked instruments. The extent to which that change actually aligned manager and shareholder interests is controversial, but it at least skewed top executives' incentives toward shareholders as opposed to stakeholders.[6]

The Tax Cuts and Jobs Act (2017) made two important changes in the § 162(m) regime. First, it increased the number of executives potentially subject to the cap. Second, it eliminated the exemption for performance-based pay. Despite the latter change, however, the bulk of executive pay remains linked to the company's stock price performance. Among the companies whose CEOs signed the Business Roundtable corporate purpose statement, for example, 91 percent of their pay consists either of stock-based compensation or cash bonuses that are based largely on the employer's financial performance. A survey of S&P 100 companies, an index that includes most of the largest US corporations, found the mean percentage of CEO pay contingent on the achieving performance goals was 85.5 percent. The median was 91 percent.[7]

Among large companies in general, about 60 percent of CEO pay is directly linked to how well the company's stock performs. At smaller companies, 75 percent of the average CEO's pay comes in the form of stock options, restricted stock grants, and performance-based cash bonuses. Only a relatively small number of companies factor ESG metrics into executive pay and then only in rather limited ways.[8]

The dominance of pay formats skewed toward shareholder profits should not be surprising. First, it has long been the case that shareholders get an indirect vote on executive pay due to the short-swing profit rules under Securities Exchange Act § 16(b). Section 16(b) provides that a corporate director or officer must forfeit to the company any profit the officer or directors makes on a matching purchase and sale that occur within six months of each other. Suppose a CEO buys 1,000 shares at $8 per share on January 5. On May 5, the CEO sells those shares at $10 per share, making a $2,000 profit. The CEO would have to forfeit that profit to the company. Transactions approved by the company's shareholders or effected pursuant to a plan approved by the company's shareholders are exempted, however, as a result of which shareholder votes on compensation plans have become routine. As with other corporate governance matters, stakeholders do not get a vote. The design of a compensation plan thus can ignore stakeholder opinions, but must be structured so as to attract support from the holders of a majority of the stock.

Second, the Dodd-Frank Act (2010) gave shareholders a direct – albeit advisory – vote on executive pay. The so-called say on pay rule mandates that at least once every three years public companies must allow shareholders to vote on the compensation paid to the corporation's named executive officers (NEOs). Those officers are defined by SEC rules as the CEO, CFO, and the next three most highly paid executive officers. The SEC's periodic disclosure rules require that extensive disclosures about NEO compensation be included in the company's annual proxy statement. Even though shareholders routinely approve almost all say on pay proposals, "mandatory say-on-pay seems to have encouraged management be more responsive to shareholder concerns about executive pay and corporate governance."[9]

Finally, in the early 1980s, the Department of Labor expressed concern that pension and other fund managers either failed to vote the shares of companies held in portfolios they managed or simply voted those shares as recommended by those companies' management. To alleviate that concern, the Labor Department issued an interpretation of the Employee Retirement Income Security Act (ERISA) that was understood as requiring managers of funds subject to ERISA not only to vote such shares but to make informed voting decisions.[10] Recognizing that most pension and mutual fund managers try to minimize back office and overhead costs, the Labor Department allowed managers to outsource voting to third party advisors.[11] Two proxy advisory companies – Institutional Shareholder Services and Glass Lewis – now dominate the market for proxy advice, with ISS alone having over 2,000 institutional investors as clients.[12] Empirical studies differ as to the extent to which those clients rely on ISS or Glass Lewis recommendations in making voting decisions,[13] but there is no doubt that such "recommendations have at least some power to move investors' votes in ways that cannot be explained by other factors."[14] Indeed, one study found that a negative ISS recommendation on say-on-pay votes resulted on average in a 25 percent decrease in yes votes.[15]

In assessing whether or not to recommend a favorable say-on-pay vote, ISS focuses exclusively on metrics keyed to shareholder value.[16] ISS will advise a negative vote if the company has "an unmitigated misalignment between CEO pay and company performance," "significant problematic pay practices," or the board is uncommunicative or unresponsive to shareholders.[17] ISS will further recommend that its clients vote against members of a company's compensation committee or even the entire board of directors, among other things, if "the board fails to respond adequately to a previous [say-on-pay] proposal that received less than 70 percent support of votes cast."[18] Stakeholders appear nowhere in ISS's say-on-pay policy.*

A major proponent of the Business Roundtable corporate purpose statement, JPMorgan Chase CEO Jamie Dimon, ran afoul of those trends in the 2022 proxy

---

* In addition, ISS recommends that its clients vote against any "proposals that ask the board to consider non-shareholder constituencies or other non-financial effects when evaluating a merger or business combination." ISS, PROXY VOTING GUIDELINES FOR 2021: BENCHMARK POLICY RECOMMENDATIONS 30 (2020).

season. Dimon chaired the Roundtable in 2019, when the corporate purpose statement was adopted, and was widely credited with having promoted it. JP Morgan
Chase's 2022 proxy statement made much of Chase's commitment to "sustainable
business practices," "including our engagement in communities and commitment
to provide economic opportunity to underserved communities, and address environmental and social issues such as climate change and racial equity" and "creating a diverse, inclusive, respectful and accountable environment." But that high
profile commitment failed to prevent Dimon and Chase from losing a say on pay
vote in 2022.

To be sure, the proxy statement also stressed how Chase's pay practices "focus
on risk-adjusted performance," but that claimed focus had not prevented Chase
from underperforming both the S&P 500 and the KBW Nasdaq Bank Index in 2021.
Despite that underperformance, Chase paid Dimon $34.5 million in standard com-
pensation for 2021 and gave him a one-time $50 million retention bonus. Dimon's
total 2021 pay was 917 times that of Chase's median employee and, excluding the
retention bonus, 346 times that of the median employee.

In 2022, when Dimon's pay package was subject to a say on pay vote, both ISS
and Glass Lewis recommended a negative shareholder vote because Dimon's pay
package was inadequately linked to firm performance. At the annual meeting,
unlike typical shareholder say on pay votes, which receive 90 percent-plus favorable votes, only 31 percent of Chase's shares were voted in favor of the bank's pay
plans. Although it would be pure speculation to suggest that Dimon's and Chase's
high profile commitment to ESG was a factor in the negative shareholder vote, it
is safe to say that that commitment did not prevent shareholders from objecting to
Dimon's pay.

The bottom line is that "executive pay arrangements, and their evaluation by
shareholders and proxy advisors, provide executives with incentives not to ever sacrifice shareholder value to provide benefits to stakeholders."[19] The bulk of these
arrangements are not dependent on *Dodge* or its progeny. Instead, as with the corporate governance arrangements discussed above, they are based on legal rules that
would remain in place even if *Dodge* were overturned.

5.4 SUMMING UP

We've seen three sets of rules that, taken together, buttress shareholder value
maximization independently of *Dodge* and its progeny. In doing so, we've barely
scratched the surface:

- Only shareholders are entitled to inspect a corporation's books and records,
  which means only they have access to critical information about the corporation's activities.[20]
- Only shareholders are entitled to dividends.[21]

- Only shareholders have standing to sue under the various corporate governance provisions under federal law, with some minor exceptions for certain creditors.[22]
- Just as shareholders have the sole right to elect directors, "Delaware law considers the right to remove directors to be a fundamental element of stockholder authority."[23]

In sum, *Dodge* does not stand alone. Instead, *Dodge* is the logical culmination of the entirety of corporate law. As such, when we say that shareholder value maximization is the law, we mean the law writ large.

6

What about the Benefit Corporation?

The business corporation is just one of many types of corporations, each of which typically has its own statute. In my home state of California, for example, we have the general (a.k.a. business) corporation, the nonprofit corporation, the nonprofit religious corporation, the nonprofit medical corporation, the professional services corporation, the employee-owned corporation, and a small host of others. The list in other states varies slightly, but is usually equally comprehensive.

Since 2010, 35 states have adopted statutes creating a new form of corporation: the public benefit corporation (PBC). Although the details vary somewhat from state to state, in general PBC statutes are intended to provide a limited liability entity through which for-profit businesses could lawfully pursue stakeholder capitalism and ESG without running afoul of the shareholder value maximization rule laid down in *Dodge* and *eBay*. Although I am focused herein on business corporations, a few words should be said about the implications of the PBC for our subject matter. In particular, the adoption of PBC statutes tends to confirm a number of conclusions reached in the preceding chapters.

6.1 A BRIEF HISTORY OF THE BENEFIT CORPORATION

In the beginning, there was the "B Corp." In 2006, a nonprofit organization called B Lab was formed to provide third party certification of companies that comply with specified "standards of social and environmental performance, accountability, and transparency."[1] Companies may voluntarily submit to an evaluation by B Lab and, if they pass, be certified as a B Corp. The hope is that such certification enables consumers committed to various social justice causes to identify and patronize socially responsible companies. As a legal matter, however, certification as a B Corp is meaningless. In states like Delaware or Michigan, where shareholder value maximization is demonstrably the law, becoming certified as a B Corp does not change the directors' fiduciary obligation to maximize shareholder value. Even in states in which a constituency statute was on the books, there was considerable doubt about whether a certified B Corp's board of directors could make tradeoffs between shareholder and stakeholder interests.[2]

To resolve those doubts, B Lab began lobbying states to adopt PBC statutes that would allow boards of corporations formed under those statutes rather than under a general corporation statute to pursue the public benefit rather than exclusively focusing on shareholder value. The first such statute was adopted by Maryland in 2010. Three years later Delaware embraced the trend, amending the state's corporation statute to authorize companies to incorporate as public benefit corporations.

Delaware General Corporation Law § 362 defines the PBC as a "for-profit corporation ... that is intended to produce a public benefit or benefits and to operate in a responsible and sustainable manner." The "public benefit" must be specified in the firm's certificate of incorporation and consist of "a positive effect ... on one or more categories of persons, entities, communities or interests (other than stockholders in their capacities as stockholders) including, but not limited to, effects of an artistic, charitable, cultural, economic, educational, environmental, literary, medical, religious, scientific or technological nature." Existing for-profit corporations may convert to PBCs only with the approval of 90 percent of the outstanding shares, with any dissenting shareholders entitled to appraisal (that is, the right to be cashed out at fair market value). The PBC must, at least biennially, provide its shareholders with a statement that includes "objective factual information ... regarding [its] success in meeting [its] objectives for promoting [its specified] public benefits and interests." Other states have adopted similar provisions, with variations, particularly as to public disclosure, and third-party assessment, of the public benefit.[3]

In general, unlike companies incorporated under traditional business corporation statutes, those incorporated under a PBC statute are not just allowed but are required to deviate from the shareholder wealth maximization norm. Directors of a PBC must balance shareholder profit, stakeholder interests, and the company's stated public benefit. Thousands of PBCs have been formed and a small number have even gone public.[4]

6.2 IMPLICATIONS FOR *DODGE*

Although it has not done so to date, the widespread availability of PBCs as an alternative to the traditional business corporation could alleviate the growing pressure on the latter to pursue ESG, since they provide an alternative by which social justice activists can pursue their ESG goals while still making a profit. In any case, the widespread adoption of PBC statutes confirms that *Dodge* is corporate law's general rule. After all, if *Dodge* were not the law, PBCs would be unnecessary. Boards of business corporations would be free to pursue public benefits without violating their fiduciary duties. The perceived need for PBC statutes suggests that boards are not free to do so absent the statute.[*]

---

[*] The drafters of the California PBC statute presumably had such an argument in mind when they including the following qualification in the statute: "The existence of a provision of this part shall not of itself create any implication that a contrary or different rule of law is or would be applicable to a business corporation that is not a benefit corporation." CAL. CORP. CODE § 14600 (b).

6.3 IMPLICATIONS FOR CONSTITUENCY STATUTES

The widespread adoption of PBC statutes likewise tends to confirm the essential meaningless of constituency statutes. If the constituency statutes had any real significance with respect to the legal obligations of directors, the PBC statutes would be unnecessary. Yet, as noted, there was considerable doubt as to whether constituency statutes allowed B Corps to function as such.

6.4 IMPLICATIONS FOR THE REST OF CORPORATE LAW

Just as one cannot expect directors to begin making tradeoffs between shareholder and stakeholder interests just by changing the general rule as set forth in *Dodge* (see the preceding chapter), "it is arguable that, despite the rhetoric of public benefit contained in the orthodox benefit corporation model, the directors of a benefit corporation … will ultimately serve the private interests of the shareholders rather than some broad social good."[5] After all, PBC statutes typically incorporate by reference the provisions of the state's general business corporation statute.[6] PBC directors are exclusively elected by shareholders.[7] Directors of PBCs owe no fiduciary duty to stakeholders.[8] Shareholders of PBCs typically retain the exclusive right to bring derivative litigation, even if the gravamen of the suit is that the directors failed to adequately take into account social and environmental factors relevant to the PBC's stated public benefit.[9][*]

---

[*] Professors Fisch and Solomon contend that PBC statutes actually perpetuate "the shareholder primacy norm by vesting shareholders – as in the traditional corporation – with ultimate power and control over the PBC and the implementation of its purpose." Jill E. Fisch & Steven Davidoff Solomon, *The "Value" of a Public Benefit Corporation, in* RESEARCH HANDBOOK ON CORPORATE PURPOSE AND PERSONHOOD 68 (Elizabeth Pollman & Robert B. Thompson, eds., 2021). In addition, they point out that most PBC's purpose statements are "too vague and aspirational to be legally significant, or even to serve as a reliable tool for evaluating whether corporate decisionmakers are adhering to the PBC's social mission." *Id.*

PART II

The Merits

7

Possible Merits of the Business Roundtable's Embrace of Stakeholder Capitalism

There are a lot of points at which one could begin reviewing the century-old debate over corporate social responsibility and shareholder value maximization. Although the famous Berle–Dodd debate in the early 1930s is often cited as the opening round of the debate, earlier eruptions worthy of study include the late Nineteenth Century populist and the early Twentieth Century Progressive critiques of corporate capitalism. Alternatively, one could start with the intellectual ferment that gave rise to *Smith Manufacturing*. Milton Friedman's 1970 essay on the social responsibility of business would make a sensible starting point, as would the constituency statutes of the 1990s. We will have occasion to touch on all of these.

Given the voluminous literature that each of those moments generated, however, it makes sense to start with the more recent incident that triggered the need for this book; i.e., the Business Roundtable's 2019 statement reversing course on corporate purpose. The trouble is that the statement doesn't actually make any arguments. Instead, it relies on a couple of platitudes:

> Americans deserve an economy that allows each person to succeed through hard work and creativity and to lead a life of meaning and dignity. We believe the free-market system is the best means of generating good jobs, a strong and sustainable economy, innovation, a healthy environment and economic opportunity for all.
>
> Businesses play a vital role in the economy by creating jobs, fostering innovation and providing essential goods and services. Businesses make and sell consumer products; manufacture equipment and vehicles; support the national defense; grow and produce food; provide health care; generate and deliver energy; and offer financial, communications and other services that underpin economic growth.[1]

That's it.

If the drafters of the Business Roundtable statement had tried to justify their reversal, what serious arguments might they have offered up in lieu of platitudes? The positive commentary that followed in the wake of the statement lets us identify a number of claims of varying merit. So, let's do the work the Business Roundtable CEOs couldn't be bothered to do.

7.1 EXTERNALITIES

Corporate social responsibility advocates contend that business corporations are to blame for a host of social ills. Harvard Business School Professor Malcolm S. Salter, for example, blamed corporations for a laundry list that includes environmental degradation, income inequality, crony capitalism, evasion of regulation, pervasive cheating by business, lack of accountability for corporate misdeeds, and systemic unemployment.[2] Famed corporate lawyer Martin Lipton offered a slightly different list, which includes "short-termism, hostile takeovers, extortion by corporate raiders, junk bond financing and the erosion of protections for employees, the environment and society generally, all in support of increasing corporate profits and maximizing value for shareholders."[3] Michigan business school professor Gerald Davis offered yet another list, including the opioid epidemic, obesity, nicotine addiction, the depression and anxiety experienced by young users of social media, and climate change. He concluded that it seems as though "business executives somehow believed that 'companies should produce addictive products, minimize their wage bills and costs of employment, pollute the environment, avoid paying taxes so long as this raises their share price and does not undermine their share price for reputational or other risk reasons.'"[4]

Stakeholder theorists contend that, as corporations grow ever larger, such negative externalities will grow both in size and complexity.[5] Continued globalization will compound the problem, both because companies can locate activities generating the most externalities in countries with weak regulatory systems and some issues – such as carbon emissions – transcend national boundaries.[6] Indeed, globalization itself is blamed for creating corporate externalities, such as the carbon put into the atmosphere by transportation vehicles deployed in global supply chains.

As we saw in the Introduction, corporate conduct undoubtedly generates negative externalities. In appropriate cases, such externalities should be constrained through general welfare legislation, tort litigation, and other forms of regulation. Yet, it is easy to overstate the significance of those externalities. There is a notion abroad in the land, abetted by much of popular culture and typified by the Salter, Lipton, and Davis' critiques, that corporate managers and lawyers unwind from a hard day of nefarious skullduggery by torturing puppies. If the stereotype were true, it might justify an expansive approach to corporate social responsibility. Yet, there is no evidence that businessmen and women are any less ethical than, say, the Hollywood types who make such movies as *Erin Brockovich* or *A Civil Action*.[7]

7.1.1 *Stakeholder Capitalism Produces Greenwashing Not Change*

The existence of corporate externalities can be conceded without conceding that the Business Roundtable CEOs and other corporate social responsibility proponents are correct. In the first instance, voluntary corporate social responsibility and ESG efforts are likely to result in more greenwashing than real change.[8]

ESG in its current form is more a buzzword than a solution. Each of its three domains presents different measurement opportunities and challenges, a fact not adequately addressed by existing disclosure standards. As a consequence, few ESG reports engage meaningfully with the moral trade-offs within the three domains and with the company's profits. Companies also selectively present metrics that portray themselves in a favorable light, resulting in the widespread perception that ESG reporting is awash in greenwash. Not surprisingly, auditors of these reports often resort to double negatives—"We found no evidence of misreporting in the company's ESG report"—and the reports themselves have had little impact on either corporate actions or external stakeholders.[9]

This is not a new complaint. Critics of corporate social responsibility, especially those on the left, have long argued that purportedly pro-social corporate actions function mainly as public relations masking an ongoing commitment to the profit motive. The most vociferous of these critics view corporate social responsibility as a capitalist plot to co-opt or distract efforts to tame and humanize the corporation.

A widely discussed example of purported misuse of corporate social responsibility was the 1991 controversy over oil company ARCO's much ballyhooed announcement that it had developed a less polluting gasoline formulation. ARCO announced it would produce gasoline using the new formula only if California mandated that all gasoline sold in the state be made using the formula. Critics quickly pointed out that the supposedly environmentally friendly development was not motivated by social responsibility but by the fact that ARCO's crude oil supplies and refineries were better suited to producing the new formula than those of ARCO's competitors. Instead of being socially responsible, ARCO was trying to score points with the environmental community while simultaneously getting an advantage over its competitors by raising their costs.

As we will discuss in more detail in Chapter 10, much greenwashing is driven by the incentives of CEOs and other top managers. But even if we set aside those individuals incentives, corporations today would still have strong financial incentives to engage in greenwashing. Empirical research shows that where corporate activism is aligned with the preferences of customers, sales increase. The same research found that, in such cases, the activist company's stock price rose. Conversely, when corporate activism was misaligned with customer preferences, both sales and the stock price declined.[10] Not surprisingly, "there has been a worrying increase in the amount of misleading information produced by companies, including information on environmental and social aspects."[11]

Those findings are corroborated by examining the social performance of portfolio companies of ESG investment funds. European corporations with major operations in Russia prior to the outbreak of the Russo-Ukrainian war typically had higher ESG ratings than those who were not operating in Russia. Doing extensive business in an increasingly authoritarian and militaristic country apparently had little, if any, impact on the ESG industry's perceptions of those companies. Perhaps even more instructively, however, is that companies with lower ESG ratings were more likely to divest or suspend any Russian operations than companies with higher ESG ratings. All of which tends to call into question the merits of the ESG industry's claims to be socially responsible.

An academic study of ESG investment fund portfolio companies likewise found that they had significantly more labor and environmental violations than portfolio companies of non-ESG funds.[12] The supposedly ESG friendly portfolio companies also paid higher fines for those violations than the non-ESG fund portfolio companies. The former also exhibited worse performance on carbon emissions. The authors conclude that their "results undermine such funds' claims that they are picking socially responsible stocks for inclusion and suggest substantial greenwashing on the part of ESG funds."[13] Noting that "ESG funds (i) obtain lower stock returns but (ii) charge higher management fees," the authors posit that "ESG funds may simply represent a way for asset managers to command higher management fees in what has increasingly become a low-fee industry."[14]

7.1.2 *Shareholders Are More Vulnerable to Director and Manager Misconduct than Stakeholders*

Even if the business community's response to the problem of corporate externalities issue were not mostly greenwashing, concern for externalities still would provide only weak support for the Business Roundtable's change of position. First, shareholders are more vulnerable to director misconduct than are most non-shareholder constituencies. To be sure, Professors Margaret Blair and Lynn Stout asserted that "when directors use their corporate position to steal money from the firm, every" constituency suffers.[15] But that is not necessarily the case. Consider a classic case of self-dealing at a solvent corporation able to pay its debts and other obligations (especially employee salaries) as they come due in the ordinary course of business. Further assume that the corporation has substantial free cash flow. If the directors siphon some portion of the corporation's free cash flow into their own pockets, shareholders are clearly hurt, because the value of the residual claim has been impaired. Yet, in this case, there is no readily apparent injury to the value of the fixed claim of all other corporate constituents.

Second, to the extent corporate externalities impose costs on stakeholders, it is easier for most of them to hedge that risk by owning stock than for shareholders to protect themselves by becoming non-shareholder constituents. Even employees can hedge some risk by investing in their employer's stock via a 401(k) plan. Such hedging is analytically important because wealth transfers from stakeholders to shareholders are less problematic if stakeholders are on both sides of that transaction. Such wealth transfers also become less likely because stakeholder concerns with issues like working conditions, wages, environmental protection and so on are more likely to be viewed as corporate priorities when stakeholders make up a substantial percentage of shareholders.[16]

7.1.3 *Stakeholders Have Contractual Protections Unavailable to Shareholders*

The externalities argument also fails because stakeholders have forms of protection largely unavailable to shareholders; namely, mobility, contracts, and general welfare legislation.[17] Starting with contractual protections, it is the case that protecting stakeholders by contract is far more feasible than protecting shareholders by contract.[18] The most obvious example is that of bondholders and other substantial creditors, whose relationship with the firm is memorialized in complex contracts containing various representations, warranties, covenants, and conditions designed to protect the bondholders from conduct by the corporation that puts their interests at risk.[19]

Like bondholders, employees regularly bargain with employers both individually and collectively. So do other stakeholders, such as local communities that bargain with existing or prospective employers, offering firms tax abatements and other inducements in return for which they could and should extract promises about the firm's conduct. In general, the interests of such constituents lend themselves to more concrete specification then do the open-ended claims of shareholders. Those non-shareholder constituencies that enter voluntary relationships with the corporation thus can protect themselves by adjusting the contract price to account for negative externalities imposed upon them by the firm.

Unlike shareholders whose contractual rights are typically set in the corporation's organic documents and are mostly fixed thereafter, stakeholders' contracts are often renegotiated. If management treats stakeholders opportunistically, the stakeholders can punish the corporation when the contract next comes up for renegotiation. If a particular corporation abuses its bondholders, for example, the investment community may demand that future bonds contain protective covenants.

Granted, the extent of negotiations between the corporation and stakeholders is likely to vary widely. In addition, because companies and stakeholders must operate under conditions of uncertainty and complexity, bounded rationality precludes complete contracting.* As a result, in many cases, such as hiring shop floor employees, the only negotiation will be a take-it-or-leave-it offer. But so what? Is a standard form contract any less of a contract just because it is offered on a take-it-or-leave-it basis? If the market is competitive, a party making a take-it-or-leave-it offer must propose price and other terms that will lead to sales despite the absence of particularized negotiations. As long as the firm must attract inputs from non-shareholder

---

* The term bounded rationality was coined by Herbert Simon. See Herbert A. Simon, *Rational Choice and the Structure of the Environment, in* MODELS OF MAN: SOCIAL & RATIONAL 261, 271 (1957). According to the theory of bounded rationality, economic actors seek to maximize their expected utility, but the limitations of human cognition often result in decisions that fail to maximize utility. Decisionmakers inherently have limited memories, computational skills, and other mental tools, which in turn limit their ability to gather and process information. *See generally* Roy Radner, *Bounded Rationality, Indeterminacy, and the Theory of the Firm,* 106 ECON. J. 1360, 1362–68 (1996) (providing an especially detailed taxonomy of the various forms bounded rationality takes, with special emphasis on the theory's relevance to corporate governance).

constituencies in competitive markets, the firm similarly will have to offer those
constituencies terms that compensate them for the risks they bear.

In the employment market, for example, various market mechanisms evolved to
protect employee investments in firm-specific human capital, such as ports of entry,
seniority systems, and promotion ladders. Although these are not negotiated with
individual employees, they are a common feature of collective bargaining.[20] Given
the decline of private sector unions, of course, collective bargaining no longer provides the protections for employees that it formerly offered. Likewise, the rise of
the gig economy has resulted in broad swaths of the economy in which employees
have minimal contractual protections. Employee handbooks and policy manuals
provide, at best, modest protections. Compared to other stakeholders, contractual
protections for employees admittedly are modest and, moreover, declining. The difficulty, of course, is that stakeholder theory is not limited to employees.

Like employees, moreover, shareholders are poorly positioned to extract contractual protections. Unlike bondholders, for example, whose term-limited relationship
to the firm is subject to extensive negotiations and detailed contracts, shareholders
have an indefinite relationship that is rarely the product of detailed negotiations.
The dispersed nature of stock ownership, moreover, makes bilateral negotiation of
specialized safeguards especially difficult.

7.1.4 *General Welfare Legislation Protects*
Stakeholders Even Post-Citizens United

Stakeholders receive important protection against corporate externalities in the
form of general welfare legislation. Recall my story about growing up in the early
1960s near the heavily polluted Nashua River. To the extent the river and its counterparts around the country are cleaner today, it is largely not thanks to stakeholder
capitalism but because governments passed environmental laws.

Corporate compliance with these and other regulations intended to protect stakeholders and society in general is a standard assumption of *Dodge's* progeny. The American
Law Institute's Principles of Corporate Governance, for example, provide that "a corporation should have as its objective the conduct of business activities with a view to
enhancing corporate profit and shareholder gain," but further provide that corporations
are obliged "to act within the boundaries set by law."[21] In an opinion written while he
was Chancellor of the Delaware Chancery Court, Leo Strine explained that "Delaware
law does not charter law breakers. Delaware law allows corporations to pursue diverse
means to make a profit, subject to a critical statutory floor, which is the requirement that
Delaware corporations only pursue 'lawful business' by 'lawful acts.'"[22] One can therefore achieve many of the stated social justice goals of stakeholder capitalism – including
both remediating negative externalities and inducing corporations to generate positive
externalities – through regulation without the need to reject shareholder value maximization. Or, at the very least, as my friend the late law professor Larry Ribstein argued,

"external regulation can be viewed as an important limitation on the discretion of those who hold power in the firm to decide whether to be socially responsible."[23]

Indeed, in today's conditions, targeted legislative and regulatory responses to the externalities created by corporate conduct are preferable to stakeholder capitalism. By virtue of their inherent ambiguity, fiduciary duties are a blunt instrument. There can be no assurance that specific social ills will be addressed by the boards of the specific corporations that are creating the problematic externalities. General welfare laws designed to deter corporate misconduct through criminal and civil sanctions imposed on the corporation, its directors, and its senior officers thus are more effective ways of achieving specific outcomes than tweaking director fiduciary duties to overturn *Dodge*, *Revlon*, and their ilk.

Numerous studies by scholars in finance, accounting, and economics support that claim by documenting that financial markets impose a significant penalty on companies that break the law. The types of corporate misconduct that have been studied include litigation involving corporations as defendants in environmental regulations, product liability, antitrust, financial disclosure violation, financial fraud, employment and age discrimination. The penalty imposed by the financial markets tends to be several times larger than the administrative or legal fines the companies pay for the foregoing types of misconduct.[24]

Leo Strine and his coauthor Nicholas Walter nevertheless rejected the claim that regulation effectively constrains corporate misconduct. Their argument had four basic parts. First, they claimed that corporations inherently generate externalities, imposing some costs on both specific outsiders and society at large. This point is uncontroversial, of course. Second, in appropriate cases, society uses law to force corporations to internalize at least some of those costs. Again, this point is basically uncontroversial, although obviously there is considerable debate over when regulatory intervention becomes appropriate. Third, they contend that corporations have incentives to resist regulation. Yet again, this point is unremarkable. Regulation imposes costs on corporations, which managers spurred by the profit motive will seek to minimize. Finally, Strine and Walter argued that the U.S. Supreme Court's *Citizens United v. FEC*[25] decision unleashed a torrent of corporate political campaign contributions intended to undermine general welfare legislation that function as constraint on the externalities caused by corporate conduct.[26] It is on this point that I depart company with their analysis.

Strine and Walter assert that, after *Citizens United*, the very success of the corporate form as a wealth-generating tool is in tension with shareholder value maximization because if the wealth impounded in corporations can be used in unlimited amounts to influence who is elected to the offices that determine the "rules of the game" the range of policy options is likely to move in a direction where there is greater danger of externality risk ....[27] As a result, they contend, the law should allow directors to "put a value on things like the quality of the environment, the elimination of poverty, the alleviation of suffering among the ill, and other values that animate actual human beings."[28] As we'll see below, however, placing a value on such things is essentially a political decision, which boards and executives are poorly equipped to make. On top of which, it is one thing when directors and executives decide to spend their own money on such social goods, but it is quite another when they spend someone else's money on them. Lastly, as we will also see below, preserving a democratic society requires that such decisions be left to the political process.

Of course, Strine and Walter's argument is precisely that the political process no longer functions as a constraint on corporate externalities and social ills. Obviously, corporations have both incentives and the resources to resist some or even most regulation. Nevertheless, Strine and Walter's argument that regulation is ineffectual post-*Citizen's United* is unpersuasive. First, despite their description of money flooding the political system, the absolute amounts being spent seem unremarkable. In the 2020 election cycle, the total amount spent on all political campaigns by all actors was, according to OpenSecrets.org, $14.4 billion. To put that figure in context, industry publication Ad Age reported that Amazon alone spent over $11 billion on advertising in 2020. In perspective, corporations simply are not spending all that much money on affecting regulation.

Second, contrary to Strine and Walter's argument that corporate political spending is deployed to erode regulations necessary to constrain the externalities inherent in corporate business activity, much corporate political spending in fact is defensive. As The Economist magazine reported, the United States originally recognized just three federal criminal offenses; namely, treason, counterfeiting and piracy.[29] Today, the list is almost endless. A study from the early 1990s estimated that there were at least 300,000 statutes and rules the violation of which carried criminal penalties. In the intervening decades, the number has surely grown, as the domain of federal criminal law has grown exponentially during that period, "propelled primarily by agency regulations."[30] On top of which, federal civil regulation has grown exponentially over the decades.[31]

The resulting costs are staggering. A study of global financial firms found that they spend $213.9 billion worldwide on regulatory compliance.[32] In 2018, half of surveyed financial firms estimated they spent between six and ten percent of annual revenues on compliance costs.[33] Compliance with all federal regulations in 2012 cost firms almost $10,000 per employee.[34]

In this environment, much corporate political spending likely goes to stave off additional regulation rather than to repealing existing laws. In the absence of a showing that the benefits of foregone regulations exceed their costs, there is no reason to assume that corporate political spending increases the extent to which corporations can externalize costs. Strine and Walter offered no convincing evidence that corporate political spending in fact has the effect they posit.

Strine and Walter also fail to take into account the likelihood that much corporate political spending will simply cancel out spending by other corporations. It seems intuitively obvious that specific regulations rarely advantage all businesses. If so, spending by opponents of particular laws or rules likely will be countered by those who benefit from them.[35] Accordingly, *Citizens United*'s alleged anti-regulatory effect will be self-minimizing.

Lastly, Strine and Walter fail to explore the implications of the fact that large corporations dominate corporate campaign spending.[36] Spending by such corporations is highly constrained by reputational considerations due to "the seriousness with which large corporations treat any potential threats to their goodwill arising from … negative publicity" generated by unpopular contributions.[37] More importantly, while Strine and Walter assume corporations use political spending exclusively to externalize the negative costs of their activities, the reality is that large corporations frequently support regulations that force corporations to internalize social costs. They do so because such regulation can create significant costs for smaller competitors and barriers to entry for startups. Regulatory costs frequently do not scale, so their costs often are borne disproportionately by small businesses and startups.

Let us suppose, however, that Strine and Walter are correct about the consequences of *Citizens United*. Is the answer to throw up our hands, admit the inadequacy of social efforts to control corporate externalities, and depend on the goodwill of executives? Would not allowing corporate executives to behave as though corporations are just like natural persons and allowing to make decisions as though they were sole proprietors spending their own money simply function as a mask for privilege? Corporate law is simply not the right tool for preventing negative corporate externalities or promoting positive ones.

7.1.5 *Who Does Mobility Protect?*

The question of whether mobility protects shareholders or stakeholders is controversial, complex, and nuanced. On the one hand, it is certainly true that shareholders often can withdraw their investment in a public corporation at relatively low cost by selling their stock on the secondary market. Hence, the old Wall Street Rule advised that it was easier to switch than fight. But that rule developed in the days when most investors were individuals holding portfolios consisting of shares in a relatively small number of companies. Those investors had plenty of other companies into which to shift their funds. Today, by way of contrast, individuals typically invest through mutual funds. Increasingly, investors are focusing on index funds that hold the entire market or, at least, broad tranches of the market such as the S&P 500. Such investors cannot exit a single firm and thus are essentially immobilized.

On the other hand, many stakeholders lack meaningful mobility. This is particularly true of labor. The transaction costs of switching jobs are non-trivial, although employment websites have reduced some of those costs. In addition, some stakeholders – especially but not limited to employees – make investments in firm-specific human capital that would be lost if they tried to leave a corporation that was imposing costs on them.

Having said that, however, the mobility problem is not quite as bad as some stakeholder capitalism proponents claim. Many corporate constituencies do not make firm-specific investments in either human capital or otherwise. Many corporate employees, for example, lack significant firm specific human capital. For such employees, mobility may be a sufficient defense against opportunistic conduct, because they can quit and be replaced without productive loss to either employee or employer.[38]

7.2 SOCIETY EXPECTS BUSINESS TO SOLVE SOCIAL PROBLEMS BECAUSE GOVERNMENT CAN'T OR WON'T

The polarization of national politics and resulting political gridlock have encouraged activists to turn to corporations to effect social change they are unable to obtain politically.[39] Activists increasingly expect corporations to do more than tend to their own knitting. Instead, along with dealing with the externalities their business activities create, corporations are expected to use public statements, lobbying, political contributions, sponsorships of nongovernmental organizations, and so on to solve social problems generally.[40] Almost two-thirds of global consumers, for example, reportedly think CEOs should take the lead on issues like climate change.[41] The percentages may vary, but similar expectations now exist with respect to many other social issues.[42]

The mainstreaming of this expectation was highlighted by BlackRock CEO Laurence D. (Larry) Fink's February 2018 letter to the CEOs of BlackRock's portfolio companies, which posited that long-term business success required that "every company must not only deliver financial performance, but also show how it makes a positive contribution to society."[43] Indeed, Fink's annual letters to CEOs have become a steady goad for CEOs to be more socially proactive. In 2022, for example, he emphasized that it is "essential for CEOs to have a consistent voice, a clear purpose, a coherent strategy, and a long-term view."[44] In his view, this requires CEOs to make clear where they stand on social issues pertinent to the company's mission. To be sure, Fink acknowledged that successful corporations need to produce value for shareholders but he also insisted that in order to do so companies must create value for their stakeholders.

This is hardly a new argument. Back in the 1930s Professor Dodd's pro-corporate social responsibility argument rested in large part on the belief that society demanded that business assume social responsibilities.[45] Forty years later, liberals were still arguing that society was plagued by a host of urgent social ills and that, there being no time to wait for the political process to solve them, business should take the lead. They believed that business could effect social change faster and more effectively than politics.[46]

Setting aside until Chapter 10 the inconsistency of this argument with democratic principles, what justifies drafting the corporation to tackle social ills? Some stakeholder theorists will point to concession theory to justify effectuating stakeholder capitalism. Concession theory has its roots in Chief Justice of the United States John Marshall's 1819 *Dartmouth College* decision. In his opinion, Marshall described the corporation as an "artificial being" that is a "mere creature of law."[47] This understanding gave rise to concession theory, a.k.a., grant theory, which posits that because the corporation can only come into existence if the state grants the business a certificate of incorporation the state can require the corporation to be socially responsible rather than single-mindedly pursuing shareholder value.[48] Put another way, concession theory proponents argue that businesses are the creation of society and thus have a moral obligation to work in the best interest of society.

Concession theory may have made sense in the very earliest days of the Republic, when incorporation required individualized special legislative charters. Incorporation at that time literally was a privilege granted by the state. Once general incorporation statutes came onto the books, however, the notion of incorporation as a special privilege or grant quickly faded away. Instead, the state's role became purely ministerial. As a result, it has been decades since either courts or scholars took concession theory seriously as a rationale for regulating corporations.[49] It thus proffers a week reed, at best, for the dramatic change in the law that would be required to effect the Business Roundtable's statement.

In contrast to the weakness of the argument in favor of using corporations to solve social ills, there are potent reasons to be dubious of doing so.[*] First, business lacks the skill set necessary to address broad social ills. Consider, for example, the question of climate change, which has become a – if not the – central ESG issue. If we ask companies to comply with environmental regulations and to take into account costs such as carbon taxes, we are asking them to do things for which business executives are trained. In contrast, asking them to evaluate the adequacy of existing government policies to solve climate change and, if not, to decide how to keep global warming within tolerable limits is asking them to deal with questions far outside their wheelhouse. "It is far beyond the capabilities of most companies to determine the appropriate tax on shareholders in order to pursue climate change objectives."[50]

As another example, consider the question of corporate patriotism.[51] Should an American company sell dual-use technology to a potential adversary such as Russia (I am writing this Chapter during the Russo-Ukrainian War of 2022)? Who is better positioned to decide what is in the country's best interest? A corporate executive or a government expert in international relations and military affairs? It is precisely for this reason that the U.S. government created regulatory agencies such as The Committee on Foreign Investment in the United States (CFIUS) to review business transactions that might adversely affect U.S. national security. Granted, a vast number of cross-border transactions remain unregulated. But this is an argument for improved government regulation rather than an argument for leaving such decisions to the goodwill and expertise of business executives. Some will argue that cross-border transactions are beyond the reach of domestic regulation, of course, but the sanctions imposed on Russia after its invasion of the Ukraine rather forcefully demonstrated the long reach of American law.

---

[*] Some critics of using business to solve social ills also argue that business is already too powerful and that power would only increase if responsibility for dealing with such ills shifts from government to business. I address that argument in the next section.

A core problem thus is that most directors and officers likely lack the skill set necessary to make decisions about ESG issues. If asked to resolve the more complex and difficult questions required by stakeholder capitalism, managers would "need to acquire much new information and expertise."[52] As long as they lack such information and skills, asking managers to focus on such questions will inevitably distract them from ensuring that their company makes money for the shareholders.

Larry Ribstein aptly framed the problem as follows:

> Should firms sell genetically modified (GM) foods? What weight should managers give to scientific evidence supporting the value and safety of GM foods? Should a socially-responsible manager consider, among other things, whether GM foods reduce world hunger or whether, given the current state of the scientific evidence, such a benefit is outweighed by the long-term costs, including potential genetic contamination? What types of genetic manipulation should managers be concerned about in their sales or manufacturing decisions? By contrast, a profit-maximizing manager need only make the simpler (though still difficult) calculation of whether the firm would gain or lose from selling GM foods.[53]

In short, developing "rules for the public good, including, where appropriate, to restrain private avarice," is not what corporations were designed to do,[54] nor for which executives are trained. Even today, the standard undergraduate and MBA corporate finance texts assume that shareholders are the corporation's residual claimants and that the firm should be run for their benefit.[55]

This is so in large part because answering those sort of questions is more a matter of politics than of business. As Robert Miller observed, even some prominent proponents of stakeholder capitalism have acknowledged that it requires directors to make what are in effect political decisions.[56] Merrick Dodd, for example, believed that directors should be guided "by the attitude of public and business opinion as to the social obligations of business."[57] Lynn Stout and Margaret Blair accepted that "the returns to any particular corporate stakeholder from participating in the corporation will be determined not only by market forces but by *political* forces."[58] Yet, as making business decisions becomes more like political decisions, we not only ask managers to step outside of their wheelhouse but to juggle increasing demands by increasing numbers of constituencies.

Even if managers had the requisite knowledge and skills, they probably have a very weak idea of what shareholders would prefer with respect to social issues.[59] Of course, some large shareholders can communicate their preferences to management. Larry Fink's annual letters to the CEOs of BlackRock's portfolio companies are but the best known example of this phenomenon. Yet, as we'll see below, those shareholders often act in ways that are inconsistent with the messages they are sending. Should management pay attention to what these investors say or what they do? In addition, it is hardly clear that Larry Fink's preferences are representative of that of investors as a class, especially that of small retail investors.

Finally, corporate executives lack incentives to solve social ills especially insofar as those ills fall outside their enterprise's business. Put another way, while business may have incentives to deal with the negative externalities produced by the enterprise's activities, they lack incentives to generate positive externalities that bestow benefits on society without generating a return for their shareholders.[60] To the contrary, as we'll discuss in more detail in Chapter 10, managers' incentives are aligned more closely with the shareholders' interest in value maximization than with ESG concerns. Of course, managers' incentives are even more closely aligned with their own self-interest.

Suppose the corporation has substantial free cash flow – i.e., funds in excess of that needed to pay current expenses and maintain capital assets. Due to the business judgment rule, boards and managers will have largely unfettered discretion to expend free cash flows, so long as they avoid egregious self-dealing. Is it more reasonable to expect boards and officers to expend such funds on saving the planet or on higher salaries and perquisites for the company's officers? In a very real sense, after all, corporate expenditures on ESG concerns do not come out of the pockets of either shareholders or stakeholders. Instead, they come out of management's pockets. As such, those who expect managers to voluntarily expend corporate funds on ESG concerns are likely to be disappointed.

Consider, for example, the problem of social and wealth inequality. The top third of Americans who are skilled, college-educated workers and managers in successfully globalized industries such as finance, technology, and electronics have done well. The bottom two-thirds are low-skilled workers whose jobs have been lost or threatened by globalization and technology. Foreign trade, foreign direct investment, immigration, and declining union participation have also played a role in their declining fortunes.[61] Big business has seemed to be neither able or even very interested in addressing their concerns.[62]

The lack of corporate interest should not be surprising. We cannot realistically count on corporations to train and retrain workers to deal with the emerging economy. Despite some credible efforts at privatization, education in general remains a public good.[63] Likewise, the benefits of retraining of workers – especially when it involves teaching complex skills – are sufficiently diffuse and widespread that individual businesses are unlikely to undertake it at the level society will require.[64]

Accordingly, as economists Sanjai Bhagat and Glenn Hubbard observe, "shareholders could use the profits of the corporation for social purposes if they wished, less wastefully than if management pursued such activities with, perhaps, more self-interest on its part."[65] Professors Bhagat and Hubbard cite as but one example, albeit an extreme one, Bill Gates, who "having founded a very successful company, Microsoft, now uses his share of the profits from this company to engage in significant philanthropic activities across the globe."[66]

7.3 CORPORATIONS HAVE TOO MUCH POWER

The power of corporations in society takes several forms, as Martin Petrin explains:

> First, corporations have instrumental or direct power; that is, they have the power
> to make decisions that affect others or the discretion to choose between different
> decisions that will affect others. Second, corporations have structural power by
> being able to set the agenda and by their ability to shape the economic environ-
> ment. Relatedly, they also have political power, which is tied to their structural
> power, and more specifically refers to their disproportionate influence over the
> political process, their superior ability to mobilize political resources, to influence
> the political agenda with threats of exit from the country, as well as their ability to
> set the rules themselves through the growing practice of corporate self-regulation.
> Finally, corporations have the power to influence and shape the wants of others
> through social conditioning or advertising, and by framing the public discourse.[67]

As we saw in the preceding section, some corporate social responsibility proponents
want corporations to use their wealth and influence to solve social problems. Other
corporate social responsibility proponents, however, reject that argument. They
claim that corporations already have too much power and corporate social responsibility is a necessary constraint on that power.

Complaints about excessive corporate power are not new. Like Jeffersonians of
the early 1800s, populist movements in the late 1800s and early 1900s objected to
concentrated corporate power.[68] There is a certain amount of irony in the populists'
opposition to corporate power, as the expansion of the availability of the corporate
form in the middle of the nineteenth century had been an outgrowth of mid-century
populist democratic theory. The mid-nineteenth century legislators who made the
limited liability corporation widely available via the enabling statutes did so precisely to encourage small and impecunious entrepreneurs to start and grow new
businesses.[69]

By the end of the nineteenth century, however, it had become populist doctrine
that their predecessors, "effort to control big business by popularizing the corporate
form" had backfired by "facilitating the rise of corporate robber barons."[70] As a result,
populists concluded that the growing power of corporations was a significant threat
to their economic and even political liberty. The Southern Agrarians of the 1930s,
for example, believed that "the corporate form of our economic system makes possible a scale of exploitation unheard of in history."[71] Frank Lawrence Owsley typified
the Southern Agrarian belief that the people's common enemy was "a system which
allows a relatively few men to control most of the nation's wealth and to regiment
virtually the whole population under their anonymous holding companies and corporations, and to control government by bribery or intimidation."[72]

In particular, the Agrarians saw large corporations as leviathans trampling on agricul-
ture and labor. The concentration of economic power in large corporations had created
"a plutocratic corporate capitalist class" that effectively ruled the country and thus stood

ready to fully exploit their power over farmers and workers.[73] Labor, especially, lacked security. Workers toiled under dehumanizing conditions. Yet, the Agrarians argued, the law protected capital by enshrining the rights of corporations into the Constitution.[74]

Today's populists have revived these concerns. On the left, movements such as Occupy Wall Street focus on corporate power. But we also see similar concerns on the populist right, which is considerably less friendly towards big business than have been traditional center-right movements. Since Pat Buchanan's presidential campaigns in the 1990s, right-wing populists have come to believe that large corporations and crony capitalism are undermining America's exceptionalism and America's national identity through globalization, while simultaneously impoverishing the working class and enriching the financial and technology oligarchs. This concern reached a peak in the wake of the post-financial crisis bailouts. In response to the *Citizens United* decision,[75] for example, Tea Party co-founder Dale Robertson complained that "[c]orporations are not like people. Corporations exist forever, people don't. Our founding fathers never wanted them; these behemoth organizations that never die …. It puts the people at a tremendous disadvantage."[76] Tea Party activists also tend to be uncomfortable with business' political agenda and business' lack of support for Tea Party social issues.[77] The inability or unwillingness of large corporations to assist in addressing the political alienation and economic instability felt by many thus helped elect Donald Trump. As Sarah Smarsh explained in a New York Times op-ed, her white, pro-Trump working class father was mainly angry "at bosses who exploit labor and governments that punish the working poor – two sides of a capitalist democracy that bleeds people like him dry. 'Corporations,' Dad said. 'That's it. That's the point of the sword that's killing us.'"[78]

Outside populist circles, we also hear similar claims today from pro-corporate social responsibility academics. As Petrin argues, for example, corporations have "become 'completely dominant' elements of our society."[79] The proposition that with great power comes great responsibility is not just a famous comic book aphorism, but is a truism for proponents of corporate social responsibility such as Petrin.[80]

These arguments may justify restraints on the use of corporate power, but they do not justify relying on stakeholder capitalism to constrain that power. If it is correct that corporations are unlikely to exercise their powers to solve social ills, as we saw in the preceding section, it seems even less likely that corporations will voluntarily adopt corporate social responsibility-based constraints on their use of those powers in the pursuit of profit. As we've seen, voluntary corporate social responsibility is likely to be more about greenwashing than constraining corporate power.

7.4 MILLENNIALS AND CENTENNIALS WILL ONLY WORK FOR WOKE COMPANIES

As the Millennial and Centennial (a.k.a. Generation Z) generations move into prime working and investing years, with their ages ranging from 25 to 41 in 2022, the business community naturally is becoming increasingly responsive to their prefer-ences. Conventional wisdom is that Millennials and Centennials are both consid-erably to the left of prior generations and more willing to scrutinize the firms with which they interact as consumers, workers, and investors.[81] As investors, Millennials supposedly embrace progressive policy preferences and are using their growing wealth and demographic predominance to drive corporate social responsibility and ESG.[82] As consumers and workers, Millennials and Centennials supposedly prefer to work for and purchase from companies that are perceived as socially and environ-mentally responsible. Accordingly, business pundits claim that companies must proj-ect an image as social justice activists in order to attract Millennial and Centennial workers and customers.[83] Indeed, as Larry Ribstein pointed out even before the rise of Millennials and Centennials as consumers, corporations do not just have incen-tives to respond to consumer demands for social responsibility but "even have an incentive to create a consumer demand for social responsibility so that they can distinguish their goods in the market and earn competitive rents."[84] Nike's embrace of Colin Kaepernick is probably the most widely cited example of these phenomena, but even such heartland companies as Walmart are embracing some socially progres-sive stances, despite the risk of alienating their Red State customer base.[85]

Granted, in the past, corporations often were engaged in social issues. As Professor Tom Lin explains in reviewing corporate involvement in the civil rights movement of the 1960s, however, corporate engagements spread across a wide political spec-trum. Some corporations actively supported civil rights, but others passively sat out the struggle, while still others actively opposed the movement.[86]

Contemporary corporate activism differs from that of earlier periods in important respects. In particular, it is no longer enough for corporations to avoid taking posi-tions deemed anti-social. Instead, young progressive activists increasingly demand that corporations take a proactive position in affirmatively supporting progressive causes and opposing conservative ones.

Corporations today are uniquely pressured to comply with the Millennials and Centennials' demands. Of course, it has long been true that left-of-center corpo-rate social responsibility campaigners used "boycotts, shareholder activism, negative publicity, and so on" to pressure corporate managers to act in ways those campaign-ers deem socially responsible.[87] As a result, in some circles corporate social respon-sibility became "a kind of 'credence' good for which reputational bonding through brand names is particularly important."[88]

The explosive growth of social media, however, has exposed companies perceived as social laggards to massive new costs. Young progressives routinely use Facebook, Twitter, Instagram and other social media platforms to organize boycotts and pro-tests. Indeed, social media "campaigns against brands have become one of the most powerful forces in business, giving customers a huge megaphone with which to shape corporate ethics and practices, and imperiling some of the most towering figures of media and industry."[89]

8

Was There a Business Case for the Business Roundtable's Embrace of Stakeholder Capitalism?

There have been countless studies of corporate social responsibility and ESG across many disciplines. Law, economics, business administration and management, sociology, ethics, and theology, among others, have all made contributions. One might hope that a compelling business case for either corporate social responsibility/ESG or shareholder value maximization would have emerged from all that work. In fact, however, the results have been all over the map.

At the outset, it is critical to take empirical research in this field with a grain of salt. There is a well-known bias in favor of publishing studies that find statistically significant correlations as opposed to those finding no correlations. There is a similar bias in favor of publishing surprising results. Conversely, however, there is a bias against publishing studies that contradict the prevailing paradigm. Data in published studies can be skewed by selection biases. In sum, as sociologist Katja Rost found by doing a meta-analysis of 162 empirical corporate social responsibility studies published between 1975 and 2015, many positive correlations between corporate social responsibility and corporate financial performance can be traced back to the bias toward publication of positive results or other publication biases. Because most researchers had preconceived pro-corporate social responsibility biases, moreover, some studies had been manipulated to produce positive correlations.[1] The same likely is true of ESG studies.

8.1 IS THERE A BUSINESS CASE FOR CORPORATE SOCIAL RESPONSIBILITY?

Whether one would expect there to be a business case for embracing corporate social responsibility depends in large part on which of our potential definitions of corporate social responsibility one adopts. If one uses Henry Manne's narrow definition of corporate social responsibility, which requires corporations to voluntarily undertake actions for which the marginal returns are less than those of other available options, there should be no gains in shareholder wealth or value. As Manne explained, "no producer will be able voluntarily to increase his own costs and survive if his competitors do not act in the same way."[2] He offered what is now a somewhat dated example of the problem:

One clear illustration comes with the independent effort of one or more, but not all, companies along a river voluntarily to control pollution killing the fish population of the river. One uncooperative company may supply all the effluent necessary to kill all the fish, and, therefore, the additional costs to the socially minded corporations would have been incurred with no real benefit being realized at all.[3]

In contrast, if we accept the definition of corporate social responsibility claiming that corporate social responsibility may be costly in the short run but can be profitable in the long run, there should be a business case for corporate social responsibility, which should be reflected in various measures of firm performance. There is not. Some studies find positive correlations between corporate social responsibility and various performance metrics, others find no relationship, and some find negative correlations.[4] In addition to the problems discussed above, the corporate social responsibility literature suffers from a number of field specific issues.

Studies differ radically in their specification and measurement of dependent and independent variables.[5] As a result, "using a particular corporate social responsibility rating, company A would be rated higher than company B; however, quite the opposite would be the case using a different corporate social responsibility-rating."[6]

A particularly significant methodological problem is that many studies are derived from self-appraisals by managers. Given that those same managers presumably were responsible for adopting the program in the first place or report to those who adopted it, management-derived data is likely to be biased so as to justify their decision. Relatedly, because firms self-select whether to participate in corporate social responsibility, there is an inherent selection bias problem in that firms most likely to gain from corporate social responsibility are the ones most likely to adopt and retain it. In addition, because corporate social responsibility activities often attract positive media attention, financial results can be distorted.

Given that results are likely to be skewed in favor of positive findings about the effect of corporate social responsibility, it is telling that two recent literature reviews concluded that the business case remains uncertain at best. One 2020 meta-analysis of studies of the impact of corporate social responsibility on firm performance found that the impact "is either statistically insignificant or marginally positive."[7] A separate 2020 literature review similarly concluded that the impact of corporate social responsibility on firm financial performance remains uncertain.[8]

8.2 IS THERE A BUSINESS CASE FOR ESG?

If socially responsible firms are superior performers, one should see evidence that investment portfolios weighted toward such firms outperform the market on a risk-adjusted basis. Yet, there is little evidence that socially responsible investment funds outperform relevant market indices. Perhaps this should not be surprising. Professor Robert Miller observes that:

Advocates of the environmental, social and governance ("ESG") movement typically hold that the relevant business decisions benefiting other corporate constituencies actually benefit shareholders too in the long run.... Given that, a couple of decades earlier, virtually the same kinds of decisions were recommended by advocates of corporate social responsibility who argued that they were good and right in some strong normative sense while conceding that they did not increase value for shareholders, the claim of ESG advocates in this regard may seem implausible to the point of being disingenuous.[9]

In fact, there is some evidence that purportedly antisocial corporate conduct can result in superior stock market performance. Firms with high carbon emissions have higher stock market returns than low carbon emitters, for example, although the result may reflect liquidity issues arising from divestment campaigns.[10] In general, there is no evidence that SRI investment funds – standing alone – improve portfolio company performance on environmental or social metrics, probably because such funds prefer investing in firms that already score high on those metrics.[11]

In addition to casting additional doubt on whether there is a business case for corporate social responsibility, such findings cast doubt on the business case for ESG. Indeed, whether ESG benefits shareholders remains a hotly debated question. A 2019 survey of CEOs and CFOs of large corporations, for example, found them almost equally divided between those who thought their companies' ESG efforts would produce long-term gains and those who thought it would increase long-term costs.[12] A 2021 literature review of over 1,100 peer-reviewed studies and 27 published meta-analyses determined that the risk-adjusted financial performance of ESG investing was indistinguishable from that of conventional investing.[13]

Turning from stock market data to corporate practice, a study of US-based ESG mutual funds from 2010 to 2018 relative to non-ESG funds offered by the same fund family found that the former's portfolio companies had worse records for environmental and social compliance. The same study further found that ESG funds' portfolio companies had higher carbon emissions per unit of revenue than their non-ESG siblings, Finally, the study found that ESG funds charged higher fees and underperformed – on a risk-adjusted basis – their non-ESG siblings.[14]

Of course, ESG is not just an investing tool but also purports to be a management tool for use by operating companies. One can draw important inferences about the effectiveness of ESG-based management from examining the way boards responded to the COVID-19 crisis. A 2020 study found that companies with high ESG ratings were less likely to cut CEO pay in response to the crisis than firms with lower ESG scores.[15] As the study's authors explain:

> The concept of ESG (environmental, social, and governance) centers on the fact that companies that truly embrace their stakeholders and invest in their needs have lower risk and higher performance. These companies are expected to suffer less economic loss in a downturn, and also to "do the right thing" by their employees. However, we found no observable difference in the ESG scores of companies that

voluntarily reduced CEO/director pay and those that did not—despite differences in performance. Nor did we find a difference in ESG scores based on whether or not they chose to lay off employees. What does this say about our ability to accurately measure ESG?[16]

Another interesting data point is provided by a study of green patent applications. These applications seek patents for new technologies designed to reduce pollution, conserve water, protect biodiversity, and mitigate climate change. The study's authors found that oil, gas, and other energy companies with low ESG scores – many of which are excluded from the portfolios of ESG-focused funds – produced more and higher quality green patents than highly ESG rated firms engaged in green research.[17] Taken together with the other studies discussed above, it thus seems as though the business case for ESG remains unmade.[*]

---

[*] In any case, if there was a business case for ESG, there would be no need for a change in the law. Professor Robert Miller explains:

> [I]f ESG advocates are correct about [the business case supporting it], then there is no conflict between ESG and a shareholder primacy model or ESG and Delaware law. ESG advocates are merely arguing that they know how to make money for shareholders better than directors do, and if they are correct, their views will prevail in the market on the merits and without the clamorous advocacy of so many ESG supporters. As Manne remarked long ago, if a corporate expenditure made for reasons of corporate responsibility is value-maximizing for shareholder, then "we are left with nothing significantly different from Adam Smith's unseen hand, which, by virtue of selfish individual behavior, guides all economic resources to their socially optimal use."

Robert T. Miller, *How Would Directors Make Business Decisions Under A Stakeholder Model?*, 77 Bus. Law. 773, 776 n.8 (2022) (citation omitted).

9

Why Did the Business Roundtable
CEOs Shift Their Position?

Given that neither the legal rules nor the governance environment in which the Business Roundtable's members must operate were changed by the new statement, and given that the new statement makes less policy sense than the older ones, what purpose was served by issuing the statement? What are the signers up to? Answering that question is critical to deciding whether there really has been an abandonment of the profit motive by business, as some stakeholder capitalism advocates claim. We begin with two plausible, but perhaps less likely explanations, and then progress to several more likely possibilities. I regard all of these explanations as complementary rather than competing. Some combination of them all – albeit to varying degrees – is likely the most plausible explanation.

9.1 WERE THE BUSINESS ROUNDTABLE CEOs WOKE?

In the 1990s, corporate officers and directors largely accepted shareholder value maximization as their guiding principle. A 1995 National Association of Corporate Directors (NACD) report, for example, identified shareholder value maximization as the primary corporate goal. The next year a NACD report on director professionalism set out the same objective, but this time without any qualifying language on non-shareholder constituencies. A 1999 Conference Board survey found that directors of US corporations generally defined their role as running the company for the benefit of its shareholders. The 2000 edition of Korn/Ferry International's annual director survey found that when making corporate decisions, directors most frequently ranked shareholder interests as their primary concern, although it also found that a substantial number of directors felt some responsibility toward stakeholders.[1]

The Business Roundtable's own periodically restated *Principles of Corporate Governance* embraced shareholder value maximization in every version starting in 1997 and continuing through 2016. The 2016 edition, for example, affirmed that business corporations "are for-profit enterprises that are designed to provide sustainable long-term value to all shareholders."[2] The 2016 edition's list of eight guiding principles of corporate governance referenced the directors and CEOs' obligation to generate long-term value no fewer than six times. The profit motive seemed secure as the accepted corporate purpose. But then came the 2019 Business Roundtable statement reversing its long-held position on corporate purpose.

It is true that the Business Roundtable statement on corporate purpose jibed with other recent statements issuing from America's C-suites. A 2019 NACD report on board leadership, for example, took note of increasing pressure on corporate executives to articulate a corporate purpose going beyond profits to address social problems.[3] A 2020 NACD survey of public company governance reported that almost "80 percent of public-company boards now engage with ESG issues in some meaningful way."[4] A 2019 survey found that over three quarters of directors did not view generating value for shareholders as being more important than protecting stakeholders.[5] Various reports from other entities and public statements by corporate leaders during the 2015–2020 time period mirror this change in sentiment as well.[6]

Professor Lipshaw recently reported on two sets of corporate statements reflecting the same changing attitudes. First, he examined CEO letters accompanying annual reports to shareholders for the 2017 fiscal year, finding that "ninety-one of the 100 sample letters contained at least one commitment to a constituency other than the shareholders."[7] Second, he examined the CEOs' response to COVID-19 as stated in first quarter 2020 earnings announcements. A significant majority of the sampled firms mentioned protecting employees as being their highest priority in responding to the pandemic.[8]

At least some CEOs have gone beyond words to deeds, embracing various forms of social activism. We can loosely divide CEO activism into three broad categories: socially responsible business practices, corporate philanthropy, and advocacy.[9] The former further subdivides into practices that are intended to be profit maximizing and those that are intended to be profit sacrificing. Managing by ESG metrics is the principal example of CEO decisions that are conventionally assumed to be profit maximizing, although we saw reasons in Chapter 8 to be dubious of that claim. In contrast, decisions that put stakeholder interests ahead of profit for shareholders may sacrifice profits.

Corporate philanthropy long has been tilted toward the CEOs' pet charities.[10] Increasingly, however, corporate giving has been directed toward political campaigns and organizations that promote left-wing social policies. Having said that, critics claim such contributions are intended mainly "as a kind of shell game disguising the sins of the top one percent behind an ostentatious facade of do-gooding."[11]

As for CEO speech, it can take the form of cause marketing, advocacy marketing, and personal advocacy. Cause marketing involves a firm pursuing profit by highlighting the socially responsible nature of its products or services in its advertising, such as "when The Body Shop, a retailer of 'cruelty-free' cosmetic products, promoted a ban to stop testing cosmetics on animals."[12] Advocacy marketing entails the expenditure of corporate funds on to promote issues that are unrelated to the firm's goods and services. Examples include the Nike "Dream Crazy" campaign featuring Colin Kaepernick and Gilette's #MeToo campaign. Personal advocacy consists of CEOs speaking out on political and social issues in their personal capacity, purportedly using their corporate title solely for identification. What differentiates cause and advocacy marketing from personal advocacy is that both of the former are oriented toward profitmaking albeit typically through an embrace of left-leaning causes. Our focus here is therefore on the latter.

9.1.1 *CEO Politics*

In April 2021, Yale Management School Dean Jeffrey Sonnenfeld convened 90 CEOs of prominent US corporations to create a common front against newly enacted voting legislation in Georgia and proposed similar legislation in Texas and elsewhere. In a Wall Street Journal op-ed patting himself on the back, Dean Sonnenfeld characterized the gathering as the start of a new "spiritual awakening," akin to the historic Great Awakenings.[13] In doing so, he defined the CEO's job as including maintenance of social peace and cohesion.

As Dean Sonnenfeld's op-ed pointed out, this was not the first time CEOs of large corporations had intervened in political controversies in recent years. There was the North Carolina "bathroom bill" brawl in 2016, opposition to various Trump actions on immigration and climate change, the Parkland shooting in 2018, and so on. Although some of the participating CEOs protest that their actions were non-partisan, critics have pointed out that in every case the CEOs came down on the progressive side of the dispute.

Both individual executives and groups of CEOs have openly spoken out in favor of abortion rights, climate change regulation, and voting rights.[14] According to one study, for example, half of activist CEOs promoted gender, racial, or sexual-orientation diversity. Over 40 percent supported pro-environmental policies. And, 23 percent issued statements in support of immigration and human rights.[15]

Are such statements driven by the CEOs' personal political views? In some cases, the answer is probably yes. A 2017 Slate essay claimed that "Fortune 500 companies today are socially liberal, especially on areas surrounding diversity, gay rights, and immigration; they are unabashedly in favor of free trade and globalization, express concern about climate change, and embrace renewable energy."[16] Robert Miller similarly concludes "that, at the current time, a sizeable majority of individuals in the socio-economic class from which public company directors, partners at elite law firms, senior officers at institutional investors and proxy advisory firms, politicians, and academics are drawn overwhelming favors one particular political agenda – i.e., the largely progressive political agenda that emphasizes issues such as climate change, environmental concerns, racial and gender diversity, systematic racism, and so on."[17] Salesforce.com CEO Marc

Benioff, to cite but a single prominent example, energetically promotes social responsibility and woke activism.[18]

So what's happened? Have today's CEOs transformed from profit-maximizers to woke social justice warriors? Perhaps in some cases, but there is some evidence suggesting that perceptions that C-suites are now dominated by woke capitalists are exaggerated.

The perception that CEOs have embraced social activism appears to be driven by high profile Democratic-leaning CEOs. But the reality is that most CEOs remain right-of-center. Campaign contributions by Fortune 500 executives and directors skew Republican. Interestingly, while contributions by corporate PACs skew toward winners, suggesting they are motivated by a desire for influence rather than ideological preferences, individual contributions by CEOs are less skewed toward winners, suggesting that their Republican skewed contributions reflect personal political preferences.[19] Of particular interest for our purposes is a study of political contributions by Business Roundtable CEOs, which found that Republican Business Roundtable CEOs outnumber Democratic ones by anywhere from a low of 47 percent to 13 percent, with the rest being neutral, to a high of 77 percent to 23 percent, depending on what percentage of political contributions you require to determine a CEO's affiliation.[20] It is not exactly a Jacobin club.

The relatively small number of Democratic-leaning CEOs are more likely to engage in personal advocacy by issuing activist statements than are the larger cohort of Republican-leaning CEOs. The Democratic-leaning CEOs are also likely to issue such statements more frequently than their Republican-leaning counterparts.[21] As a result, public CEO personal advocacy tends to skew sharply to the left, creating the misimpression that the few speak for the many.

9.1.2 *CEO Activism Leans Left but the Profit Motive Survives*

What people do matters more than what they say. The COVID-19 pandemic provided an immediate test of the stakeholder capitalism commitments of the CEOs who signed the 2019 Business Roundtable corporate purpose statement. Despite what the CEOs said in Professor Lipshaw's analysis of earnings statements issued at the start of the pandemic, CEOs failed to put deeds to words according to most stakeholder theory proponents.

One useful analysis of actual CEO behavior is provided by the Test of Corporate Purpose (TCP), which is an initiative formed to study the impact of COVID-19 on corporate governance. In contrast to what one might have expected if one believed the Business Roundtable's CEOs took seriously the statement's new rhetorical emphasis, companies remained focused on maintaining shareholder returns even as employees and other stockholders were losing jobs and dealing with a dangerous virus. Relatively few CEOs lost their jobs or took a pay cut as a result of the pandemic.[22] Those CEOs who did take a pay cut often took a purely symbolic cut. Two thirds took a cut of ten percent or less.

The proposition that CEO's actions do not match their words is further supported by Lucian Bebchuk and Roberto Tallarita's analysis of recent going private transactions. They found no evidence that CEOs or boards negotiated for protections for non-shareholder constituencies, despite the well-known evidence that such transactions are often harmful to stakeholder interests. In contrast, management and shareholders both benefited considerably from such transactions.[23]

An even more recent study lead authored by Bebchuk looked at merger deals negotiated during the COVID-19 pandemic.[24] Bebchuk and his coauthors looked at 100 public corporation acquisitions valued at $1 billion or more. The total value of the deals exceeded $700 billion. As with their prior study, the authors assumed that if boards and managers were truly worried about non-shareholder constituents, those directors and managers would allocate some of the gains from the deals to stakeholders and negotiate post-acquisition protections for stakeholders. The authors further assumed that if stakeholder theory dominated corporate leaders' thinking that the havoc being wreaked on employees, consumers, communities, and other stakeholders by the pandemic would especially motivate socially responsible and ESG-focused corporate leaders to take such measures to protect such constituencies. They found that those leaders looked out for the interests of shareholders and their own interests, but gave little or no attention to the interests of stakeholders. The average premium over market paid by the shareholders was 34 percent. All of the deals included termination fees ensuring that the target would be paid if the deal failed to go through and most included other deal protection terms intended to make sure the acquisition happened. As for corporate leaders, many received contractual guarantees of continued post-acquisition employment. Turning to stakeholders, however, there were few benefits or protections. In none of the 22 largest deals (those with a value of $10 billion or more), for example, did the target negotiate for terms preventing employees being fired after the acquisition or providing severance benefits for any who were fired. The absence of such provisions is especially telling because some of the deals were flagged as posing significant risks of post-closing job losses. Nor did any of those deals have an contractual protections for customers, suppliers, creditors, or the environment. Instructively, despite the centrality of climate change concerns to the ESG movement, none of the deals had any climate-related provisions. The authors conclude:

> [T]he most likely driver of our findings is the lack of incentives for corporate leaders to deliver value to stakeholders at the expense of shareholders. In fact, given the design of their compensation arrangements, the structure of the labor and corporate control markets, and the other operative factors, corporate leaders have incentives not to deliver value to stakeholders beyond what is instrumentally useful to increase shareholder value.[25]

The policy implication seems clear. Relying on CEOs to behave like social justice warriors is a naïve hope, at best. As the authors observe, "if corporate leaders chose not to protect the environment, employees, or other stakeholders in a time when stakeholders needed extraordinary protection and shareholders enjoyed a booming market, it is not reasonable to expect them to protect stakeholders in normal times."[26]

Studies of how the Business Roundtable CEOs behave in running their companies outside the COVID-19 context further confirm that the majority are not exactly social justice warriors. Research by Aneesh Raghunandan and Shiva Rajgopal found that companies whose CEOs signed the Business Roundtable statement had a higher incidence of federal regulatory compliance violations than companies whose CEOs had not signed the statement. Signatory firms also had more stock buybacks, which many social responsibility advocates claim are antisocial, and a weaker association between CEO pay and performance. They draw the reasonable conclusion that "Business Roundtable signatories aren't leaders in socially conscious environmental, social or governance practices or stakeholder orientation."[27] In subsequent work, moreover, they found that there was no stock market reaction to the announcement of the BRT statement, which suggests that investors did "not perceive the Statement as a true commitment to improve ESG practices in the future."[28]

9.1.3 *Profits Trump Politics*

The shallowness of the Business Roundtable signatories' commitment to stakeholder capitalism is hardly surprising. Even true social justice warrior CEOs like Marc Benioff abandon their stakeholder capitalism commitments when push comes to shove. "What sets apart the new activist CEOs is how they use their names and corporate muscle to campaign directly against specific laws governing social issues, often on short notice, sometimes by threatening to withhold business."[29] But when it comes to dividing up the pie between shareholders and stakeholders, even the activist CEOs still commonly put shareholders first. "Corporations are engines of profit making, and they seek profit at every opportunity," even when run by the purportedly woke.[30]

To cite but a single high profile example, the Wall Street Journal reported on August 29, 2020, while the pandemic was still raging, that one day after "Salesforce. com Inc. posted record quarterly sales, the business-software company notified its 54,000-person workforce that 1,000 would lose their jobs later this year."[31] As John Stoll opined in the Journal, Salesforce CEO and Business Roundtable 2019 statement signatory Marc "Benioff called the company's strong earnings a victory for stakeholder capitalism." Benioff claimed to have done "a great job" for both shareholders and stakeholders. One might reasonably ask, however, as Stoll did, "how does the billionaire founder justify this claim when shortly after that interview Salesforce notified staff of plans for around 1,000 layoffs? This despite Mr. Benioff's no-layoff pledge in March on Twitter and the challenge to other CEOs to follow his lead."[32] One might add to that inquiry a question about how Benioff would justify telling Salesforce employees that in a few months down the road two percent of them would be fired, leaving them to twist slowly in the wind for months while worrying whether they would be among those who get fired.

Over the years, we have seen many such examples. Focusing just on CEO decisions that adversely affected employees, consider such common decisions as downsizing and offshoring. These decisions almost always were intended for the benefit of shareholders. The impact on employees and communities in which the companies did business were commonly given short shrift.[33]

Why have supposedly woke CEO activists put shareholder interests ahead of those of stakeholders when forced to make a choice between them? Perhaps they recognize the risk of backlash that will negatively impact the bottom line. When corporations take sides, they inevitably alienate some of their constituents. "Activists for some issues that are not aligned with those of powerful progressive corporate interests – issues like religious and conservative social causes – probably feel like their voices and views are already marginalized in contemporary society, and this movement has the potential to further crystalize that marginalization."[34]

The risk of a backlash against CEO activism is not just a theoretical possibility. In fact, there have already been several examples of a backlash against CEOs using their bully pulpits to support progressive causes. In May 2021, for example, conservative-leaning research and educational organization Consumers' Research ran a series of television ads targeting Nike, Coca-Cola, and American Airlines for their support of such causes. The American Airlines ad asked:

> Why is CEO Doug Parker trying to appease the radical left? To distract from billions in taxpayer bailouts, from his $10 million payday, from American's record layoffs. The ad further took the airline to task for losing baggage, shrinking leg room amid the pandemic, and attacking Texas's voter ID law even as it requires identification from its passengers.[35]

Such backlash can adversely impact corporate bottom lines. As The Economist reported, for example, when Walmart banned sales of certain types of ammunition in response to a mass shooting, "footfall in Walmart stores in Republican districts fell more sharply as a result than it rose in Democratic ones."[36]

Of course, CEO activism can have an adverse impact on corporate profits regardless of whether the CEO is truly woke or just greenwashing. As popular culture critic Jordan B. Peterson opined:

> It's staggering to me to watch the corporate elite types kowtow to the radical Marxists. They do it to virtue signal or because they're feeling guilty or maybe because they're facing genuine pressure and don't want to stand up against it. But they're playing a game that will punish them intensely.[37]

If so, it seems probable that truly woke CEOs will be punished even more severely.

9.2 WERE THE BUSINESS ROUNDTABLE CEOs RESPONDING TO CHANGES IN CONSUMER, INVESTOR, AND LABOR DEMANDS?

If the Business Roundtable CEOs themselves are not woke, perhaps they were catering to those who are. In other words, the Business Roundtable's 2019 statement could be a mass effort at cause marketing. As we saw in Chapter 7, according to conventional wisdom, Millennials and Centennials prefer to work for and purchase from companies that are perceived as socially and environmentally responsible. Likewise, conventional wisdom holds that members of these post-Boomer generations prefer to invest in companies whose CEOs project an image as social justice activists. As we saw, conventional wisdom overstates the case. Nevertheless, it's plausible that some CEOs thought supporting the Business Roundtable's change of position would help them attract Millennial and Centennial customers, investors, and workers.

There certainly have been many cases in recent years of CEOs seeking to placate angry young employees. One thinks of Google employees' successful 2018 effort to derail the company's work for the Defense Advanced Research Projects Agency. Or the successful employee effort to force Hachette Book Group to cancel publication of Woody Allen's memoir. Employee pressure contributed to Delta's decision to publicly oppose Georgia's voting law in 2021. Spotify's CEO felt obliged to apologize to the company's employees for hosting Joe Rogan's podcast. The list goes on and on.

As we'll see below, however, many such CEOs likely were engaged in insincere greenwashing. After all, many – if not most – CEOs probably agree with Michael Jordan that Republicans buy shoes too. And they have seen the backlash that increasingly comes with appeasement. Hence, as we saw above, many – almost all – CEOs still put profits ahead of politics.

Examples abound. Spotify's CEO may have apologized to the company's employees, but Joe Rogan's podcast is still on the platform. Despite widely publicized outrage and protests by Simon & Schuster's employees, company management refused to cancel a seven figure two-book deal with former Vice President Michael Pence. The latter example prompted a publishing consultant to observe that "publishers want to publish what they think will make money …. They're not in this to teach anybody a lesson or espouse particular principles. They recognize they make money off many different audiences with different political beliefs."[38]

9.3 WERE THE BUSINESS ROUNDTABLE CEOs RESPONDING TO GREEN ACTIVIST INVESTORS?

Shareholder activism is not limited to Millennials and Centennials, of course. Some institutional investors long have offered some funds that focus on corporations perceived as socially responsible, which generally has been understood to mean companies pursuing progressive goals. A few smaller fund families even specialize in socially responsible investing. True, this is changing. As we have seen, a growing number of major institutional investors have embraced social activism in support of progressive goals with respect to all of the funds they manage. As we also saw, however, much of this seems to be greenwashing. In any case, as the Etsy story discussed below suggests, profit-oriented investors still out punch ESG oriented investors. Accordingly, something else also must be going on.

9.4 WERE THE BUSINESS ROUNDTABLE CEOs TRYING TO FEND OFF REGULATION?

One pragmatic justification for corporate social responsibility and stakeholder capitalism is that embracing them enables business to ward off government regulation.[39] The claim is that if business does not self-police, government will intervene. In the past, corporate social responsibility proponents argue, business failures to act led to government intervention in areas such as the environment, consumer protection, workplace safety, and civil rights.[40]

If government is as gridlocked as proponents of using business to solve social ills claim, avoiding government regulation would not play a particularly significant role in the thinking of top CEOs. In the real world, however, as the examples we just cited suggest, avoiding government regulation may be an important motivator. Indeed, as we saw in Chapter 7, corporations have strong incentives to fend off regulation. Despite claims that *Citizens United* left government helpless before an onslaught of corporate lobbying expenditures, which we have seen were grossly overstated, the regulatory state continues to grow apace.

It thus seems entirely plausible that the Business Roundtable's members were trying to head off regulation by progressive politicians. As Wall Street Journal columnist David Benoit observed when the Business Roundtable issued its 2019 statement, "Democratic presidential candidate Elizabeth Warren has argued that the primacy of shareholder returns has worsened economic inequality, enriching wealthy investors at the expense of workers."[41] With the mainstream of the Democratic Party seemingly moving in Warren's direction on business and finance issues, the Business Roundtable's members may have hoped that a voluntary – and perhaps intentionally ambiguous – embrace of corporate social responsibility platitudes would help them fend off more intrusive regulation in the event of a Democratic presidential victory in 2020.[42]

9.5 WERE THE BUSINESS ROUNDTABLE CEOs JUST CYNICAL OLIGOPOLISTS?

As we saw in Part I, both Merrick Dodd and the *Smith Manufacturing* opinion pointed to pro-corporate social responsibility statements by corporate leaders as support for their arguments. Some claim that the embrace of corporate social responsibility by those leaders was – and remains today – profoundly cynical. Drug development entrepreneur Vivek Ramaswamy, for example, argues that in the wake of the 2008 financial crisis "a bunch of big banks got together with a bunch of millennials, birthed woke capitalism, and then put Occupy Wall Street up for adoption." As a result, he argues, "big business makes money by critiquing itself."[43]

This is not a new phenomenon. In fact, corporate social responsibility frequently has been coopted by corporate managers to justify and defend concentrated corporate power, monopolies, and rent seeking. Indeed, the industry titans upon whom Dodd and *Smith Manufacturing* relied most heavily, were the bosses of some of the pre-war era's largest and most monopolistic enterprises.[44] Again, this is the flip side of an argument we have already encountered. Instead of arguing that large and successful businesses should embrace corporate social responsibility so as to offset their power, this line of argument claims that it is precisely their size and success that allows such businesses to do so.

As businesses mature, growing size and profits supposedly give management what some call "the 'luxury of philosophizing,' but which other commentators refer to 'less charitably' as 'monopoly power.'[45] Only a monopolist enterprise can afford corporate social responsibility. If there is vigorous competition, companies that accept lower profits in the name of corporate social responsibility will be unable to compete with profit maximizing firms. In a competitive market, directors and officers concerned with keeping their jobs will thus be motivated mainly be value maximization. But in a market where one or a few firms are dominant, firm management may indulge in social justice causes without worrying about a resulting decline in profits that might threaten their positions.

This line of analysis prompted Milton Friedman to argue that businesspeople who boast about corporate social responsibility expenditures "should be regarded as asking for an investigation by the Antitrust Division of the Justice Department."[46] Friedman held up President Lyndon Johnson's call for banks to voluntarily restrict foreign lending as a leading example of the problem. In order to reward banks that voluntarily cooperated, President Johnson offered to seek exemptions for them from the antitrust laws. Friedman argued that the bank's "voluntary exercise of 'social responsibility'" thus resulted in "a governmentally approved cartel to raise the price to foreign borrowers – which helps to explain why leading New York bankers were among those who developed the program and why so many banks heavily involved in foreign lending have been so favorably disposed towards it."[47]

The decline in antitrust enforcement in recent decades thus may help explain the resurgence in interest in corporate social responsibility. Indeed, Harvard law professor Mark Roe attributes the success of increased pressure for expansive views of corporate purpose to declining competition in key US industries.[48] Increasing firm profitability makes it easier for large companies to afford corporate social responsibility, while declining competition makes doing so less risky. Conversely, populist resistance and resulting social pressure rises in response to the vast size and wealth of huge quasi-monopolies.

9.6 WERE THE BUSINESS ROUNDTABLE CEOs PINING FOR THEIR IMPERIAL DAYS?

For much of American business history, boards of directors were largely supine. Instead, public corporations were run by a hierarchical bureaucracy of professional managers. The era of managerial capitalism reached its highwater mark in the post-war period as executives who learned their leadership skills in the military rose to the top.[49] In an era thus dominated by the proverbial men in gray flannel suits, titans of industry tended to be quietly dependable bureaucrats rather than showmen.[50] The top management team really was a team, at least compared to prior periods such as the era of the Robber Barons.

As the Me Generation of the 1970s evolved into the Yuppie era of the 1980s, however, flamboyant business leaders like Lee Iacocca increasingly became prominent celebrities.[51] This new breed of CEO broke free of fetters from both above and below, with neither boards nor the rest of the top management team providing significant constraints. They were thus largely free to run their corporations as they saw fit, which gave rise to the apt moniker "Imperial CEOs." As a result, the predecessors of the CEOs who signed the Business Roundtable statement had broad discretion to make decisions that put the interests of stakeholders ahead of those of shareholders.

In the 1980s, Imperial CEOs faced a serious challenge in the form of hostile takeover bids by so-called corporate raiders like Sir James Goldsmith, Ron Perelman, T. Boone Pickett, Carl Icahn, and their ilk, whose access to the emergent phenomenon of junk bonds gave them the financial resources to make credible efforts to buy even very large firms. Martin Lipton rose to fame by defending Imperial CEOs from the raiders.[52] Lipton's invention of what he called the shareholder rights plan – better known as the poison pill – was a major reason the brief hostile takeover era fizzled out by the early 1990s.

Although the Imperial CEOs survived the so-called merger mania of the 1980s, they finally ran into a series of insurmountable hurdles in the first two decades of the new millennium. The scandals at Enron, WorldCom, Tyco and other high profile companies with Imperial CEOs significantly undermined their status as admired celebrities. The financial crisis of 2007–2008 called their abilities into question. The passage of the Sarbanes-Oxley Act in 2002 and the Dodd-Frank Act in 2010 imposed new obligations on CEOs and created new liability risks for them. Independent boards of directors and activist shareholders created new centers of power within the corporation.

In the last 20 years, partly as a response to legal changes such as Dodd-Frank and Sarbanes-Oxley and partly because of changes in director compensation and socialization, boards of directors have become more significantly independent and more engaged.[*] It is increasingly the case that the board is the boss and the CEO

---

[*] To be sure, some board members are CEOS of other companies. In 2018, for example, 13.7 percent of S&P 500 directors were active CEOs of other corporations. Just under twenty-three percent were former CEOs of other corporations. THE CONFERENCE BOARD, CORPORATE BOARD PRACTICES IN

works for the board instead of the other way around.[53] Boards of directors are less willing to acquiesce to a CEO's wishes and more willing to actively question CEO proposals.[54]

Shareholder activism – especially by hedge funds – has become more common and a much more potent threat. Such investors are constantly on the lookout for managers who are failing to maximize shareholder value and are willing to exert pressure for changes intended to reverse that failure.[55] Their influence has been multiplied by the increasing willingness of traditionally passive institutional investors, such as mutual and pension funds, to support activist hedge fund campaigns.[56] The resulting pressure to maximize shareholder gains not only directly constrains CEO discretion, but also incentivizes boards to exercise greater oversight of CEO decision making.

One cannot help suspecting that at least some of the Business Roundtable CEOs would welcome a return to the days of the Imperial CEOs. Indeed, their support for stakeholderism may well be strategic: an attempt to advance a managerialist agenda dressed up in stakeholder clothing to make it more appealing to the general public.[57] Business professor Robert Eccles notes that only a tiny percentage of the Business Roundtable CEOs whose company responded to a survey had gotten their board of directors' approval for signing the 2019 corporate purpose statement. He concludes "the Imperial CEO lives on in America!"[58]

Tellingly, preeminent corporate lawyer Martin Lipton has morphed from anti-takeover warrior into a vigorous advocate of what he calls "the New Paradigm," which "conceives of corporate governance as a collaboration among corporations, shareholders and other stakeholders working together to achieve long-term value …."[59] Lipton complains that:

> For several decades, there has been a prevailing assumption among many CEOs, directors, scholars, investors, asset managers and others that the sole purpose of corporations is to maximize value for shareholders and, accordingly, that corporate decision-makers should be very closely tethered to the views and preferences of shareholders. This has created an opportunity for corporate raiders, activist hedge funds and others with short-termist agendas, who do not hesitate to assert their preferences and are often the most vocal of shareholder constituents. And, even outside the context of shareholder activism, the relentless pressure to produce shareholder value has all too often tipped the scales in favor of near-term stock price gains at the expense of long-term sustainability.[60]

But it is difficult to take Lipton's arguments at face value.

When you look closely at The New Paradigm it quickly becomes apparent that Lipton is still in the business of defending corporate managers. The only difference

THE RUSSELL 3000 AND S&P 500 (2019). Given that a majority of directors are neither current nor former CEOs, however, it would be wrong to suggest that the Business Roundtable speaks for directors generally.

is that the corporate raiders of the 1980s have been replaced by hedge fund activists. Accordingly, one suspects that Lipton's goal is not to empower his CEO clients to be more prosocial, but to use stakeholder capitalism as a lever for restoring the CEO's former imperial powers.[61] Those suspicions find confirmation in Bebchuk's study of deals negotiated during the COVID-19 pandemic. Lipton's law firm, Wachtell, Lipton, Rosen & Katz, represented target companies in 15 percent of the studied deals. Despite Lipton's frequent pronouncements about the need to embrace stakeholder capitalism, none of the Wachtell Lipton deals contained any contractual protections for labor, customers, creditors, or the environment.[62]

9.7 WERE THE BUSINESS ROUNDTABLE CEOS GREENWASHING?

The explanations we have considered so far reflect three accounts of managerial incentives. The CEOs might be (1) honestly seeking to protect stakeholders, (2) seeking to enhance shareholder value, or (3) pursuing their own preferences and self-interests. Each of the foregoing explanations could be consistent with at least two of those motivations. All of them are thus plausible reasons why the Business Roundtable CEOs claimed to embrace stakeholder capitalism.

Without meaning to exclude those possibilities, however, we turn now to the explanation I find most plausible. Theologian and philosopher Michael Novak wrote of the CEOs who signed an earlier British statement of corporate purpose embracing stakeholder theory that "[n]o doubt, being pragmatic gentlemen, they intend to grant the opposition a victory in rhetoric, while afterwards hoping to muddle through more or less as always."[63] Such statements are, Novak opined, "acts of intellectual appeasement."[64] Today we call it greenwashing.

9.7.1 *Some Very Speculative Theories about CEO Motives for Greenwashing*

Why would CEOs engage in disingenuous puffery? I have long treasured a pet personal theory that wealthy CEOs send their children to posh private schools where they are indoctrinated in social justice politics. The children then come home and pressure their CEO parent to be socially responsible as they have learned at school to define the term. I recall one CEO saying the company initiated a recycling program back in the early 1990s after one of the CEO's children did a science fair project on the merits of recycling.

An alternative theory advanced by some is that most CEOs live in blue state bubbles – albeit sometimes embedded within red states – and everyone they know in politics, the culture, the media, and society embraces some version of stakeholder theory. If so, perhaps such CEOs simply want to keep their friends happy. Alternatively, perhaps such CEOs perceive woke-ism to be the inevitable future and believe resistance is futile. In either case, appeasement may seem the least bad alternative.[65]

Novak advanced a third speculative theory premised on the notion that CEOs secretly feel guilty about their wealth. Appeasing stakeholder capitalists is a form of self-flagellation by which these CEOs expunge their guilt feelings. Novak explained that he does not believe that to be the case, but reported it because it was a commonly held theory.[66] Personally, the persistence of huge CEO pay packages leads me to doubt the merits of this theory. I find it hard to believe that large numbers of US CEOs are so masochistic that they enjoy being beaten up over the size of their paychecks.

9.7.2 *Theories Grounded in Self-Interest*

Let us turn, however, to more serious explanations for why CEOs practice greenwashing. If one shares the economists' basic assumption that people are rational actors who try to maximize their utility, explanations consistent with the self-interest of CEOs will be most attractive. In turn, setting aside conflict of interest situations, the incentive schedule faced by CEOs and other managers aligns their interests with those of the shareholders rather than that of the various stakeholders. Gerald Davis observes that:

> As documented by a generation of financial economists under the rubric of "corporate governance," the capital markets in the Anglo-American world have evolved a vast matrix of institutions to ensure that corporate managers seek to increase share price. These include outsider-dominated boards of directors selected for their expertise at serving shareholder interests; rigorous financial auditors whose reputations depend on their integrity; activist investors who stand to profit from share price increases; hordes of equity analysts who call out any decisions that don't increase shareholder value; executive compensation systems tied to share price; shareholder-friendly corporate law; stock markets with rigorous pro-shareholder listing standards; and a market for corporate control that punishes firms with undervalued shares. All these mechanisms combine to enforce a monomaniacal executive focus on share price.[67]

Indeed, as we saw in Chapter 5, considerable effort has gone into various legal and market efforts to link the CEO's self-interest with that of the shareholders. A CEO negotiating a new pay package or faced with a hostile takeover bid is nevertheless likely to put the CEO's own welfare ahead of that of either shareholders or stakeholders. A CEO faced with an ordinary business decision is likely to choose the most profitable option, however, as the CEO's incentives are all about the profit motive.

9.7.3 *The Impact of CEO Compensation Practices*

As we saw in Chapter 5, the rules governing executive compensation are intended to address the principal–agent problem by aligning the C-suite's financial incentives with maximizing shareholder value. At most companies, half or more of a CEO's pay comes in the form of restricted stock grants or stock options, which gives the CEOs strong incentives to maximize shareholder wealth.[68] Another large chunk of CEO pay comes from non-equity performance bonuses. Although there are a growing number of companies using ESG and/or EDI metrics in measuring CEO performance for the latter purpose, those metrics have not replaced financial metrics.

Useful recent data on this issue is provided by Lucian Bebchuk and Roberto Tallarita's survey of CEO compensation practices at S&P 100 companies as disclosed in those companies' 2020 proxy statement.[69] As we saw in Chapter 5, federal rules require public corporations to provide extensive disclosures of executive compensation, the bulk of which are to be made in the issuer's annual proxy statement. The compensation of the CEO, CFO, and the company's other three most highly compensated executive officers must be disclosed in detail. In addition to detailed tabular breakdowns of total pay and the various components of the officers' pay packages, the company must provide detailed narrative information in a Compensation Disclosure and Analysis (CD&A) statement. The CD&A must identify each element of the pay package and explain why the company chose those elements and how they determined the amounts payable on each of those elements. The CD&A thus must disclose and discuss each of the named officer's salary, bonus, and equity compensation. Along with the required Compensation Committee report, the tabular data and C&A allow one to draw a comprehensive picture of how companies pay CEOs, including how they use ESG metrics and benchmarking to assess performance-based pay.

The S&P 100 companies studied by Bebchuk and Tallarita have an aggregate market capitalization of $26 trillion, representing over half of the entire US stock market. If any set of companies were likely to embrace stakeholder capitalism, the S&P 100 seems the most probable candidate. After all, as we have seen, larger companies are more likely to be able to afford stakeholder capitalism.

Given their substantial number of workers and other stakeholders, the potential impact of such firms embracing stakeholder capitalism would be enormous. Given their high visibility and influence, moreover, how S&P 100 companies treat their executives, shareholders, and stakeholders can have huge ripple effects by setting best practice norms and otherwise influencing how smaller companies behave. Accordingly, a survey of the huge companies in the S&P 100 should be quite informative as to the extent and effectiveness of stakeholder capitalism. If they have not adopted effective ESG-based compensation programs for their C-suite executives, it seems unlikely that smaller companies will have done so.

Almost all of the surveyed companies based the vast majority of their CEOs pay on achievement of contingent performance bonuses. Bebchuk and Tallarita's survey found that just over half (52.6 percent) of the companies in their survey used ESG-based metrics in setting CEO pay, which means almost half of the largest and most powerful companies do not. Instructively, the CEOs of 62 of the companies in their survey were signatories of the 2019 Business Roundtable statement, but 26 of those firms used no ESG-based metrics in setting CEO pay. We can infer that the CEOs of those 26 companies were motivated by something other than financial incentives when they signed the Roundtable statement. We can also infer that, if push comes to shove and those firms' CEOs are faced with choosing between shareholder and stakeholder interests, the CEOs of those companies will have no financial incentive to prefer the latter and considerable financial incentive to prefer the interests of their shareholders.[*]

If one assumes boards and CEOs really value stakeholder capitalism, one would assume they would want to give ESG-based metrics substantial weight and also want the proxy statement to disclose the weights given those metrics. But that is not consistent with what Bebchuk and Talarita found. In most cases, the companies using ESG-based metrics incorporated them into calculating the CEO's annual bonus. In 2020, bonuses amounted to just 21.5 percent of the pay of CEOs of companies included in the Russell 3000 index.[70] The remainder typically consisted of cash salaries and equity compensation in the form of stock options or restricted stock grants. As a result, almost 80 percent of the typical CEO's pay is determined without regard to ESG considerations. To the contrary, the bulk remains linked to share performance.

As for the portion of CEO pay to which ESG considerations are potentially relevant, relatively few firms in Bebchuk and Talarita's survey disclosed the weight given those metrics in setting their CEO's bonus (just over 27 percent). Among those who disclose the weight they give ESG-based metrics, those metrics account for a tiny percentage of the CEO's total performance-based pay (1.5 to 3 percent). There are a few firms that give ESG metrics a higher weight, but 12.5 percent is the highest Bebchuk and Talarita report.

A study by law professor David Walker examined the compensation of CEOs who were current and recent members of the Business Roundtable's board. Walker determined that the median percentage of CEO pay that was based on ESG metrics was just 0.2 percent of the value of the CEO's shares, outstanding equity awards, and other forms of variable compensation. The median ESG-based compensation amounted to just 1.1 percent of the CEOs' total incentive compensation. The trivial amount of ESG-based compensation is especially striking considering that the same companies devoted, on average, 10 percent of their proxy statements to ESG issues. Walker concluded that "ESG talk far outweighs ESG walk, at least as far as executive incentives go, and ESG based pay seems more like window dressing than a serious attempt to incentivize executive behavior."[71]

---

[*] The mean compensation of the CEOs in Bebchuk and Tallarita's survey was $25 million. The median was $21 million. Lucian A. Bebchuk & Roberto Tallarita, The Perils and Questionable Promise of ESG-Based Compensation 11 (Mar. 1, 2022), https://papers.ssrn.com/sol3/papers.cfm?abstract_id=4048003. Recall from Chapter 5 that the mean percentage of surveyed companies CEO pay contingent on performance was 85.5 percent and the median was 91 percent. The CEOs of the signatory companies that do not use any ESG-based metrics thus would face potential personal financial losses on the order of eight figures if they preferred the interests of stakeholders to shareholders.

We know that for most people monetary rewards are a powerful – if not the most powerful – motivator.[72] The importance of pay is illustrated by a study of Methodist minister compensation. If anyone could be expected to be operating primarily from altruistic motives, one assumes it would be religious ministers. Yet, the study's authors found that the Methodist Church appears to use a pay for performance compensation system. The Church set ministerial pay according to "a type of sharing rule, by which the pastor is paid close to 3% of the revenue that accrues to the church when a new member joins."[73] One might assume that pay is an even more potent motivator for executives of for-profit businesses.

In sum, current CEO pay practices incentivize CEOs to favor shareholder interests over stakeholder interests. The vast bulk of their pay comes from performance-based elements such as bonuses and equity compensation. The metrics used to assess the performance of almost half of CEOs have no ESG-based components. The weight given those metrics by companies that use them is typically a tiny percentage. If we assume that pay is the primary motivator for CEOs, the rampant talk of stakeholder capitalism coming from Business Roundtable members and other CEOs likely should be taken with more than just a grain of salt.

9.7.4 *The Influence of CEO Job Prospects*

In addition to their pay, CEOs care deeply about their current and future job prospects, which incentivizes them to focus on shareholder interests. With the growing independence and power of corporate boards of directors, this incentive is becoming increasingly important. As we will see in our discussion of Etsy below, the easiest way for directors to show loyalty to shareholder interests is to fire a CEO whose performance is displeasing to activist shareholders. Consistent with that prediction, there is considerable evidence that CEO turnover is closely related to stock performance.[74]

9.7.5 *Evidence of Greenwashing*

We saw in Chapter 7 that corporations have substantial incentives to engage in greenwashing. When those enterprise-level incentives are coupled with the personal incentives on the part of CEOs that we just reviewed, it would be surprising if the embrace of stakeholder capitalism by both companies and CEOs did not have an element of puffery. Indeed, Lucian Bebchuk and Roberto Tallarita conclude that the Business Roundtable CEO's "statement was mostly for show, largely representing a rhetorical public relations move, rather than the harbinger of meaningful change."[75] In other words, the answer to the question of why the Business Roundtable CEOs changed position is that the CEOs in fact had only changed position rhetorically. Put another way, the Business Roundtable statement was a collective exercise in greenwashing.

There is considerable evidence that that was what motivated the Business Roundtable statement. Recall that Aneesh Raghunandan and Shiva Rajgopal's research showed that companies run by CEOs who had signed the 2019 Business Roundtable statement had a higher incidence of federal regulatory compliance violations than did companies whose CEOs had not signed the statement.[76] Companies run by signatory CEOs had more stock buybacks and a weaker association between CEO pay and performance. They concluded the signatory CEOs are not actively engaged "in socially conscious environmental, social or governance practices or stakeholder orientation."[77] As was the case with Novak's British CEOs, it thus seems plausible that many if not most of the signatory CEOs were willing to give their critics a rhetorical victory without changing their actual behavior.

The greenwashing explanation is further supported by another study of the companies of the Business Roundtable signatory CEOs, which found that those companies paid out 20 percent more in dividends and stock buybacks during the COVID-19 pandemic than did comparable corporations whose CEOs had not signed it. Similarly, signatory companies were 20 percent more likely to lay off workers than non-signatory firms. Overall, signatory companies "were less likely to donate to relief efforts, less likely to offer customer discounts, and less likely to shift production to pandemic-related goods."[78] Business commentator Barry Ritholtz sarcastically summed up these concerns, noting that if one scans "the list of 181 signatories … it's a Who's Who of corporate behavior that has burdened and disadvantaged the very stakeholders they will now champion."[79]

Still more support for the greenwashing explanation comes from Bebchuk and Tallarita's "review of all the corporate governance guidelines of public companies joining the Business Roundtable statement, including the many companies that revised their guidelines in the year since the issuance of the statement."[80] These guidelines are official corporate documents that are typically approved by the board of directors or the board's Nominating and Corporate Governance committee. They are typically posted to the section of the corporation's website dealing with information for investors. They are updated on a regular basis to reflect evolving corporate governance legal requirements and best practices. They often include a statement of corporate purpose.[*]

Bebchuk and Tallarita concluded that these "guidelines mostly continue to reflect a shareholder primacy approach,"[81] despite the fact that their CEOs signed the Business Roundtable statement. Out of a sample of 20 companies whose CEO had signed the Business Roundtable statement, not one had changed its corporate governance statement to bring it into line with the Business Roundtable statement.

---

[*] The New York Stock Exchange requires all listed companies to "adopt and disclose corporate governance guidelines," but does not require that the guidelines include any reference to corporate purpose. NYSE, LISTED COMPANY MANUAL § 303A.09 (2022). Best practice recommendations urge that such guidelines "be revisited on a regular basis." ALAN S. GUTTERMAN, BUSINESS TRANSACTIONS SOLUTIONS § 344:41 (2020).

Tellingly, they found explicit endorsements of shareholder primacy even "in the corporate governance guidelines of the two companies whose CEOs played a key leadership role in the Business Roundtable's adoption of its statement."[82]

Bebchuk and Tallarita's review makes a particularly striking contrast to a survey of CEO statements conducted by Professor Lipshaw. As noted above, Lipshaw reviewed a sampling of CEO letters to shareholders included in corporate annual reports for 2017, many of which reflected concern for stakeholders rather than an exclusive focus on shareholder profits.[83] He also reviewed COVID-related communications and earnings announcements for the first quarter of 2020. He found "the consistent message … was that employees and customers were either explicitly or implicitly the company's highest priority, companies were diverting resources to employees, customers, and communities by way of enhanced benefits, relaxation of contractual limitations, and significant charitable contributions of cash and resources."[84]

I find Bebchuk and Tallarita's analysis much more compelling than Lipshaw's. It is one thing to say a few positive words about one's ESG commitments in a shareholder letter. It is quite another to embed such commitments in the corporation's corporate governance guidelines. To be sure, Professor Lipshaw dismisses Bebchuk and Tallarita's findings because, "given [his] view that the Statement itself reflected very little change in what companies had been doing all along," the lack of changes to corporate statements of their governance principles is not surprising.[85] Yet, if ESG commitments are as mission critical as the Business Roundtable statement implies, it would be reasonable to expect them to be expressly incorporated into corporate governance guidelines.

As Harvard Business School professor Robert Eccles observes:

> Flowery words were contained In the August 2019 Business Roundtable's (BRT) much ballyhooed (at least by them) "Statement of the Purpose of a Corporation"…. In reflecting on that one year later, not a single one of these signatories, to the best of my knowledge, had written a company-specific simple one or two-page "Statement of Purpose" signed by every member of the board. Doesn't seem to me this should be so hard to do if the board has agreed with this multi-stakeholder model. Or maybe the board never did.[86]

9.8 SUMMING UP

Although it is possible that at least some Business Roundtable CEOs were sincerely concerned with stakeholder interests, the most plausible accounts of the CEOs' incentives and interests suggest that they will focus on shareholder interests at least where there is no managerial conflict of interest incentivizing them to pursue personal concerns inconsistent with shareholder interests. As we have seen, the structure of management compensation, board of director oversight, and the threat of shareholder activism constrain management discretion in important ways. Merely allowing directors to consider stakeholder interests thus guarantees nothing, because management can – and likely will – exercise its discretion to favor shareholders in true zero-sum settings. After all, the idea that the same managers who have driven private sector unionism virtually to the point of extinction will suddenly become workers' protectors is risible, at best.

A regime in which managers and directors are not just allowed but affirmatively required to consider stakeholder interests when making decisions likewise offers no guarantees absent some enforcement mechanism by which employees and other stakeholders can hold management accountable. As we saw in Chapter 5, creating such a mechanism would require remaking vast chunks of corporate law. It thus seems highly unlikely.

10

Why the Business Roundtable CEOs
Should Have Stayed the Course

This Chapter opens with two arguments for shareholder value maximization that are routine in the literature but which fair minded shareholder value maximization proponents have to admit are problematic. One is the common assertion that shareholders' ownership rights require that their agents – i.e., the directors and officers – maximize the value of the company to its owners. The other is that a rising tide will lift all boats, which is mostly true but requires qualification.

Then we will move to four arguments that are much stronger. First, we'll consider the argument from accountability. Directors and officers are hired to manage other people's money and must be accountable for how they do so. Shareholder value maximization is an essential part of any viable accountability scheme. Second, we note the serious implementation problems involved in making stakeholder capitalism a workable system of corporate governance. Third, we turn to the argument that stakeholder capitalism threatens democracy. Finally, we will evaluate the argument that shareholders would bargain for shareholder value maximization as the default rule of corporate law.

10.1 NO SOUL TO DAMN AND NO BODY TO KICK

Since its earliest days, the corporation has been "a person within the law."[1] Corporate law statutes operationalize that conception by granting the corporation "the same powers as an individual to do all things necessary or convenient to carry out its business and affairs."[2] Indeed, albeit controversially, the corporation's separate legal personality has even entitled it to certain constitutional rights.[3]

Put another way, "in "the eyes of the law a corporation is a separate and distinct entity from its stockholders,"[4] not to mention its directors, officers, employees, and other constituents. The corporation is thus sometimes said to be a real entity.[5] In turn, some contend that the corporate entity is a thing capable of being owned.*

---

* Conversely, as we saw in our discussion of *Smith Manufacturing*, some have argued that the corporation's legal personhood entitles it to "assume the modern obligations of good citizenship in

In his famous essay on the social responsibility of business, for example, Milton Friedman opined that "a corporate executive is an employé of the owners of the business."[6] Those owners are the shareholders of the corporation, who purportedly possess most of the incidents of ownership, such as "the rights to possess, use, and manage, and the rights to income and capital."[7]

Because private property is such a profound part of the American ethos, the normative implications of the conception of the corporation as property have long dominated corporate governance discourse. In particular, Friedman and others have premised their arguments against a stakeholder-centric conception of corporate purpose on the moral claims of private property.[8] According to Friedman, directors and officers have a responsibility to their employers – i.e., the shareholders – to maximize the value of the firm for the owners within the bounds of the law and accepted ethical customs. In pursuing their own conception of socially responsible conduct, the directors and officers would be spending their employers' money. As stewards charged with conducting the business to the benefit of its owners, such largesse is impermissible.[**]

The trouble with Friedman's argument is that a corporation – despite its separate legal personality – simply is not a thing capable of being owned. Those who view the corporation as a real entity are engaged in a form of reification. In other words, they are treating an abstraction – in this case, a legal fiction – as if it has material existence. Reification is often essential in discussing corporations, because it permits us to utilize a form of shorthand. Indeed, it is very difficult to think about large firms without reifying them. After all, it is easier to say Apple introduced a new iPhone than to attempt in conversation to describe the complex process that actually took place. Unfortunately, reification can be misleading, because it allows one to lose sight of the fact that corporations do not do things, people do.[9] Or, as English Jurist Edward, first Baron Thurlow, reportedly quipped, the corporation "has no soul to be damned, and no body to be kicked?"[10]

This insight gave rise to what is known as the nexus of contracts model of the corporation. The contractarian model of the corporation came to prominence in the 1980s.[11] By 1993, no less an authority than Delaware Chancellor William Allen noted "the dominance of the nexus of contracts model of the corporation in the legal academy," albeit not uncritically.[12] Although it has never achieved unanimous

---

the same manner as humans do." A. P. Smith Mfg. Co. v. Barlow, 98 A.2d 581, 586 (N.J. 1953). As Professor Adam Winkler explains, however, corporations are "not the same as natural persons" and, as a result, "are not truly 'free' in the way that individuals can be." Adam Winkler, We the Corporations: How American Business Won Their Civil Rights 388 (2018).

[**] Like Friedman, Merrick Dodd believed that shareholders owned the corporation. Also like Friedman, Dodd recognized that ownership and control had separated in public corporations. *See* E. Merrick Dodd, Jr., *For Whom Are Corporate Managers Trustees?*, 45 Harv. L. Rev. 1145, 1156 (1932) (arguing that "leadership of industry is in the hands of those who do not own"). Although Dodd acknowledged that "orthodox theory" held that "managers are elected by stockholder-owners to serve their interests," *id.* at 1157, he argued that managers were properly understood as fiduciaries of the institution as a whole and thus may take into account the interests of all the corporation's constituencies. *Id.* at 1162–63.

acceptance, the contractarian approach remains the dominant paradigm among corporate law scholars.[13]

In the contractarian model, the corporation is viewed as a nexus of the complex web of contracts between the corporation's various inputs.[*] Obviously, there are many factors of production that must come together in order for a corporation to provide goods and services. Labor, capital, land, and entrepreneurship are the classic four broad categories that virtually all firms require. As a result, within any firm, there will be a complex set of relationships between constituencies such as employees, creditors, shareholders, managers, and others. But that web must have a nexus.

If there is no nexus with which these constituencies could contract, employment contracts would cascade – looking rather like a standard hierarchical organization chart – with each employee contracting with his or her superior. Debt contracts would be even more complex. Such a cascade would be costly to assemble, if not impossible. Most corporate constituents lack any mechanism for communicating with other constituencies of the firm – let alone contracting with one another. Accordingly, constituencies must be (and are) linked to a central nexus and not each other. The corporation serves as that nexus, providing a (fictional) legal counterparty for the explicit and implicit contracts establishing rights and obligations among the various inputs making up the firm.

Although the concept of "ownership" of the corporation is prevalent in some contractarian accounts, the use of the term is in some respects a misnomer. No one owns a fiction, and asserting property rights over a nexus would stretch the limits of logic and imagination. Thus, the separation of control and ownership is more properly conceptualized as the separation of management and control. Ownership in this context is thus simply the right to specify the terms not specified in an incomplete contract. Put another way, shareholders do not own the corporate entity but rather simply possess contractual rights to the residual claim on the corporation's assets and cash flows. For the same of semantic simplicity, however, I use the term separation of ownership and control in its conventional sense herein as a shorthand.

Basic rules of corporate law reflect that distinction. For example, shareholders have no right to use or possess corporate property. As one court explained, "even a sole shareholder has no independent right which is violated by trespass upon or conversion of the corporation's property."[14] Likewise, corporate law statutes long have assigned management rights solely to the board of directors and those officers

---

[*] As used by contractarians, the term "contract" is not limited to relationships constituting legal contracts. Instead, contractarians use the word contract to refer generally to long-term relationships characterized by asymmetric information, bilateral monopoly, and opportunism. *See* Oliver Williamson, *Corporate Governance*, 93 YALE L.J. 1197 (1984) (discussing the transaction cost economics variant of the contractarian theory of the firm). Hence, I have elsewhere opined, "the nexus-of-contracts model is properly viewed as a metaphor rather than as a positive account of economic reality." Stephen M. Bainbridge, *Community and Statism: A Conservative Contractarian Critique of Progressive Corporate Law Scholarship*, 82 CORNELL L. REV. 856, 871 (1997). Many stakeholder theorists reject the nexus of contracts model. For an analysis of their objections, *see id.* at 858–71.

to whom the board properly delegates such authority. Accordingly, to the extent that possessory and control rights are the indicia of a property right, the board is a better candidate for identification as the corporation's owner than are the shareholders. As an early New York opinion put it, "the directors in the performance of their duty possess [the corporation's property], and act in every way as if they owned it."[15]

All of which is pertinent to our inquiry, because understanding that the corporation is not a thing capable of being owned but simply a legal fiction, suggests that Friedman's property rights-based argument has no traction.[16] Shareholders are not owners, so their rights are not grounded in property. Instead, as contracting parties, their rights are bargained for terms of their contract with the corporation. As we'll see below, shareholder value maximization is one of those rights.

10.2 DOES A RISING TIDE LIFT ALL BOATS?

Of all the corporation's many stakeholders only shareholders hold a fixed claim on the corporation's assets and earnings. Employees are entitled to the wages and, in some cases, performance-based pay. Creditors are entitled to interest and return of principal. And so on. After all of the corporation's fixed claimants have been paid, anything left over goes to the shareholders.[17] Likewise, only shareholders are entitled to distributions of the corporation's profits in the form of dividends.[18] When a company is sold, only shareholders get paid. As such, shareholders own the so-called residual claim on the corporation's earnings and assets (which is not the same as owning the firm itself).[19]

Since a residual claim is paid only after every other stakeholder's fixed claim has been satisfied, some argue that shareholder value maximization means that a rising tide will lift all boats. After all, if there is money left over for shareholders, everyone else must have been paid in full. So long as general welfare laws prohibit the corporation from imposing negative externalities on those constituencies, the shareholder wealth maximization norm redounds to their benefit. The goal of maximizing shareholder value thus is pro-stakeholder, in the sense that shareholders, as residual claimants have incentives to maximize the total value of the firm, which benefits the fixed claimants as well. Maximizing shareholder value is thus the most socially responsible thing a corporation can do.[20]

This argument formed an implicit part of the justification for journalists John Micklethwait and Adrian Wooldridge's perspicuous claim that the for profit corporation is "the basis of the prosperity of the West and the best hope for the future of the rest of the world."[21] As they explain:

> Henry Ford's $5 wage was a force for good; but his cheap cars helped change the lives of the poor in ways that socialists could only dream about. Boeing has spent millions of dollars financing good works in Seattle, but the real boost to the region has been the jobs that it has provided. Johnson & Johnson's behavior with Tylenol was exemplary—but its main contribution to American well-being has been all the pills and profits that it has made. The central good of the joint-stock company is that it is the key

to productivity growth in the private sector: the best and easiest structure for individuals to pool capital, to refine skills, and to pass them on. We are all richer as a result.[22]

Those who hold this position view the chief social responsibility of the corporation as being an engine of economic development and progress. It does so by making money. But a corporation cannot make money on a sustainable, long-term basis if it routinely mistreats its workers, cheats customers and suppliers, defrauds creditors, or pillages the environment. A tide of rising profit thus will lift all of our boats.

Some critics reject this argument, arguing that shareholders are not the sole residual claimants. Lynn Stout, for example, argued that outside of a liquidation in bankruptcy, the shareholders claim on corporate assets and earnings is exclusively paid via distributions in the form of cash dividends. Whether dividends get paid depends not on shareholders but on the directors.[23] "This rule seems to strike a fatal blow to the notion that corporate law treats shareholders as sole residual claimants, entitled to every penny of profit left over after the firm's contractual obligations to creditors, suppliers, and employees have been met."[24] In fact, however, it is a make-weight argument. The residual claim argument does not require that every left over penny be paid out to shareholders as opposed, for example, to being retained and reinvested in the business for the long run benefit of the shareholders.

Stout also argued that successful firms not only return profits to shareholders but also to employees in the form of higher wages and managers in the form of higher salaries and perquisites. Likewise, creditors gain because claims become less risky.[25] Professor Macey concedes the point, but explains that Stout's argument nevertheless fails because "shareholders are not distinguished by being the only corporate constituents with residual claims to the profits of the firm. What distinguishes shareholders is that they are the only claimants to the cash flows of the firm whose only economic interests in the firm are residual."[26]

Personally, I come down on the other side of the debate from Stout. But regardless of whether shareholders are the sole residual claimants or not, a rising tide does not lift all boats. As we have seen, the ability to externalize costs is baked into the corporation's DNA. As a result, it is entirely plausible that in some cases the tide will lift the shareholders' boat while swamping those of society and the company's non-shareholder constituencies. Although we rejected that argument as a justification for stakeholder capitalism, it must be admitted that it does limit the validity of the rising tide argument for shareholder value maximization. As Micklethwait and Wooldridge acknowledged:

> You don't have to be a hard-core opponent of globalization to worry about corporate heartlessness. There is a widespread feeling that companies have not fulfilled their part of the social contract: people have been sacked or fear that they are about to be sacked; they work longer hours, see less of their families—families—all for institutions that Edward Coke castigated four hundred years ago for having no souls.[27]

Even corporations that do not intentionally impose externalities on stakeholders and societies at large often need to make risky decisions, which can disadvantage non-shareholder constituencies. The increased return associated with an increase in risk does not benefit non-shareholders, because their claim is fixed, whereas the simultaneous increase in the corporation's riskiness makes it less likely that non-shareholder claims will be satisfied. Hence, the rising tide argument cannot be a complete explanation for the shareholder wealth maximization norm.

10.3 THE ARGUMENT FROM ACCOUNTABILITY

Having disposed of two weak arguments for shareholder value maximization, let us turn to stronger arguments in its favor. The first requires us to understand that much of the debate is conducted in isolation. Discerning the proper corporate purpose requires us not just to consider limited liability and the externality problem that results but also to account for another defining characteristic of the corporation: namely, the separation of ownership and control.

10.3.1 *The Separation of Ownership and Control*

Although shareholders are often said to "own" the corporation, they have virtually no decision-making powers – just the right to elect the firm's directors and to vote on an exceedingly limited – albeit not unimportant – number of corporate actions.[*] Rather, management of the firm is vested by statute in the hands of the board of directors, who in turn delegate the day-to-day running of the firm to its officers, who in turn delegate some responsibilities to the company's employees.[28]

Although he was not the first observer to identify the separation of ownership and control in American corporations, which dates back into the early nineteenth century, Adolf Berle is commonly credited for raising the issue to the prominence it now holds in corporate law scholarship.[29] In what is probably still the most influential book ever written about corporations, *The Modern Corporation and Private Property*, Berle and his coauthor Gardiner Means argued that it had become common for corporations to have dispersed ownership in which no one shareholder (or group of shareholders acting together) owned sufficient stock to have working control of the firm.[30] As a result, these corporations exhibited a complete separation of ownership and control in which the directors and their subordinate employees controlled the corporation.[**]

---

[*] As we just saw, ownership is not a useful concept with respect to the corporation. Shareholders do not own the corporation, they simply have contractual rights that include some weak ownership-like rights. Nevertheless, the "separation of ownership and control" is an accepted term of art and is used as a shorthand here for describing the limited control rights of shareholders.

[**] At the time Berle and Means wrote, boards of directors were almost universally dominated by the corporation's officers, especially the company's CEO. As a result, it was the senior executives that really ran the company. Today, reforms such as board independence requirements, have shifted some power back towards the board. *See* Stephen M. Bainbridge & M. Todd Henderson, Outsourcing the Board: How Board Service Providers Can Improve Corporate Governance 23–28 (2018) (tracing the evolution of the board-executive relationship). Accordingly, I will use the term "managers" and "management" herein to refer to the board and top executive team inclusively.

The growth of managerial control occurred, according to Berle and Means, because stock ownership was dispersed amongst many shareholders, no one of whom owned enough shares to affect materially the corporation's management. In turn, Berle and Means believed that dispersed ownership was inherent in the corporate system. Important technological changes during the decades preceding publication of their work, especially the development of modern mass production techniques, gave great advantages to firms large enough to achieve economies of scale, which gave rise to giant industrial corporations. These firms required enormous amounts of capital, far exceeding the resources of most individuals or families. They were financed by aggregating many small investments, which was accomplished by selling shares to many investors, each of whom owned only a tiny fraction of the firm's stock.

Separation of ownership and control thus proved an essential prerequisite to corporate success. This conclusion is premised on two observations: (a) most investors in corporations prefer to be passive holders of stock; and (b) separating ownership and control results in various efficiencies in making decisions. Vesting decision-making power in the corporation's board of directors and managers allows shareholders to remain passive, while also preventing the chaos that would result from shareholder involvement in day-to-day decision making.

10.3.2 *The Principal–Agent Problem a.k.a. Agency Costs*

While separation of ownership and control facilitated the growth of large industrial corporations, that separation also created the potential for shareholder and managerial interests to diverge. As the residual claimants on the corporation's assets and earnings, the shareholders are entitled to the corporation's profits. But it is the firm's management, not the shareholders, which decides how the firm's earnings are to be spent. Thus, there is a risk that management will expend firm earnings on projects that benefit management, rather than shareholders.

Put into economic terms, the separation of ownership and control creates the principal–agent problem we noted in the Introduction. In turn, the principal–agent problem gives rise to agency costs.[31] Economic theory tells us that agency costs are composed of three elements. First, principals expend time and effort monitoring their agents and sanctioning those agents who underperform or act selfishly. Second, because agents have *ex ante* incentives to credibly promise to work hard and to refrain from cheating, agents will incur bonding costs to make that commitment more credible. Third, because no system is perfect, some agent malfeasances and misfeasances will go unprevented, resulting in residual losses.[32] Many commentators argue that minimizing agency costs is the central problem of corporate governance.[33]

Accordingly, accountability is an essential component of corporate governance.[34] In turn, shareholder value maximization is an important component of corporate governance's accountability system. Shareholder value maximization provides a quantifiable metric by which to assess whether directors and officers have used their authority responsibly or for their own selfish benefit.[*] It requires one to ask such simple questions as: "Is the company profitable? Are its profits increasing? Is the share price going up? Are new customers being obtained on a profitable basis?"[35]

A common error made by stakeholder theorists is to assume that the profits to which those questions refer are historical earnings. Properly understood, however, value maximization looks to the future. Maximizing value is a matter of maximizing the present discounted value of the firm's future earnings.

It is of course true that there will be a certain amount of uncertainty associated with those questions, as there is with any attempt to predict future outcomes. That uncertainty is one reason courts invoke the business judgment rule and defer to board decisions in most cases absent disabling conflicts of interest or completely uninformed decision making. But, having said that, those questions remain simpler and more certain than those associated with the multi-factor analysis required by stakeholder theory.

10.3.3 *The Bainbridge Hypothetical and Win-Win Cases*

As an example of the argument, consider what some commentators have termed the Bainbridge hypothetical, which has been a standard explanatory tool of my teaching and scholarship.[36] The hypothetical assumes that a board of directors has concluded that an obsolete plant is no longer viable. One option under consideration is building a new plant in the current Rust Belt location in which construction, compliance, and labor costs are very high. The other option is to build a new plant in an off-shore location in which construction, compliance, and labor costs are much lower. The latter option would harm the plant's current workers and the local community in which it is located. But that option would benefit shareholders and creditors by reducing costs and, moreover, provide jobs for the workers who build the new plant and the employees hired to work at it. Assume that the latter groups cannot gain except at the former groups' expense.

To be sure, many business decisions do not pose such stark trade-offs. Many business decisions are potentially win-win scenarios, such that the proverbial rising tide

---

[*] As Eugene Fama explained, such a metric is also essential to workable systems of executive compensation:

> The max shareholder welfare rule for the decisions of firms also poses contract problems between shareholders and managers. Even with a one-dimension max shareholder wealth rule, manager decisions are subject to uncertain outcomes that make evaluating and compensating managers difficult. In a multidimension max welfare regime, the contract problem is more complicated. How do we write and enforce a payoff function in which managers are evaluated on wealth along with multiple dimensions of welfare, with the likelihood of randomness in outcomes on all dimensions?

Eugene F. Fama, *Contract Costs, Stakeholder Capitalism, and ESG* 5 (Chicago Booth Paper No. 20–46, 2020), http://ssrn.com/abstract=3722179.

usually does lift all boats. This is true even of decisions that in the short run seem to favor stakeholders at the expense of shareholders. Providing health benefits for employees may increase expenses and reduce profits in the short term, for example, but often leads to greater productivity in the long term. In other words, companies can do well by doing good. Happy and healthy employees are more productive than unhappy and unhealthy ones. Good pay and benefits thus redound to improved performance, but not only by improving the lot of existing employees but also by enabling the corporation to attract more talented employees. As John Micklethwait and Adrian Wooldridge aptly observed:

> There are plenty of hard-nosed reasons why the corporate sector has a vested interest in being seen to do good. Consider two reasons that are increasing in importance. The first is trust. Trust gives companies the benefit of the doubt when dealing with customers, workers, and even regulators.... The second reason is the "war for talent." Southwest Airlines is one of the most considerate employers in its business: it was the only American airline not to lay people off after September 11. In 2001, the company received 120,000 applications for 3,000 jobs.[37]

Even the stakeholder theorists' ultimate bête noire, Milton Friedman, acknowledged that "it may well be in the long-run interest of a corporation that is a major employer in a small community to devote resources to providing amenities to that community or to improving its government."[38] Another major stakeholder theorist bête noire, Michael Jensen, likewise acknowledged that corporations "cannot create value without good relations with customers, employees, financial backers, suppliers, regulators, communities, and the rest."[39]*

Market forces will thus often induce firms driven by the profit motive to behave in pro-social ways. If customers have a preference for goods and services that are environmentally friendly, for example, firms will have an incentive to mitigate their environmental impact. If investors have a preference for ESG friendly investments, capital will flow toward corporations with strong pro-ESG reputations and those firms' stock price should rise to reflect their lower cost of capital. Managers of such

---

* Put another way, shareholder value maximization does not encourage directors and executives to treat employees and other stakeholders as mere automatons whose knowledge, expertise, and feelings are irrelevant. To the contrary, shareholder value maximization encourages managers to treat employees and other stakeholders with consideration precisely because that is usually the best way of maximizing shareholder value. In other words, concern for stakeholders is a means to the end of shareholder value maximization rather than an end in and of itself.

It may be objected that one should not use others as a means to an end. Indeed, for Kantians this is a moral imperative. Yet, Kantian philosophy does not privilege stakeholder theory over shareholder value maximization. Corporate social responsibility treats shareholders as a means of accomplishing social ends that the shareholders may or may not share.

In the real world, moreover, people treat each other as means rather than ends all the time. If I go to a restaurant for dinner, I am using the waiter to obtain food. At the same time, the waiter is using me to earn a living. Just so, shareholders use stakeholders to obtain a return on their investment while stakeholders use the shareholders to make a living.

corporations will have an incentive to develop such reputations, especially given how much of their pay comes from equity and other performance-based compensation arrangements.[40]

Market forces can even incentivize corporations to internalize costs they might otherwise seek to externalize. Consumers who care more about price than sustainability or human rights will prefer cheap coffee, but those who value sustainability and ensuring that growers get fair compensation will opt for higher-priced fair trade coffee. Obviously, unless consumers have homogeneous preferences not all firms will internalize those costs.[41] In addition, of course, some corporations will respond to such incentives not by actually changing their behavior but by greenwashing. This is why society backstops market forces by contractual protections and general welfare legislation designed to incentivize corporations to internalize costs that would otherwise be borne by specific stakeholders or society at large.

Having said all that, however, even win-win situations require a decision-making norm. The expanded pie must still be divided. In seeking to do so, a singular maximand remains essential, because it "is logically impossible to maximize in more than one dimension at the same time unless the dimensions are what are known as 'monotonic transformations' of one another."[42]

> A name for this problem is the "double maximand": the aim is to maximize two aims, despite there being an inevitable trade-off between them. A popular way of presenting this is to call it a "balance." Balance can, of course, be a good thing, but it can also be a plausible excuse for missing the point. For, example if someone told you to "run as far as possible as fast as possible," you would be left wondering whether to jog for 26 miles or sprint for 100 meters, or to compromise between the two. Actually, those instructions leave you with freedom to do whatever you want, and if asked how you come to be lying in the grass listening to the skylarks, you could explain that you were striving to achieve a balance.[43]

Extending the analogy to the corporate context, directors authorized to balance shareholder value maximization, stakeholder interests, and ESG considerations are being authorized to do the equivalent of lying in the grass listening to skylarks. To be sure, we nevertheless allow the business judgment rule to insulate most such decisions from judicial review because we assume that managerial concern for stakeholders and society usually results in gains to the company and that after the stakeholders' fixed claims are satisfied the remaining gains go to the shareholders. But the key point is that the accountability problem does not go away even in win-win cases.

10.3.4 *The Bainbridge Hypothetical and Zero Sum Cases*

As we saw above, "[b]usiness life is not somehow miraculously limited to win-win decisions."[44] To the contrary, decisions requiring boards to assess "potential trade-offs between shareholders and stakeholders are ubiquitous."[45]

Consider a company that provides its employees with compensation and benefits at levels that fully enable it to attract and retain talented and productive employees. And suppose that this company has, as many major public companies do, a significant stream of profits that enables it to fund all necessary investments and to also pay dividends. In this common situation, if the directors were to follow pluralistic stakeholderism, they would face a trade-off. Financing an increase in employee compensation by reducing dividends would make employees somewhat better off and shareholders somewhat worse off. Trade-offs and conflicts of this kind are likely to be very common.[46]

It is these sort of cases that are truly instructive and which the Bainbridge Hypothetical is designed to explore.

By what standard should the board make the decision posed in the Bainbridge hypothetical? Shareholder value maximization provides a clear answer to this otherwise difficult situation – close the plant. Absent shareholder value maximization, the board would lack a determinate metric for assessing its options.

10.3.5 *Stakeholder Theory Needs Metrics but Offers None*

To be sure, stakeholder theorists believe "that directors should allocate benefits among corporate constituencies fairly or justly, in a manner that is right and good – that is, according to some normative criterion."[47] The problem is that stakeholder theorists have reached "no consensus … about what this normative criterion is."[48] The absence of such a consensus means that stakeholder theory provides no criteria for determining which of potentially multiple options are superior to others, let alone determining which is best.[*] In other words, even if the directors have perfect information and the outcome of the various options available to the board could be known with certainty – conditions that are never satisfied in the real world – stakeholder theory still would not provide them with a mechanism for sorting and ranking those options.

---

[*] Although moral and ethical considerations may be pertinent to the decision whether or not to adopt shareholder or stakeholder capitalism, they do not provide a determinate criterion for making specific business decisions:

> The problem … is that directors are not moral philosophers and we cannot reasonably expect that they will become moral philosophers, and until they become moral philosophers—and moral philosophers all of the same stripe—they cannot resort to moral philosophy to make business decisions together in an effective manner.

Robert T. Miller, How Would Directors Make Business Decisions Under A Stakeholder Model?, 77 Bus. Law. 773, 799 (2022). A further difficulty is that while some commentators contend that "[s]takeholder capitalism relies on a relatively homogeneous society with largely similar moral preferences," Karthik Ramanna, *Friedman at 50: Is it Still the Social Responsibility of Business to Increase Profits?*, 62 CAL. MGMT. REV., no. 3, 2020, at 28, 34, we live in a time in which moral preferences are seen as contestable and politically partisan.

It seems most unlikely that anyone could design a workable version of such a mechanism. Although it is true that shareholders do not have completely homogenous preferences, stakeholder interests are far more heterogeneous. Not only do different stakeholder categories have different interests, but within each category some members will have different interests from other members of the same category. Employees care about job security, their absolute compensation, their compensation relative to other employees, their benefits, diversity and inclusion, occupational safety, and so on. Within firms, different categories of employees will have different concerns. Overseas employees may have different concerns than domestic ones, for example. Gig employees will have different concerns than those with job security. Creditors care about the return on their money but care even more about, as Will Rodgers put it, the return of their money. Within a single firm, long-term creditors will have different concerns than short-term ones. Suppliers care about have a continuing demand for their products or services and timely payment. Customers traditionally cared mostly about low prices but increasingly also care about things like sustainability, the human rights of producers, and so on. Recall that appealing to customers concerned with the latter is what benefit corporations were designed to do. Recall also that Millennials and Centennials supposedly have different preferences as consumers than do older customers.

In the foregoing list, of course, we identified just a few of the most prominent of the many classes of stakeholders with which firms must engage. Likewise, we have not considered the need for firms to take into account social concerns beyond those of stakeholders, such as the environment. Reconciling all of those interests seems likely to be a task beyond the ability of boundedly rational humans.[49] As we saw above, given the constraints on managerial resources, gathering the information and expertise necessary to make decisions under such conditions "is likely to divert managers' efforts from the kinds of business decisions they are better able to make."[50] Not only do managers lack incentives to do so, society logically should not want managers to stray outside their wheelhouse.

The task of reconciling the relevant interests will be compounded by competition between the various constituencies. Although stakeholder theory often is framed in communitarian terms, the multiplicity of competing interests suggests that a corporation run according to stakeholder theory would be a most fractious community. As Eugene Fame observed, "if all stakeholders have rights to influence the firm's decisions, they are unlikely to agree about which decisions maximize combined wealth, and they are unlikely to agree about how combined wealth is split among stakeholders."[51] It is hard to imagine Wall Street bankers and workers, to cite but two polar extremes, sitting around a campfire singing Kumbaya after a friendly session of whacking up the pie in fair shares. Each constituency will have an incentive to extract as much wealth from the firm as possible. Those stakeholder groups best able to organize and reach agreement as to their goals will fare best, while more diffuse groups likely will fare less well. The former will be better able to bring pressure to bear on management or to persuade management that their interests coincide.

Bebchuk and Tallarita's study of the role ESG-based metrics play in compensation decisions at S&P 100 companies demonstrates the difficulties firms are already having in attempting to take such metrics into account. Among the companies that consider ESG-based factors, most used metrics relating to employee concerns and many used metrics relating to consumers and the environment. Few companies discussed the interests of local communities and only a tiny number took supplier concerns into account. As a result, it seems fair to conclude that companies are finding it difficult to take into account the full breadth of their constituencies.[52]

In addition, Bebchuk and Tallarita found that the ESG-based metrics used by firms in their sample took into account only some of the interests of the various constituencies. Most companies disclosed considering how the CEO performed on diversity, equity, and inclusion. Most also disclosed weighing the CEO's performance on occupational health and safety. But none based the CEO's pay on increasing employee pay or benefits or improving employee job security. They conclude "that companies choose only a few groups of core stakeholders and focus on a limited number of aspects of their welfare," which seems entirely predictable.[53]

Even if we assume that proponents of stakeholder capitalism manage to define the necessary metrics, however, the inherent conflicts not just between shareholder and stakeholder interests but also between the interests of various stakeholder classes mean that any such metrics would inevitably consist of indeterminate balancing standards. As Bebchuk and Tallarita observe, "the economics of multitasking [coupled with] the fact that many important dimensions of employee welfare are hard to measure means that CEOs might be pushed to focus on some factors and ignore others, based on criteria that depend not on the importance of these factors but on their measurability."[54] Put another way, the Biblical aphorism that no one can serve two masters becomes even more apropos when the number of masters increases to double digits. In turn, the inherent ambiguity of such standards would deprive directors of the critical ability to determine *ex ante* whether their behavior comports with the law's demands, thereby raising the transaction costs of corporate governance.[55] In addition to depriving the board of workable guidance, allowing directors to eschew shareholder value maximization complicates efforts to hold boards accountable, since a "single objective goal like profit maximization is more easily monitored than a multiple, vaguely defined goal like the fair and reasonable accommodation of all … interests."[56]

A useful analogy is provided by the problem lawyers encounter when they represent multiple parties. Consider the example of Louis Brandeis, who coined the term "lawyer for the situation" to rebut accusations that his practice had been replete with conflicts of interest. After a thorough examination of Brandeis' professional conduct, legal ethics professor John Frank concluded:

[T]he greatest caution to be gained from study of the Brandeis record is, never be "counsel for a situation." A lawyer is constantly confronted with conflicts which he is frequently urged to somehow try to work out. I have never attempted this without wishing I had not, and I have given up attempting it. Particularly when old clients are at odds, counsel may feel the most extreme pressure to solve their problems for them. It is a time-consuming, costly, unsuccessful mistake, which usually results in disaffecting both sides.[57]

Even authorities who are disposed more favorably toward the idea of lawyers for the situation acknowledge that that role "is not easy, may fail, and will often bring recrimination in its wake."[58] Despite many years of refinement, the relevant rules of legal ethics are still viewed as inadequate, vague, and inconsistent. They are hardly the stuff of which certainty and predictability are made.

10.3.6 *Standards and Accountability*

The absence of workable standards gives rise to the central accountability problem associated with stakeholder capitalism, because in the absence of clear standards directors will be tempted to pursue their own self-interest. After all, directors who are responsible to everyone are accountable to no one.[59] In the Bainbridge hypothetical, for example, if the board's interests favor keeping the plant open, we can expect the board to at least lean in that direction. The plant likely will stay open, with the decision being justified by reference to the impact of a closing on the plant's workers and the local community. In contrast, if directors' interests are served by closing the plant, the plant will likely close, with the decision being justified by concern for the firm's shareholders, creditors, and other benefited constituencies.

Cases in which CEOs use ESG concerns to justify underperformance will be even more common than cases in which they use them to camouflage self-dealing and conflicts of interest. As SEC Commissioner Hester Peirce observed in opposing proposed SEC regulations mandating extensive climate-related disclosures by public companies:

> Executives, for their part, might not mind the new regime that elevates squishy climate metrics. After all, how wonderful it will be for an executive who has failed to produce solid financial returns to be able to counter critics with a glowing report on climate transition—"Dear Shareholders, we fell far short of our earnings target this year, but you will be pleased to know that all in all it was a fantastic year since we made great progress on our climate transition plan." If the CEO's compensation is tied to lower greenhouse gas emissions, she can forgo the focus on company financial value—so 20th century!—and spend her time following the proposal's urging to convince suppliers to shift to electric transport fleets and customers to freeze their jeans instead of washing them.[60]

As evidence supporting that claim, consider Professors Ryan Flugum and Matthew Souther's study of management communications during the two weeks following an earnings announcement. They looked for statements that the managers' firms consider "the interests of stakeholders as opposed to shareholders, citing terms such as 'stakeholder value,' 'the benefit of stakeholders,' or 'stakeholder interests.'"[61] They found "that managers are 34 to 43 percent more likely to cite stakeholder value maximization during periods following earnings announcements that fall short of market expectations."[62] Conversely, they also found that, after mentioning stakeholder objectives in a prior quarter, managers are more likely to not mention them in a quarter where the firm's performance exceeds analyst expectations. In other words, managers use stakeholder interests as camouflage for their own poor performance, while reverting to a focus on shareholder interests when firm performance improves.

To be sure, as we saw in Chapter 4, an unintended consequence of the business judgment rule is to insulate directors from liability in many cases resembling the Bainbridge hypothetical. As we also saw, however, that does not mean that shareholder value maximization should be abandoned as the underlying legal rule. Indeed, the case law provides "no support for [the] argument that the business judgment rule is intended to allow directors to mediate between competing interest groups."[63]

In addition, the trouble with requiring directors to multi-task by juggling the interests of multiple constituencies becomes especially pronounced when we turn to those cases in which the business judgment rule does not apply with full force. As we have seen, in ordinary business decisions governed by the business judgment rule, management's incentives are more closely aligned with shareholder rather than stakeholder interests. Suppose, however, that our hypothetical corporation receives a takeover bid from a bidder with a history of closing obsolete plants. The board rejects the bid, citing the bidder's history. All of the practical problems discussed above are present. More important, while an honest concern for the threatened workers may have motivated the directors' decision, so too might a concern for their own positions and perquisites. Indeed, corporate managers are much more likely to suffer losses as a result of takeovers than are other non-shareholder constituencies. Accordingly, it is not at all difficult to imagine a target CEO and board using non-shareholder interests as nothing more than a negotiating device to extract side payments from the bidder. Under current law, the business judgment rule would not protect the directors' decision unless they could show that it also benefited the shareholders. As we saw in discussing the constituency statutes, however, extending the business judgment rule to such decisions was the central motivating factor behind the one serious legislative effort to embrace a form of stakeholder capitalism. Because applying the business judgment rule to takeover decisions permits managers to play one constituency off against another, the accountability provided by current law is lost. The same would be true if the business judgment rule were extended to other conflict of interest situations, which also tend to have strong management conflicts of interest. Hence, stakeholder capitalism likely would result not in protection of stakeholders but in a transfer of wealth from both shareholders and non-shareholders to managers.

Support for that supposition is provided by a study of non-shareholder constituency statutes. Adoption of these statutes increased managerial entrenchment, while reducing shareholder wealth. Managers of companies incorporated in states with a constituency statute engaged in more earnings management than those incorporated in states lacking such statutes. Conversely, the study found that non-shareholder constituencies received at most marginal benefits (if any) from the statutes' adoption.[64] The bottom line is that stakeholder capitalism reduces managerial accountability without providing measurable gains for stakeholders.

10.3.7 *Accountability and Human Nature*

Some stakeholder theorists assume away the accountability problem by making highly optimistic assumptions about human nature. Merrick Dodd posited just such a view, in which power does not corrupt, but rather "tends to create on the part of those most worthy to exercise it a sense of responsibility."[65] In my view, however, that understanding of human nature is naïve at best. "Indeed, one of the reasons the law is suspicious of self-dealing transactions in general is that '[h]uman nature tells us the director will advance her own interests in the transaction, to the detriment of the corporation.'"[66] Even where managers do not intentionally pursue their self-interest, they likely will choose the option that benefits themselves. As Chancellor Allen pointed out, "human nature may incline even one acting in subjective good faith to rationalize as right that which is merely personally beneficial."[67]

10.3.8 *ESG Is Already Creating an Accountability Problem*

Bebchuk and Tallarita point out that we are already seeing ESG creating an accountability problem. There has been a longstanding legislative and regulatory trend toward increasing transparency with respect to executive compensation. Ideally, companies should set out clear and objective goals to be achieved by their compensation arrangements, disclose the extent to which those goals were achieved, and provide sufficient context for assessing the success of those arrangements in improving firm performance. Many ESG-based compensation disclosures fail to satisfy those criteria. Instead, as predicted above, they offer "vague and underspecified goals, such as increasing sustainability, diversity, inclusion, or employee well-being, without any specific targets or additional information." Widespread proliferation of such vague metrics would further reduce CEO accountability, "as it gives them the opportunity to get rid of painful incentives and increase their pay while at the same time pretending to steer the company toward social responsibility and stakeholder welfare."[68]

10.4 THE IMPLEMENTATION PROBLEM

As we saw in the preceding section, shareholder value maximization provides a quantifiable metric by which to assess whether directors and officers have used their authority responsibly or for their own selfish benefit. Berle was the first to point out that the absence of such a metric means that stakeholder capitalism has an essentially insoluble practical problem. Specifically, he contended that society could not abandon "'the view that business corporations exist for the sole purpose of making profits for their stockholders' until such time as you are prepared to offer a clear and reasonably enforceable scheme of responsibilities to someone else."[69] No such scheme existed at that time and none has been forthcoming. In fact, it is quite difficult to implement a system by which one can maximize more than a single objective. Although the implementation problem arises in large part out of concerns we have already discussed, it is worth reviewing them in the specific context of discussing whether stakeholder capitalism reasonably can be implemented.

The initial problem is that the stakeholder paradigm suffers from internal inconsistencies. Consider the stakeholder perspective of "delivering value to our customers." A company like Apple can significantly improve value to current customers by selling its high-quality products at a fraction of current prices. In the short run, this pricing will lead to higher market share and many more happier customers. In the long run, if Apple continues to maintain or increase the quality of its products, it may face financial difficulty. In other words, focusing on just short run value to customers is not a long-term sustainable practice.

Second, as we have seen, stakeholder capitalism does not eliminate conflict. "If all stakeholders have rights to influence the firm's decisions, they are unlikely to agree about which decisions maximize combined wealth, and they are unlikely to agree about how combined wealth is split among stakeholders."[70] Corporate constituencies will still prefer their interests to those of other constituencies. Likewise, conflicts within constituencies will persist.[*]

The third practical challenge of the stakeholder governance paradigm is the difficulty of operationalizing a simultaneous commitment to customers, employees, suppliers, and communities and to long-term shareholder value. How do we provide a clear directive to corporate managers and hold them accountable to it? Under stakeholder capitalism almost any management expenditure of corporate

---

[*] We see similar conflicts within the choices made by ESG investment funds. Prior to the 2022 Russian invasion of Ukraine, ESG indices typically excluded defense contractors. Companies that sell ratings of corporate ESG performance likewise downgraded defense companies. In the wake of outbreak of war, however, many rating firms, ESG funds, and index suppliers are reconsidering the exclusion of defense companies. The Russo-Ukrainian war also raised questions about whether fighting climate change was more socially responsible than dealing with inflation and the impact of energy prices on the poor. James Mackintosh, *Do Good Investing is Under Pressure*, WALL ST. J., Mar, 28, 2022, at B1. Trying to be socially responsible is exceedingly difficult when the definition of what is socially responsible involves clashing goals and rapidly changing perceptions about what is pro-social.

resources, short of outright fraud, can be justified as consistent with addressing the priorities of some stakeholder group. This is particularly the case because, as we just noted, so many ESG criteria are quite vague. At present, "most companies [are] using discretionary or underspecified goals and many others using only qualitative goals."[71] Hence, as we just saw, the lack of managerial accountability becomes a problem.[72]

The final problem is how one prevents cheating. If a substantial number of companies truly embrace meaningful stakeholder capitalism, their marginal costs of production will rise. As more and more firms do so, the competitive advantage for firms that decline to do so will steadily increase. In particular, the incentive to cheat – as by greenwashing – becomes quite strong. If consumers have difficulty distinguishing sincere embraces of stakeholder capitalism from strategic puffery, which frequently seems to be the case, one ends up with a market for lemons.[73]

10.4.1 *The Untenable Constituency Board Solution*

Harvard law professor Victor Brudney acknowledged that stakeholder capitalism inherently suffered from such implementation problems, but proposed solving them by reforming the board of directors to include "appropriately weighted representatives of each class of claimants."[74] Deciding what the appropriate weighting for each constituency class presents what law professor Amir Licht calls a "thorny issue,"[75] which surely understates the difficulties the task presents. Equally, if not more thorny, are the questions of what corporate constituencies are entitled to representation – do local communities get representation and, if so, which ones, to cite but one problematic example – and how their representatives are to be selected.

If those problems could be solved, others will arise to bedevil the project. First, why should we assume that constituency directors would be loyal to their constituency rather than being coopted? The cooption issue will be especially problematic absent changes that delink director compensation from share price and other financial metrics. Second, constituency directors may result in the same sort of destructive conflicts that occur with minority shareholder representation under cumulative voting or after successful short slate proxy contests. The problem would be even worse in constituency boards, however, because of the competition between the various constituencies for resources. Third, the presence of constituency directors on a board would compound the principal–agent problem resulting from the separation of ownership and control. As Judge Ralph Winter pointed out, in the 1970s there was concern that labor representatives on German boards formed alliances with managers against shareholder representatives.[76] Fourth, Judge Winter also pointed out the significant risk of price-fixing and other antitrust issues that would arise if a board included customer and supplier representatives.[77]

10.4.2 *The Untenable Codetermination Solution*

Codetermination is an alternative to the multi-constituency board offered by some proponents of stakeholder capitalism. Germany long has had a system of codetermination under which companies have a dual board structure. In its best known form, the Codetermination Act 1976, which governs the largest German firms (those with more than 2,000 employees), the dual board consists of a management board comprised of the top management team and a supervisory board half of whose members represent the firm's shareholders and half of whom represent the firm's employees. In smaller firms (those with between 500 and 200 employees), the Works Constitution Act gives shareholders a two-thirds majority on the supervisory board. Companies with fewer than 500 employees are allowed but not required to have a supervisory board. If present, the supervisory board's role is akin to that of US boards. The supervisory board thus appoints and dismisses members of the management board, conducts oversight of management, and ensures corporate compliance.

As we saw in the Introduction, some commentators have proposed to implement stakeholder capitalism in the United States via codetermination, as have Senators Elizabeth Warren and Bernie Sanders.[78] Yet, the German model of codetermination is at best a weak form of stakeholder capitalism. True, employees have a voice on the board. But that voice typically is only advisory. In small firms, employee representatives make up just one-third of the board, ensuring that shareholder representatives can outvote employee representatives. In larger firms, subject to the 1976 act, the president of the supervisory board is chosen by the shareholders and given a double vote so as to break ties. In addition, at least one of the employee representatives must come from management. As such, the extent to which the supervisory board model gives meaningful power to employees is often overstated.

Professors Jens Dammann and Horst Eidenmüller recently proffered a persuasive argument that codetermination would be a bad fit for US corporations.[79] They acknowledged that there are some plausible justifications for adopting codetermination. Participation in the decisions that affect one's life is widely regarded as an essential element of human dignity. This argument is a core element of Catholic social thought's support for codetermination, to cite but one prominent example.[80] Participation in board decision making also can help ensure that employees are paid a just wage, representing a fair share of corporate profits. Lastly, codetermination may help insulate society against the immense power of large corporations.

On balance, however, Dammann and Eidenmüller conclude that the costs associated with codetermination outweigh its benefits. "Crucially, these costs and benefits include not just those accruing to shareholders but also those imposed on or enjoyed by other constituencies, most notably employees."[81] Unfortunately, their survey of the empirical literature confirms that attempts to quantify those costs and benefits remain inconclusive. As they thus conclude, "decades of empirical research on codetermination lead to a sobering assessment: the results hardly yield a compelling case for or against the policy."[82] As they caution, of course, even if the empirical literature provided a compelling answer to the question of whether the benefits to German society and the German economy outweigh the costs, there is no reason to assume that the same would be true in the United States.

Turning to qualitative assessments of codetermination, Dammann and Eidenmüller point out that codetermination inexorably leads to divided loyalties within the board, because "the shareholder representatives know that they must please the shareholders to get reelected, whereas the worker representatives know that their reelection depends on keeping employees satisfied."[83] Such divided loyalties inevitably impede the effectiveness of board decision making. To be sure, some contend that a diverse board can help improve decision making by, for example, reducing the extent of groupthink and related sources of dysfunction. But assuming that racial or gender diversity has that effect, there is no guarantee that including employee representatives on the board necessarily will promote such forms of diversity. There is, however, a guarantee that including employee representatives will increase conflicts within the board that will reduce the quality of decision making.

There also is no guarantee that the knowledge and skills employee representatives bring to the boardroom table are of the sort that leads to more informed decision making. The late law professor Michael Dooley opined that workers will be indifferent to most corporate decisions that do not bear directly on working conditions and benefits. He argued that, "as to the vast majority of managerial policies concerning, for example, dividend and investment policies, product development, and the like, the typical employee has as much interest and as much to offer as the typical purchaser of light bulbs."[84] Dooley's argument is supported by a number of empirical studies. One study, for example, found that workers who did not desire participation often cited a lack of managerial expertise as the reason. Another study found that employee participation in decisions relating to shop floor issues, such as working methods, was a better predictor of enhanced employee satisfaction and performance than was employee participation in strategic decisions. A review of the literature concluded that participatory management is most effective when it is directed at employee's daily work rather than at policy issues affecting the entire firm.[85] All of which tends to suggest that employee representatives add little except increased labor advocacy to the board.

As I have argued elsewhere, inclusion of employee representatives on the board also will increase agency costs.[86] Corporate employees have an incentive to shirk so long as their compensation does not perfectly align their incentives with those of the firm's shareholders. In turn, knowing of this phenomenon, the firm's shareholders should expect management to reduce the compensation of the firm's employees by the amount necessary to offset the expected degree of employee shirking. Because *ex ante* wage adjustments are rarely fully compensatory due to bounded rationality and the resulting use of incomplete contracts, the firm's shareholders should expect management to monitor employees and punish *ex post* those who shirk.

One of the accountability mechanisms that aligns managerial and shareholder interests is monitoring by the board of directors. Allowing employee representation on the board necessarily reduces the likelihood that the board will be an effective monitoring device. Workers have an interest in supporting rules that free management from accountability to shareholders, because shareholders "could seek profits by getting highly motivated managers who sweat the labor force."[87] Managerial shirking of its monitoring responsibilities will often redound to the workers' benefit, suggesting that employee representatives on the board of directors are less likely to insist on disciplining lax managers than are shareholder representatives. If employees are entitled to voting representation on the board of directors, monitoring by the board and its subordinate managers will be less effective, which will cause agency costs to rise.

The prediction that agency costs rise when employees are represented on the board is supported by evidence from the German experience with codetermination. It is widely reported, for example, that labor's presence on the supervisory board impedes cost cutting measures that adversely affect workers.[88] Codetermination is also said to impede the market for corporate control as an accountability mechanism by making hostile takeovers more difficult.[89]

Interestingly, even in Germany – the heartland of codetermination – there has been a long-term trend away from the dual board system. The number of German corporations lacking the two key elements of codetermination – the supervisory board and the plant-level works council – rose from 50.6 percent to 60.5 percent between 1984 and 1994.[90] This decline was attributed to broader shifts in the German economy shift toward smaller firms and service industries, both of which are outside the scope of the codetermination laws.[91] Between 2002 and 2015 the number of companies subject to the 1976 Codetermination Act declined in every year. In 2016, the number ticked up to 641 from 635.[92] As of 2018, only 36 percent of German workers were employed by firms with either equal or one-third employee representation on the supervisory board.

In addition to the important work by Dammann and Eidenmüller, another recent critical take on codetermination was proffered by economists Simon Jäger, Shakked Noy, and Benjamin Schoefer's 2021 National Bureau of Economic Research working paper.[93] Their review of the currently available empirical evidence concludes that codetermination has at best small positive effects on worker and employer outcomes, although it leaves room for moderately positive results on criteria such as wages and productivity. They then offer a new study of how changes in codetermination laws affected aggregate economic outcomes and the quality of industrial relations within the countries adopting those changes. They find no positive effects. They propose three complementary reasons why codetermination seems to have very limited economic effects:

First, existing codetermination laws convey little authority to workers. Second, countries with codetermination laws have high baseline levels of informal worker voice. Third, codetermination laws may interact with other labor market institutions, such as union representation and collective bargaining.[94]

As for proposals for importing codetermination into US law, the authors argue that deep institutional differences between US and European preclude easy comparisons. Having said that, however, they do reach a clear conclusion "that codetermination is not a standalone institution. Rather, it is part of a broader institutional and cultural package whose other elements complement codetermination and supply its practical infrastructure."[95] Implementing stakeholder capitalism through codetermination thus would require massive changes in both law and business, which would exceed the changes discussed in Chapter 5.

Even if one sets all those concerns to one side, insofar as implementing stakeholder capitalism is concerned, the base problem with codetermination is that it precludes all corporate constituencies other than shareholders and labor from participating in the governance of the corporation. To be sure, there are those who will argue that labor is the most important non-shareholder constituency.[96] But others might disagree. Some will point to climate change as a critical corporate social responsibility issue and, accordingly, will emphasize the importance of various environmental stakeholders.[97] Others point to creditors "as the most important of the firm's stakeholders after shareholders, whose participation in the corporate enterprise is essential to ensuring a corporation's ability to expand and thrive."[98] As such, codetermination fails to solve the problem of viably implementing a true system of multi-constituency stakeholder capitalism.

10.4.3 *The Untenable Team Production Solution*

Presumably because of these concerns with constituency boards and codetermination, most stakeholder capitalism advocates focus instead on the issues on which we have been focused; namely, the fiduciary duties of corporate managers. Some advocate reversing *Dodge* to allow directors to consider stakeholder interests when making decisions.[99] Others go even further to argue that managers should owe fiduciary duties to core stakeholders.[100] In contrast, the central claim of this book remains that both of those propositions are irredeemably erroneous.

Perhaps the best known attempt to develop a tenable solution to the implementation problem, at least in late twentieth and early twenty-first century legal scholarship, was Margaret Blair and Lynn Stout's team production model. In several articles written around the turn of the century, Blair and Stout set out a so-called model of corporate governance somewhat resembling my director primacy model, but also differing from director primacy in key respects.[101] Recall that the two basic questions any model of corporate governance must answer are (1) who makes decisions for the corporation?; and

(2) what is the decision-making norm that should guide the chosen decision makers? As to the former question, team production and director primacy are both board-centric. Blair and Stout argued, for example, that directors "are not subject to direct control or supervision by *anyone*, including the firm's shareholders."[102] A critical difference between our respective models, however, is suggested by Blair and Stout's argument that corporate law treats directors not as hierarchs charged with serving shareholder interests, but as referees – mediating hierarchs, to use their term – charged with serving the interests of the legal entity known as the corporation. As such, they contended "that hierarchs work for team members (including employees) who 'hire' them to control shirking and rent-seeking among team members."[103] Director primacy claims this is exactly backwards – directors hire factors of production, not vice-versa.*

As for the second key question, although Blair and Stout's original work tended to downplay the normative implications of their model, they acknowledged that it "resonates" with the views of progressive corporate legal scholarship.[104] As we have seen, of course, Stout's later work arguably established her as the twenty-first century's leading critic in the legal academy of shareholder value maximization on both positive and normative grounds. In any case, Blair and Stout defined the corporation's purpose as maximizing the "joint welfare function" of all constituents who make firm specific investments.[105] They presumably adopted that standard so as to avoid the problem of directors struggling to juggle competing interests. But a standard focused on pie expansion does not eliminate the need for standards by which to divide the resulting pie.

10.4.4 *Team Production's Limited Domain*

Harvard law professor John Coates argued that Blair and Stout's mediating hierarch model fares poorly whenever there is a dominant shareholder.[106] If so, the model's utility is vitiated with respect to close corporations, wholly-owned subsidiaries, and publicly-held corporations with a controlling shareholder. In addition, Coates argues, Blair and Stout's model also fares poorly whenever any corporate constituent dominates the firm. Many of publicly-held corporations lacking a controlling shareholder are dominated by one of the constituents among which the board supposedly mediates – namely, top management. Although the precise figures are disputed, a substantial minority of publicly-held corporations still have boards in which insiders comprise a majority of the members. Even where a majority of the board is nominally independent, Coates suggests, the board may be captured by insiders.

---

*   I quibbled with Blair and Stout's terminology on grounds that although public corporations typically have many production teams embedded in various places within the corporate hierarchy, team production is an inapt model for understanding either the corporate entity or the work of the board of directors. *See* Stephen M. Bainbridge, *Director Primacy: The Means and Ends of Corporate Governance*, 97 Nw. U.L. Rev. 547, 594–96 (2003).

10.4.5 *Team Production's Erroneous View of the Board's Role*

In Blair and Stout's model, directors are hired by all constituencies and charged with balancing the competing interests of all team members "in a fashion that keeps everyone happy enough that the productive coalitions stays together."[107] In other words, the principal function of the mediating board is resolving disputes among other corporate constituents. This account of the board's role differs significantly from the standard account.

The literature typically identifies three functions performed by boards of public corporations.[108] First, and foremost, the board monitors and disciplines top management. Second, while boards rarely are involved in day-to-day operational decision making, most boards have at least some managerial functions. Broad policymaking is commonly a board prerogative, for example. Even more commonly, however, individual board members provide advice and guidance to top managers with respect to operational and policy decisions. Finally, the board provides access to a network of contacts that may be useful in gathering resources and/or obtaining business. Outside directors affiliated with financial institutions, for example, apparently facilitate the firm's access to capital. In none of these capacities, however, does the board of directors directly referee between corporate constituencies.

To be sure, dispute resolution is an important function of any governance system.[109] *Ex post* gap-filling and error correction are necessitated by the incomplete contracts inherent in corporate governance. Those functions inevitably entail dispute resolution. Corporate governance addresses the problem of incomplete contracting by creating a central decisionmaker authorized to rewrite by fiat the implicit – and, in some cases, even the explicit – contracts of which the corporation is a nexus.

As the principal governance mechanism within the public corporation, the board of directors is that central decisionmaker and, accordingly, bears principal dispute resolution responsibility. Yet, as economist Oliver Williamson explained, in doing so, the board "is an instrument of the residual claimants."[110] Hence, as we have seen, if the board considers the interests of non-shareholder constituencies when making decisions, it does so only because shareholder wealth will be maximized in the long-run.

If directors suddenly began behaving as mediating hierarchs, rather than shareholder wealth maximizers, an adaptive response would be called forth. Consistent with the predictions developed above, shareholders would adjust their relationships with the firm, demanding a higher return to compensate them for the increase in risk to the value of their residual claim resulting from director freedom to make trade-offs between shareholder wealth and non-shareholder constituency interests. Ironically, this adaptation would raise the cost of capital and thus injure the interests of all corporate constituents whose claims vary in value with the fortunes of the firm.

10.5 STAKEHOLDER CAPITALISM VERSUS DEMOCRACY

Today's stakeholder theorists claim to be working in a capitalist rather than socialist model. "They want to 'humanize' the corporation, not to expropriate it."[111] Yet, some persuasive commentators have long contended that stakeholder capitalism poses a serious threat to democratic capitalism. Michael Novak aptly observed that when stakeholder theorists ask for corporations to "become more 'responsible' … they mean dedicated to causes dear to statists."[112] In order to achieve those causes, however, the stakeholder theorists are using corporate power to bypass the democratic process. They turn to demanding corporate social responsibility precisely because they "have failed to persuade a majority of their fellow citizens to be of like mind and that they are seeking to attain by undemocratic procedures what they cannot attain by democratic procedures."[113]

The core problem was aptly laid out by Milton and Rose Friedman, who asked:

> If businessmen do have a social responsibility other than making profits, how are they to know it? Can self-selected private individuals decide what the social interest is? Can they decide how great a burden they are justified in placing on themselves or their stockholders to serve that social interest? Is it tolerable that these public functions of taxation, expenditure, and control be exercised by the people who happen at the moment to be in charge of particular enterprises, chosen for those posts by strictly private groups?[114]

In effect, the Friedmans argued that stakeholder capitalism amounts to taxation without representation. Put another way, the exercise of political power by undemocratically selected technocrats skilled predominately in business and finance amounts to authoritarianism by the wrong authorities.

As we have seen, identifying and then making the trade-offs necessary to resolve "social/political issues, including allocating capital to determine environmental/ health/safety/consumer protection standards, can only be made by those accountable through a very different kind of market test – the political process."[115] Because "questions of which social issues to address, how to address them, and the amount of resources to allocate to these issues can only be fairly dealt with through the political process" the logical conclusion "is that CSR advocates are trying to access and use corporate resources to achieve objectives that they have failed to attain through the political process."[116]

Robert Miller provides a useful example of this concern:

> Take climate change, a key issue for stakeholderists and ESG advocates more broadly. It is clear beyond dispute that significant reductions in carbon levels requires action not by one company or even one country but by substantially all companies in substantially all countries; if some or even only a good majority of business emitting high levels of carbon reduce their emissions, the net result would likely be trivial, for others can and likely will free ride on their efforts. The obvious solution is regulation

requiring all companies to reduce their emissions very substantially, the solution that has been used to control other forms of pollution for the last fifty years. But such regulation does not have broad support among the public, and such regulations have not been implemented in any major economy (whatever regulations have been imposed fall far short of what most climate change activists believe necessary). Stakeholderism provides a possible answer to this problem: it may be possible to convince corporations to do voluntarily what they are not required to do legally.[117]

In fairness, it must be noted that the problem is not limited to progressives. Shortly before the November 2016 Presidential Election, United Technologies Corporation (UTC) CEO Gregory Hayes defended the firm's decision to close an Indiana furnace factory operated by its Carrier Corporation subsidiary and transfer production to a factory in Mexico. In doing so, Hayes was responding to repeated public criticism of the decision by then Presidential candidate Donald Trump. Although Hayes claimed the decision had not been taken lightly, the decision was part of Hayes' on-going pursuit of shareholder wealth maximization. While the Indiana plant was profitable, it simply was not profitable enough to meet Hayes' goals, especially when compared to Carrier's highly profitable Mexican plants. Once Trump was elected President, Hayes backtracked and agreed to keep the plant open, but continued to insist that, "as for the initial decision to close the plant, 'we did the right thing for the business.'"[118]

Whether the request comes from the right or left, asking corporate executives to take on governmental functions not only asks them to undertake tasks for which they are untrained and for which their enterprise is unsuited, it also subverts the basis of a liberal democracy. Government efforts to solve social problems are inherently limited by the checks and balances baked into the American political system. Stakeholder capitalism bypasses those checks and balances by asking unelected executives to undertake solving social ills.[*]

In the mid-1960s, for example, Milton Friedman engaged in a close study of the Johnson Administration's efforts to reduce the country's balance of payments deficit and reduce to outflow of gold. Part of those efforts was an attempt to persuade banks to voluntarily limit foreign loans. In order to induce banks to cooperate, President Lyndon Johnson proposed legislation to exempt banks from the federal antitrust laws. In addition to that government payoff, Friedman noted that banks had a strong financial incentive to participate in the loan scheme. Restricting the number of

---

[*] In addition, if stakeholder capitalism were effective, it would weaken the case for effecting stakeholder protection through the political process. They suggest that stakeholder capitalism would provide a relief valve for political pressures for pro-stakeholder policy reforms. "In other words, if corporations are seen to be voluntarily adopting broader measures that benefit stakeholders – which may or may not be effective or sincere – politicians may hold off with introducing 'harder' legal requirements in this regard. Stakeholderism is therefore counterproductive." Martin Petrin, *Beyond Shareholder Value: Exploring Justifications for a Broader Corporate Purpose* 20 (November 1, 2020), https://ssrn.com/abstract=3722836.

foreign loans reduced the supply of funds available to foreign borrowers, which drove up the price banks could charge for the limited number of available loans. Instead of being a voluntary act of social responsibility, the program was really a government-approved cartel supported and developed by the country's largest banks.[119]

Based on his studies of that and other similar government programs, Friedman concluded that exhortations for corporations to be socially responsible "had little effect until they were backed up by coercion to enforce sanctions against those who did not comply."[120] "Relying on companies/investors to do the right thing without government action is as naive as having a professional basketball league without rules or referees, but clubs writing glossy purpose statements promising to play fair."[121] In turn, state coercion induces regulatory capture by large businesses, which results in various socially irresponsible results such as increased economic concentration. Social responsibility claims by corporations thus typically are intended to conceal such results rather than reflect true corporate altruism.[122]

Friedman and his allies therefore argued shareholder value maximization is necessary to preserving both economic and social liberty. According to Friedrich Hayek, for example:

> [O]nce the management of a big enterprise is regarded as not only entitled but even obliged to consider in its decision whatever is regarded as the public or social interest, or to support good causes and generally to act for the public benefit, it gains indeed an uncontrollable power—a power which could not long be left in the hands of private managers but would inevitably be made the subject of increasing public control.[123]

In other words, shareholder value maximization affirmatively contributes to preservation of a free society by limiting the need for political regulation of unchecked managerial power.

The Friedman/Hayek argument still holds true. Today, however, stakeholder capitalism poses a more serious threat than ever because of its potential to contribute substantially to the ongoing culture wars. To be sure, Chapter 9 concluded that the Business Roundtable's 2019 statement was not principally the result of progressive activism by social justice warrior CEOs. Indeed, as we have seen, most of today's CEOs – even those who signed the Business Roundtable statement – are not woke social justice activists. Yet, as illustrated by the backlash against CEO greenwashing and appeasement, corporate intrusion into politics substantially enflamed the culture wars. Polarization would only be enhanced if we move the political process into firms by asking managers to make what are in effect political decisions.

10.6 THE HYPOTHETICAL BARGAIN

The nexus of contracts theory of the firm is not merely descriptive but also prescriptive. It treats the law as being analogous to a standard form contract offered by the state so as to facilitate private ordering. If the law provides a set of off-the-rack rules that work well for most businesses, it reduces bargaining and other transaction costs. On the other hand, if the law creates rules that impede businesses, the businesses' owners and other stakeholders will need to bargain for alternatives or otherwise find workarounds.[*]

If transaction costs are zero, of course, bargaining of that sort would be no problem. This is simply a straightforward application of the Coase Theorem, which asserts that, in the absence of transaction costs, the initial assignment of a property right will not determine its ultimate use.[124] According to the Coase Theorem, rights will be acquired by those who value them most highly. In a world of zero transaction costs, the parties thus will opt out of suboptimal default rules by contract. In the face of positive transaction costs, however, bargaining around such a rule becomes costly and, in some cases, wholly impractical, forcing the parties to live with a suboptimal rule. The public corporation – with thousands of shareholders, managers, employees, creditors, and other constituencies, each of whom have different interests and asymmetrical information – is a very high transaction cost environment indeed.[125]

In the public corporation setting, society can reduce the transaction costs parties incur by providing the rule most people would prefer. Only a small number of idiosyncratic businesses would incur costs for bargaining or other workarounds. In effect, we must perform a thought experiment, in which we ask "if the parties could costlessly bargain over the question, which rule would they adopt?" In other words, we mentally play out the following scenario: Sit all interested parties down around a conference table before organizing the corporation. Ask the prospective shareholders, employees, contract creditors, tort victims, and the like to bargain over what rules they would want to govern their relationships. The rule that emerges is known as the majoritarian default. Adopting that bargain as the corporate law default rule reduces transaction costs and therefore makes it more efficient to run a business. Of course, we cannot really conduct such a negotiation; but we can draw on our experience and economic analysis to predict what the parties would do in such a situation.[126]

Much if not most of corporate law consists of majoritarian defaults.[127] Contractarian corporate law scholars generally conclude that shareholder value maximization – not stakeholder capitalism – is one of those majoritarian defaults.[128] Eugene Fama's summation is representative of this view:

> [The hypothetical bargain results in] a contract structure in which almost all stakeholders negotiate fixed payoffs (basically, forms of debt), and shareholders bear the

---

[*] Providing a standard form contract, of course, is not the sole function of corporation law. Law also provides institutional features that could not be effected by internal contracts. *See, e.g.*, Henry Hansmann & Reinier Kraakman, *The End of History for Corporate Law*, 89 GEO. L.J. 439, 406–23 (2001) (arguing that parties could not effect affirmative asset partitioning by contract). The firm thus has both contractual and institutional attributes.

residual risk of net cashflows—revenues minus costs. (This is why shareholders are called residual risk bearers.) In exchange for fixed payoff contracts for other stakeholders, shareholders get most of the rights with respect to decisions that affect net cashflows. Given the contrast costs of more complicated multidimensional decision rules (like max[izing] shareholder welfare), the optimal decision rule is max[izing] shareholder wealth.[129]

To see why this is so, let's consider a hypothetical bargain session between the pertinent corporate constituencies.

10.6.1 *The Board of Directors as Bargaining Party*

Let's start with the board of directors on one side of the negotiating table.[130] On the other side, we will start with the shareholders as the board's only counterparty. We will then complicate the analysis by introducing stakeholders as additional bargaining parties.

On balance, directors should prefer shareholder capitalism to stakeholder capitalism. On the one hand, as our analysis of the argument from accountability suggests, directors might prefer the rule – stakeholder capitalism – that allows them camouflage self-interested decisions by engaging in a multi-constituency decision-making process. On the other hand, however, directors have strong incentives to prefer shareholder value maximization. We saw in Chapter 5 that many of the legal rules of corporate law – not just *Dodge* and its progeny – provide such incentives. Nobody likes to lose their job, for example, but directors can be elected or removed only by shareholders. To be sure, there are substantial obstacles that make it difficult to oust directors who displease the shareholders, but at least they have the ability to do so in some cases. Stakeholders have no such ability.

Directors also have a significant stake in the financial success of the corporation. This is so because, in the first instance, there are reputational costs to firm failure. Second, to the extent the directors invest in firm-specific human capital, that investment will be lost if the directors lose their positions following a firm failure, proxy contest, or takeover. Third, the growing emphasis on stock-based director compensation gives the board a direct financial interest in the firm's returns to shareholders. Paying directors at least in part in equity rather than cash is now nearly universal among larger companies.[131] As corporate governance expert Charles Elson explains, this practice aligns the directors' interests with those of the shareholders[132] and thus tilts directors' incentives away from stakeholder interests. As far back as 2001, an independent director who owned $500,000 worth of his company's stock stated: "If this company faces a challenge, I lose sleep at night."[133]

The point is not that director and shareholder interests are always aligned. In some important cases, such as corporate takeovers, they will not be. The point is simply that, behind the veil of ignorance, directors will tend to align themselves with shareholders rather than stakeholders.

10.6.2 *The Shareholders as Bargaining Party*

Turning to shareholders, despite the acknowledged proliferation of socially responsible and ESG investors, it remains the case that when most shareholders invest "in
a corporation, they do not think that they are giving their money away."[134] To the
contrary, they expect "to receive a healthy return on their capital."[135] As a harshly
critical statement on corporate purpose signed by over 6,000 stakeholder theorists
and other progressive academics concluded, "left to their own devices, most capital
investors will not care for the dignity of labor investors; nor will they lead the fight
against environmental catastrophe."[136]

All of the standard valuation tools of corporate finance by which returns are estimated are ultimately dependent on profit, by which the reader will recall that we
refer not to historic but rather future earnings. This is especially obvious in the case
of discounted cash flow valuation, which is based on projected future free cash
flows. Yet it is also true of valuation techniques that use historical data. Capitalized
earnings value the firm by dividing earnings by a capitalization rate. Discounted
dividend methods use a formula in which dividends serve as the numerator and
some discount rate is the denominator. Although the latter two use historical data,
all three methods are attempts to estimate the true value of the firm, which is the
present discounted value of all dividends to be paid by the corporation in the future.
Similarly, all methods of capital budgeting are based on an assumption of profit
maximization. In its simplest form, for example, the corporation calculates the net
present value (NPV) of all available projects and opportunities. The corporation
first invests in the project offering the highest NPV then in the project offering the
second highest and so on until it runs out of cash to invest or it runs out of projects
offering positive NPVs (obviously, the firm should not invest in negative NPV projects or it will lose money). Accordingly, as Henry Manne observed in his debate
with Henry Wallach, "[i]f the anticipated return is diminished by 'social' expenditures, the price of a share will decline until it provides the market rate of return on
investments of the same quality."[137] As such, if *Dodge* had adopted corporate social
responsibility rather than shareholder value maximization as the default rule, "no
one would have felt comfortable investing in unprotected equity."[138] Shareholders
therefore would oppose any bargain that gives directors a license to reallocate wealth
from shareholders to non-shareholder constituencies.

Another way of stating the argument is to put it in terms of economic efficiency.
Boards of directors sometimes face decisions in which it is possible to make at least
one corporate constituent better off without leaving any constituency worse off. In
economic terms, such a decision is Pareto efficient. It moves the firm from a Pareto
inferior position to a Pareto superior position.

Other times, however, boards face a decision that makes at least one constituency better off but leaves at least one worse off. The Bainbridge hypothetical and
other zero sum decisions are just the worst-case variation on this theme. Imagine a
decision with a pay-off for one constituency of $150 that leaves another constituency

worse off by $100. As a whole, the organization is better off by $50. In economic terms, this decision is Kaldor-Hicks efficient.

The key criteria of a Pareto superior transaction is that it makes at least one person better off and no one worse off. In contrast, Kaldor-Hicks efficiency does not require that no one be made worse off by a reallocation of resources. Instead, it requires only that the resulting increase in wealth be sufficient to compensate the losers. Note that there does not need to be any actual compensation, compensation simply must be possible. With this background in mind, the shareholder wealth maximization norm can be described as a bargained-for term of the board-shareholder contract by which the directors agree not to make Kaldor-Hicks efficient decisions that leave shareholders worse-off.[139]

The shareholders' objections to stakeholder theory will be greatly compounded if Robert Miller is correct that stakeholder theory contemplates allowing boards to transfer wealth from shareholders to stakeholders but not in the other direction.[140] In other words, stakeholder capitalism does not permit tradeoffs between shareholders and stakeholders whose result is to make shareholders better off and stakeholders worse off. If stakeholder capitalism were the hypothetical bargain, shareholders thus would be signing off on a deal that leaves them systematically worse off.

Miller's argument starts off with the premise that all corporate constituents except shareholders have fixed claims set by explicit or implicit contracts. The logic of shareholder capitalism is that whatever is left over after all of those fixed claims goes to the shareholders. While it is true that the proverbial rising tide does not lift all boats, shareholder capitalism nevertheless allocates the entirety of the residual claim to the shareholders.

Miller's point is that stakeholder capitalism treats the fixed claims of non-shareholder constituencies as a floor setting the minimum to which the stakeholders are entitled:

> Consequently, any application of the stakeholder model involves paying every constituency other than the shareholders what they are legally entitled to receive under a contract with the corporation—and perhaps more. In every case in which a constituency receives more than it is due under its contract with the corporation, the additional value it receives always comes at the expense of shareholders, never at the expense of any other constituency. In other words, applying the stakeholder [model] results in a transfer of wealth from shareholders to one or more other corporate constituencies.[141]

As an example, Miller offers a hypothetical in which the corporation enters into a collective bargaining agreement with its employees setting wages and benefits. Miller contends that if the firm outperformed expectations stakeholder theorists would contend that the profits be shared with the employees. If the firm underperformed, however, stakeholder theorists would insist that the employees nevertheless get their contractually specified wages and benefits rather than having their pay cut. He concludes:

Under the stakeholder model, in other words, when the venture in which the various constituencies have an interest works out well, the bargain among the parties may be adjusted to benefit other constituencies at the expense of shareholders, but if the venture works out badly, other constituencies will get the benefit of their bargain and any unexpected losses fall on the shareholders. It should go without saying that, in other contexts, no rational commercial party would ever agree to such terms. Indeed, from the point of view of shareholders, the stakeholder model is Bugs Bunny corporate governance: heads I win, tails you lose.[142]

In competitive markets, he argues, any payments to stakeholders in excess of what they bargained for would result in super-competitive returns to those constituencies and, accordingly, sub-competitive returns to the shareholders.

Miller's claims ring true. Stakeholder capitalism is not a win-win model. His analysis thus provides further reason to believe that if the hypothetical bargain were to actually occur shareholders would insist on shareholder capitalism. After all, why would shareholders agree to a bargain that gives them returns below what they could earn in a competitive market?

In addition to earning a return on their investment, shareholders would also bargain for shareholder value maximization for multiple reasons we have already suggested. First, recall that absent the shareholder wealth maximization norm, the board would lack a determinate metric for assessing options.* Second, any legal standards developed to review such decisions would operate mostly by virtue of hindsight. Finally, absent clear standards, directors will be tempted to pursue their own self-interest. After all, directors who are responsible to everyone are accountable to no one.

10.6.3 *The Stakeholders as Bargaining Party*

The conclusion that shareholder value maximization is the majoritarian default does not change when we introduce into the mix non-shareholder constituencies as a bargaining party. Although it is true that the proverbial rising tide does not necessarily lift all boats in all cases, it is also true that director pursuit of shareholder

---

* As Professor Miller thus observes:

> [I]t is not that stakeholder theory fails to provide sufficiently determinate answers to how a board should make business decisions; it is that, for every business decision, the stakeholder model provides *no answers at all*. It is thus the exact opposite of what rational commercial parties would typically agree to when, in a complex venture, the profits of the venture must be distributed among various parties who have participated in the venture in different ways. The agreements used by such parties typically provide for elaborate cash waterfalls that determine exactly how much each party is entitled to receive. The stakeholder model is at the very opposite end of the spectrum. Worse than insufficiently determinate, it is *radically indeterminate*.

Robert T. Miller, *How Would Directors Make Business Decisions Under A Stakeholder Model?*, 77 Bus. Law. 773, 785 (2022) (emphasis in original).

wealth maximization often redounds to the benefit of non-shareholder constituencies. Even where shareholder and non-shareholder interests conflict, moreover, non-shareholders receive superior protection from contracts and both targeted and general welfare legislation. Because shareholders will place a higher value on being the beneficiaries of director fiduciary duties than will non-shareholder constituencies, gains from trade are available, and we would expect a bargain to be struck in which shareholder wealth maximization is the chosen norm.[*]

10.6.4 *Summation*

The hypothetical bargain methodology transforms the shareholder wealth maximization norm from a right incident to private property into a mere bargained-for contract term. As with the rights of other corporate constituents, the rights of shareholders are established through bargaining, even though the form of the bargain typically is a take-it-or-leave-it standard form contract provided off-the-rack by the default rules of corporate law and the corporation's organic documents. The contractarian account of this norm thus rests not on an outmoded reification of the corporation, but on the presumption of validity a free market society accords voluntary contracts.

The economic consequences of rejecting the hypothetical bargain and embracing stakeholder capitalism could be severe. If embracing stakeholder capitalism raised the cost of equity capital, as we would expect, companies may begin to "search for a more hospitable host for incorporation. The present trickle of stock expatriations, motivated by the potential for tax savings, could become a flood."[143]

---

[*] In an economic sense, fiduciary duties prevent corporate directors and officers from appropriating quasi-rents through opportunistic conduct unanticipated when the firm was formed. Quasi-rents arise where investments in transaction specific assets create a surplus subject to expropriation by the contracting party with control over the assets. *See* Benjamin Klein et al., *Vertical Integration, Appropriable Rents and the Competitive Contracting Process*, 21 J. L. & ECON. 297 (1978). A transaction specific asset is one where its value is appreciably lower in any other use than the transaction in question. Once a transaction specific investment has been made, it generates quasi-rents – i.e., returns in excess of that necessary to maintain the asset in its current use. (The asset may also generate true rents – i.e., returns exceeding that necessary to induce the investment in the first place – but the presence or absence of true rents is irrelevant to the opportunism problem.)

If such quasi-rents are appropriable by the party with control of the transaction specific asset, a hold up problem ensues. Investments in transaction specific assets therefore commonly are protected through specialized governance structures created by detailed contracts. As we have seen, however, under conditions of uncertainty and complexity, bounded rationality precludes complete contracting. Under such conditions, accordingly, fiduciary duties provide an alternative source of protection against opportunism. Both shareholders and at least some stakeholders make transaction specific investments in corporations. Both are thus subject to having their quasi-rents appropriated by the directors and officers who control the corporation. The claim here thus is not that only shareholders need protection from opportunistic conduct by management, but that shareholders would bargain for – and stakeholders would be willing to concede – the specific form of protection provided by the fiduciary duties of the corporation's officers and directors. *See* STEPHEN M. BAINBRIDGE, CORPORATION LAW AND ECONOMICS 424–29 (2002).

10.7 DOES THE HYPOTHETICAL BARGAIN HOLD
IN THE ESG ERA?

Some might concede that shareholder value maximization once was the hypothetical bargain, while arguing that it no longer does in light of the rise of Millennials,
Centennials, and other ESG-focused investors. We considered the rise of Millennials
and Centennials as workers, but now we need to focus on whether their rise as investors changes the analysis.* More precisely, because the vast majority of Millennial
and Centennial investors invest through exchange traded funds (ETFs) and mutual
funds rather than directly, we need to focus on the role of the so-called Big Three.

   The mutual funds and ETFs managed by BlackRock, State Street, and Vanguard
collectively control about 25 percent of shareholder votes at S&P 500 companies.
Importantly, although each of the Big Three's holdings are divided up among many
different funds and ETFs, each normally votes all shares controlled by all of its funds
the same way. All of which has turned the Big Three into the proverbial 800-pound
gorillas of the investment world.

   Although BlackRock CEO Larry Fink arguably has been the most vocal proponent of ESG commitments, all of the Big Three have publicly and repeatedly
emphasized their commitments in this area. There is no evidence that these commitments have had any beneficial social impact. Tariq Fancy, the former chief
investment officer for sustainable investing at BlackRock observes that:

> [T]here is no compelling empirical evidence that ESG investing mitigates climate
> change. Outside of a very small minority of private, long-term funds, such as
> venture-capital funds that back promising technological solutions to the climate crisis,
> the vast majority of funds marketed as ESG and sustainable funds today—as well as
> the nonbinding practice of ESG integration into existing investment processes—
> can't point to any real-world impact that would not have otherwise occurred.[144]

On close examination, moreover, the Big Three's commitments have often been
honored mainly in the breach. In 2021, for example, BlackRock stated that it wanted
its portfolio companies by not later than 2050 to remove as much carbon dioxide
from the atmosphere as they emit. Critics pointed to BlackRock's failure to set any
earlier goals and pointed out that BlackRock had failed to specify what proportion
of its portfolio companies would have achieved zero-emission status by 2050.[145]
More generally, the Big Three and other purportedly ESG-focused fund managers

---

* I do not believe the rise of Millennials and Centennials as investors changes the analysis. But let
us assume for the sake of argument that it does. As we saw in Chapter 7, given the constraints on
management skills, information, and incentives, it would be preferable for corporations to maximize shareholder value and allow young progressive investors to use their stock market returns to
support causes they see as socially responsible. *See* Eugene F. Fama, *Contract Costs, Stakeholder
Capitalism, and ESG* 4 (Chicago Research Booth Paper No. 20–46, 2020) (suggesting that "it is optimal for firms to make decisions that max shareholder wealth and let consumer-investors allocate
the wealth to achieve optimal consumption and portfolio allocations, including ESG exposures").

frequently vote in ways inconsistent with their stated ESG mandate, even when proxy advisory services have recommended a favorable vote.[146]

Why don't the Big Three live up to their commitments? The principal determinant of ESG fund voting decisions appears to be the fund's short-term financial performance rather than ESG-related considerations. Incorporating ESG considerations into voting – and, in the case of actively managed funds, investing – decisions entail significant costs. In particular, assessing how thousands of portfolio companies from around the globe are performing on ESG issues requires substantial numbers of expert personnel whose services are expensive. In order to hold down costs and remain competitive, large institutional investors consistently underinvest in ESG personnel. In 2020, for example, BlackRock had the largest ESG stewardship team of any asset manager. Yet, that translated into only 47 professionals, each of whom was responsible for conducting analyses of approximately 500 companies. The amount of time devoted to each portfolio company thus is inevitably limited, which is "impossible to reconcile with a detailed analysis of each company."[147]

Consider, for example, the Big Three's record in voting on ESG-related shareholder proposals made by other investors.[*] Despite the fact that the Big Three collectively own enough shares to determine the outcome of the vote on many pro-ESG proposals made by other shareholders,[148] they rarely vote in favor of such proposals. In the 2018–2019 proxy season, for example, the largest of the Big Three – Vanguard and BlackRock – supported unique shareholder E&S proposals at rates of 7.5 percent and 7.1 percent, respectively. State Street explicitly markets itself as supporting progressive environmental and social issues and supported E&S proposals at the somewhat higher rate of 22.7 percent. Some might question how much support is evidenced by voting for barely one in five such proposals.

Stock market prices provide indirect evidence that the Big Three's ESG commitments are mostly greenwashing. Corporate stock prices react to new information about a company's ESG performance only where the information in question is material to the company's financial prospects. This suggests that investors are not making purchase and sale decisions based on non-pecuniary factors. Instead, their decisions are driven by financial considerations.[149]

The Big Three get away with underperforming on ESG issues because those who invest in them do not punish the fund managers for doing so. In particular, investors in ESG funds do not exit funds that vote in ways inconsistent with their stated pro-ESG mandate.[150] There is no reason for fund managers to do more than pay lip service to ESG considerations if there is no penalty for greenwashing.

---

[*] SEC Rule 14a-8 allows shareholders meeting certain procedural requirements to place proposals on the corporation's proxy statement and have those proposals voted on at the company's annual shareholder meeting. *See generally* Stephen M. Bainbridge, *Revitalizing SEC Rule 14a-8's Ordinary Business Exclusion: Preventing Shareholder Micromanagement by Proposal*, 85 FORDHAM L. REV. 705 (2016)

Some have pointed to the 2021 proxy fight at ExxonMobil as evidence that share-holders – including the Big Three – are increasingly willing to put environmen-tal concerns ahead of profit. Engine No. 1 is a small hedge fund that purports to be focused on advancing ESG issues, especially with respect to climate change. Engine No. 1 nominated a short slate – four director candidates – in opposition to the candidate slate put forward by the incumbent board. Three of Engine No. 1's candidates were elected, which the New York Times proclaimed as a "major tri-umph" for climate activists.[151]

On closer examination, however, the ExxonMobil result actually supports the hypothesis that today's investors remain focused on profit. Two of the successful three Engine No.1 were longtime oil industry executives. Engine No.1's arguments were focused on ExxonMobil's subpar financial performance, emphasizing that over the preceding ten years ExxonMobil had lost money while stock market indices had tripled. ExxonMobil was persistently investing in expensive projects that could only pay off if oil prices increased substantially and on a sustainable basis. Finally, Engine No.1 highlighted ExxonMobil CEO Darren Woods $75 million pay over the preceding four tears. In sum, the "fight wasn't about being woke, it was about capitalists holding other capitalists responsible for results."[152]

Additional evidence that most investors have not embraced the ESG worldview is provided by the results of shareholder proposals related to ESG issues. Indeed, I believe that the best data on what investors really want comes not from surveys (as evidenced by the disastrous performance of the polling industry in recent years, which has cast doubt on all types of survey research), but from what people actually do when given the opportunity to vote on shareholder proposals relating to ESG issues. Examples of such proposals include asking the board to create board commit-tees to oversee the company's social and environmental performance, requesting dis-closure of political contributions, calling for linking executive pay to ESG metrics, disclosure of greenhouse gas emissions, and a host of similar issues. According to an evaluation by the Gibson Dunn law firm of ESG-related shareholder proposals in the 2020 proxy season, the number of proposals relating to environmental and social issues dropped by 10 and 21 percent, respectively. Average support for social propos-als was 21.5 percent, while environmental proposals average 30.2 percent support.

10.7.1 *The Hypothetical Bargain and the Persistence of Investor Heterogeneity*

The importance of the Big Three cannot be denied, but it can be overstated. As one commentator asks, "can we assume that all retail investors, family offices, mutual funds, pension funds, private equity funds, hedge funds, governments, foundations, and universities, have the same goals?"[153] To the contrary, "[i]n addition to such attributes as family, corporate, foreign, or state ownership, shareholders differ in other ways, such as whether they have a business relationship with the firm, have long-term or short-term investment horizons, use derivatives to decouple voting and economic rights, have a propensity to engage in shareholder activism, or focus on political, corporate social responsibility, or other interests that may not be shared by the firm's remaining shareholders."[154] Because various studies show the supposed Millennial and Centennial monolith is a myth,[155] these differences undoubtedly persist and will continue to do so.

10.7.2 *An Anecdote*

In April 2022, Starbucks CEO Howard Schulz announced that the company would suspend a plan that had promised shareholders a three-year program of distributing $20 billion in profits to the shareholders via stock buybacks and dividends. Although Starbucks would continue to pay dividends, it was cancelling the planned stock buy-backs. Those buybacks would have amounts to two-thirds of the $20 billion total. At the same time, Schulz announced a shift in corporate focus to employees and customers. If investors really valued stakeholder capitalism, one might have expected Starbucks' stock price to rise. It fell by 3.7 percent.[156] In commenting on Schulz's decision, one of the Wall Street Journal's Heard on the Street columnists casually remarked, almost as though it went without saying, that "Shareholders of course are less impressed by companies that seek to reward 'all stakeholders.'"[157]

10.8 HEDGE FUND ACTIVISTS ENFORCE THE HYPOTHETICAL BARGAIN

The story of Etsy, Inc., provides an excellent example of the potential futility of private ESG commitments and the probable triumph of shareholder value maximization. "In 2015, Etsy was a crown jewel of the movement for socially conscious business, simultaneously pursuing multiple objectives beyond profit."[158] Over its first decade of existence, Etsy built a distinct corporate culture that balanced multiple maximands. It treated employees well, was kind to the environment, and empowered craftspeople and artisans to profitably market their products. Etsy was a certified B-Corp. It was also reasonably profitable.

But then Etsy went public. Its registration statement asserted that "we believe that companies can and should use the power of business to create social good, which is reflected in our status as a Certified B Corporation. Our commitment to using business as a force of good manifests itself in the way we run our business."[159] From the outset, however, Etsy faced significant pressure from its shareholders to improve the company's performance and boost the stock price. Etsy thus presented an important test case of whose preferences would prevail: those of ESG investors or those of profit maximizing investors.

10.8.1 *The Rise of Hedge Fund Activism*

The Etsy story in fact stands as a paradigmatic example of the increasing pressure public companies face from activist hedge funds to improve share price performance. Hedge funds originated in the late 1960s as investment pools that were akin to equity mutual funds, but were essentially unregulated and were thus free to use short-selling, leverage, derivatives, and other techniques to hedge those investments. They provided institutions and high net worth individuals with a purportedly market neutral investment in which gains and losses were determined by the fundamentals of the chosen portfolio securities rather than factors affecting the entire market.

In the 1990s, the hedge fund industry rapidly evolved. Some retained the traditional equity fund approach. Others specialized in arbitraging price differentials between linked products. Still others focused on riding macroeconomic developments. The key category for our purposes, however, are the activist funds.

In one sense, activist hedge funds are akin to traditional value investors. They seek to identify target companies that they believe to be undervalued by the market. Unlike traditional value investors, activist funds are willing to be much more involved "hands on" investors. Although some activists seek value-enhancing changes through negotiation, the subcategory with which we are mainly concerned tend to be highly confrontational.[160] In either case, however, the standard hedge fund compensation 2-and-20 rule – i.e., an annual management fee of 2 percent of assets under management and a performance fee of 20 percent of returns above a specified benchmark – encourages managers of these funds to have a laser-like focus on the stock price of the companies in which they invest.

The activist playbook is well established. Identify an undervalued company, evaluate the shareholder base and the corporation's governance to determine its vulnerability, and, assuming the prospects for effecting change are positive, buy a substantial stake in the target. The fund will then meet with management to urge them to voluntarily adopt the changes the fund seeks. If management is resistant, the activist will threaten a proxy contest. The incumbent managers often will capitulate somewhere along the process, but if not the activist will proceed to a proxy contest, typically seeking to elect a short slate rather than the entire board of directors. If successful, the activist's board representatives will seek to influence the board to adopt the proposed changes.[161]

Activist hedge funds and their academic defenders claim that activist campaigns benefit all shareholders. They posit that targeted boards and management become more disciplined in their use of company resources and their allocation of capital. The target companies become more likely to return free cash flows to shareholders rather than spending them on empire building and management perks. If the target has underperforming assets, those assets will be sold or spun off. In some cases, the activist's board representatives will bring an external, uncompromising perspective on a company's strategic options. Finally, when appropriate, the activist campaign may lead to the sale of the target corporation at a premium.[*]

Some also claim that directors and officers who are incentivized by an activist campaign to be better and more faithful managers should raise firm value in ways that benefit all stakeholders. After all, managerial shirking that takes the form of slacking, excess compensation and perquisites, spending free cash flow on negative net present value projects and so on presumably benefits none of the firm's constituencies.[162]

There is some support for these claims. If the fund's stake in the target corporation exceed five percent, the fund must file a disclosure statement with the SEC on Schedule 13D in which the fund discloses the amount of equity securities it holds in the target and its plans for that investment, among other items. A study by Alon Brav, Wei Jiang, Frank Partnoy, and Randall Thomas of what happened to target corporation stock prices in the aftermath of a Schedule 13D found that the targets' stock prices on average sustainably rose by seven percent.[163] Another study by Brav and Jiang, along with Lucian Bebchuk, found that stock prices in targeted firms continued to rise for three years after the hedge fund had exited the investment, suggesting that changes wrought as a result of the fund's investment proved beneficial in the long run (at least for shareholders).[164] These gains appear to come from operational changes rather than financial chicanery, as other studies indicate that target firm's return on assets improves relative to their industry as a whole.[165]

Despite such evidence former Delaware Chief Justice Leo Strine argues that activist campaigns can "negatively affect a board's ability to chart a long-term course that is both profitable for stockholders and respectful of the company's workers, consumers, communities, and the environment."[166] Strine's view is a plausible interpretation of hedge fund activism. Unlike Engine No.1 and other ESG-oriented investors, activist hedge funds may occasionally pay lip service to ESG concerns, but at the end of the day they are primarily focused on maximizing shareholder returns and usually want to see the company do so in a relatively short period of time (although the average activist hedge fund holding period is two years, half are less than nine months).

Regardless of the true impact of hedge fund activism on the target company, its shareholders, and its stakeholders, there is very little doubt that activists are impacting corporate governance:

> Hedge funds have created headaches for CEOs and corporate boards by pushing for changes in management and changes in business strategy, including opposing

---

[*] Although I have been critical of hedge fund activism in the past due to its inconsistency with board-centric corporate governance, hedge fund activism is the reality under which the current corporate purpose debate must play out. *See* Stephen M. Bainbridge, *Preserving Director Primacy by Managing Shareholder Interventions, in* Research Handbook on Shareholder Power 231 (Jennifer G. Hill & Randall S. Thomas eds. 2015).

acquisitions favored by management both as shareholders of the acquirer and as shareholders of the target, and by making unsolicited bids.

This new activism by hedge funds has become a prime irritant for CEOs. Martin Lipton, the renowned advisor to corporate boards, recently listed "attacks by activist hedge funds" as a key issue for directors. Alan Murray from the Wall Street Journal calls hedge funds the "new leader" on the "list of bogeymen haunting the corporate boardroom," and his colleague Jesse Eisinger notes that these days hedge funds are the "shareholder activists with the most clout."[167]

Although activist investors formerly concentrated on low hanging fruit, which typically consisted of poorly managed small firms, they are increasingly willing to take on even the largest companies.[168] Not surprisingly, the CFOs of about half of the companies surveyed by Deloitte reported their firm "made at least one major business decision specifically in response to shareholder activism," with share repurchases being the most common.[169] In many cases, such decisions have had distinctly negative effects on stakeholders.[*]

Put bluntly, "hedge fund activists ... want ordinary, solvent companies to maximize profits for their shareholder owners, as opposed to benefiting communities, workers, or other so-called stakeholders."[170] Boards that put stakeholder interests ahead of (or even on par with) shareholder interests thus are likely to face proxy contests and other forms of activism from activist hedge funds and their allies.[171] Directors who too often shortchange shareholder value in the name of social responsibility may well find themselves on the losing end of such contests. As long as that remains the case, "CEOs who care about their job and job market prospects have strong incentives not to protect stakeholders beyond what would be useful for shareholder value maximization."[172].

10.8.2 *The Hedge Find Activists Come for Etsy*

In May 2017, activist hedge funds of the sort we have been describing began circling Etsy. On May 2, a small hedge fund – Black-and-White Capital – disclosed a two

---

[*] Corporations can do a number of things that advantage shareholders at the expense of debt holders, including draining assets out of the firm through high dividend payments, issuing new debt with a higher priority than the existing debt, significantly increasing the firm's leverage, or shifting company operations to higher risk projects. There is evidence that hedge fund activism results in precisely these sort of wealth transfers. Hadiye Aslan & Hilda Maraachlian, *Wealth Effects of Hedge Fund Activism* 18 (June 12, 2007), https://ssrn.com/abstract=993170. One study found, for example, that "target bonds underperform their benchmarks starting one year after activist filing significantly by 3 percent to 5 percent per year for the full sample. Consistent with this finding, their results reveal that there is a greater incidence of downgrades than upgrades in the same time frame as return underperformance." *Id.* The evidence about the impact of hedge fund activism on employees is mixed, but there is evidence that wages of employees at firms targeted by activists at best remain stable. *Id.* at 25. Pension funds of targeted firms are more likely to be underfunded, mainly because activist "targeted firms reduce employer contributions to the pension fund, which they justify by increasing the assumed rates of returns on plan investments." *Id.*

percent stake in Etsy and said it would push for a sale of the company or other value maximizing changes. The next day two more activist hedge funds – TPG Capital and Dragoneer – bought stakes in Etsy and also began pressuring the board for change. The funds succeeded in short order. Indeed, as the Dealbreaker website snidely put it, Etsy flipped from being a "crunchy hipster to Gordon Gekko in one afternoon."[173]

Etsy's board fired the incumbent CEO, cut eight percent of its workforce, and – perhaps most tellingly – gave up its B-Corp certification. The new CEO focused on profit rather than social justice. The switch was well received by investors. As Dealbreaker summed up the transition, Etsy "shareholders [didn't] really want to talk about third world development funds while their share price is getting brutally hammered."[174] Etsy recovered from its financial problems and again became profitable, but it functions as a normal business corporation rather than a benefit corporation.

Although Etsy's story is a particularly high profile one, it is hardly unusual. A 2020 study found that "activist hedge funds specifically target corporations with higher levels of corporate social responsibility (CSR), which they regard as a waste of shareholder resources – and that their campaigns are effective in reducing CSR."[175] When their companies are targeted by activist hedge funds, directors and CEOs often abandon their existing plans and agree to demands that may not be in what the board and executives believe to be in "the organization's best interests in the long run."[176] As a result, many other firms that started out with a strong focus on stakeholders found that they had to shift to a shareholder emphasis as they grew.[177]

Part of the problem that such companies face is that, even though the activist hedge funds remain a minority of investors, they have a disproportionately large impact on how corporations are governed. Indeed, the influence of hedge fund activism goes far beyond just the relatively small number of companies the funds target. Stories like that of Etsy lead directors and managers to fear being targeted in the future and to take present steps to avoid that outcome by focusing on shareholder value despite the purported preferences of ESG investors. Survey data confirms that "boards and managers were themselves more and more likely to propose the types of corporate finance moves, such as increasing stock buybacks, that they perceived activist hedge funds would likely advocate."[178] Likewise, several studies confirm that, "[f]or every firm targeted [by activists], several more are likely to reduce R&D expenditures in order to avoid becoming a target."[179]

But there is also a further problem, which speaks directly to our question of whether today's shareholders remain wedded to value maximization. Despite the pro-ESG rhetoric coming from firms like the Big Three and all the rest of the hoopla surrounding ESG investing, Leo Strine reminds us that "the voice of equity capital is represented most loudly by … active speculators trying to outguess the market," not by ESG investors.[180] Perhaps so, but pro-shareholder capitalism voices can also be found in more staid corners of the market. As the Council of Institutional investors observed in response to the Business Roundtable statement, "boards and managers need to sustain a focus on long-term shareholder value. To achieve long-term shareholder value, it is critical to respect stakeholders, but also to have clear accountability to company owners."[181]

The percentage of public corporation stock owned by institutional investors such as the members of the Council climbed from less than 25 percent to over 70 percent between the 1980s and the 2020s.[182] These institutions have "used shareholder value to measure performance, publicly targeted underperforming firms, strongly backed equity-based compensation for CEOs, and organized 'just vote no' campaigns in director elections to protest continued poor performance."[183] Such investors are no more likely to abandon shareholder value maximization than are the hedge fund activists.[184]

Many readers may look at the foregoing analysis and see a case for interventions intended to protect vulnerable stakeholders from the adverse effects of hedge fund activism. Whether some such intervention is appropriate is a question beyond the scope of this project. The point here is simply that corporate social responsibility and ESG are not viable solutions. Hedge fund activism aligns manager and shareholder interests, making managers less likely to opt for stakeholders when put to the test. As such, the hypothetical bargain remains shareholder value maximization.

10.9 SHAREHOLDER VALUE MAXIMIZATION IS PRO-SOCIAL

Up to this point, we have been principally concerned with making the case against stakeholder capitalism. This emphasis is perhaps inevitable. As was observed by Michael Novak, who wrote widely on ethical and moral aspects of economics and politics, the best defense of shareholder capitalism "is that the known alternatives are worse."[185] Or to paraphrase Winston Churchill's well known quip about democracy, no one pretends that shareholder capitalism is perfect. It may well be the worst way of organizing an economy except for all the other ways that have been tried from time to time. Nevertheless, there is an affirmative case to be made for shareholder value maximization and it is to that case we now turn.

10.9.1 *The Profit Motive Results in Socially Efficient Resource Allocation*

The affirmative case starts with our assumptions that shareholders prefer value maximization and that stakeholder capitalism reduces the return to shareholders by reallocating wealth from shareholders to stakeholders at least in zero-sum cases. In a regime of stakeholder capitalism, shareholders will withdrawal capital from public corporate equity and reallocate it to alternatives such as private equity, unincorporated entities, and corporate debt. Building on a version of that premise, Charles Elson and Nicholas Goossen convincingly argue that society benefits from shareholder value maximization. If investors are unwilling to invest in corporate stock, corporations will "become much more reliant on debt financing. Such an approach would have made it difficult for new, risky, and potentially socially viable ventures to have been formed and to thrive."[186]

In other words, pursuit of shareholder value maximization leads to a more efficient allocation of resources. It is simply a corporate application of Adam Smith's "invisible hand."[187] Consider, for example, how shareholder value maximization leads to more efficient resource allocation in the Bainbridge hypothetical. Assuming that general welfare legislation and contractual protections, such as plant-closing notice laws and worker retraining programs, can ameliorate dislocations caused by closing the old plant and opening the new one, the new plant will increase profits by using resources more productively.

In other words, profits send important signals to both management and the markets in which the company operates. If selling goods or services online is more profitable than through bricks-and-mortar stores, for example, firms will reallocate resources from the latter to the former. This may displace those employees who worked in the old stores, but it will benefit those who are hired to work in the online operations, as well as the company's shareholders, creditors, and customers.

> For examples confirming this hypothesis [of more efficient resource allocation], one may turn to the considerable evidence from non-centrally-managed economies that the performance of state-owned and partially-state-owned industrial firms is substantially below that of privately-owned firms in competitive markets. There are storied examples of politically-generated inefficiency in the operation of much of the subsidized industries of Western Europe, as well as the United States' experience with Amtrak, the Postal Service, the Corps of Engineers, and other agencies.[188]

10.9.2 *The Profit Motive Is an Essential Motivational Spark for Innovation*

Profits may not lift all boats, but they do grow the size of the social pie by creating new wealth. The profit motive incentivizes companies to develop new or improved goods and services, incentivizing "experimentation, which leads to break-through technologies, medicines, or consumer services, ultimately enhancing human welfare."[189] Put another way, profit is the "motivational spark" that incentivizes innovation.[190] Accordingly, as Alex Edmans observes: "Profits are a key element of a well-functioning society. Without profits, citizens can't fund their retirement, insurance companies can't pay out claims, and endowments and pension funds can't provide for their beneficiaries."[191]

> The world with capitalism, and companies that seek profit, is much brighter. As Nicholas Kristof pointed out in a New York Times op-ed, "the result of corporate shareholder value maximization mixed in with globalization" is that, "[for humanity over all, life just keeps getting better." In a world of free markets, "[p]eople living in extreme poverty fell from 42 percent of the world's population

in 1981 to below 10 percent today. That is 2 billion people who are no longer suffering extreme poverty. Absolute poverty declined substantially in the US, from 13 percent in 1980 to 3 percent today."[192]

Along the same lines, Micklethwait and Wooldridge quote German sociologist Werner Sombart's observation that "on the reefs of roast beef and apple pie socialist utopias of every sort are sent to their doom."[193] In turn, they argue, those reefs existed because of the general rise in prosperity – despite frequent panics and slumps – associated with the emergence of large industrial corporations. These "new companies plainly improved the living standards of millions of ordinary people, putting the luxuries of the rich within the reach of the man in the street."[194]

10.9.3 *The Profit Motive Promotes Freedom*

As we have seen, stakeholder capitalism is at best inconsistent with liberal democracy. In contrast, as a social decision-making norm, shareholder value maximization does more than just expand the economic pie. It affirmatively promotes freedom.

A legal system that encourages shareholder value maximization necessarily allows individuals freedom to pursue the accumulation of wealth. Economic liberty, in turn, is a necessary concomitant of personal liberty; the two have almost always marched hand-in-hand.[195] Moreover, the pursuit of wealth has been a major factor in destroying arbitrary class distinctions by enhancing personal and social mobility. Accordingly, it seems fair to argue that the economic liberty to pursue shareholder value maximization is an effective means for achieving a variety of moral ends. "Indeed, that capitalism and the corporation are at the heart of human progress seems difficult to deny – simply ask yourself to name a great civilization that was created by a stakeholder-oriented society (or, put differently, that did not look favorably on free markets, industry, and trade)."[196]

In turn, the for-profit public corporation is a powerful engine for focusing the efforts of individuals to maintain the requisite sphere of economic liberty. Those whose livelihood depends on corporate profit cannot be neutral about political systems. Only democratic capitalist societies permit voluntary formation of private corporations and maintain a sphere of economic liberty within which they may function. This gives those who value such enterprises a powerful incentive to resist both statism and socialism. Because tyranny is far more likely to come from the public sector than the private, those who for selfish reasons strive to maintain both a democratic capitalist society and, of particular relevance to the present argument, a substantial sphere of economic liberty therein, serve the public interest. As Michael Novak observes, private property and freedom of contract were "indispensable if private business corporations were to come into existence."[197] In turn, the corporation gives "liberty economic substance over and against the state."[198]

Conclusion

Shareholder value maximization is the law. It ought to be the law. This is, in part, because the chief alternative available in liberal democratic societies – stakeholder capitalism – is fundamentally flawed. If executives such as those who signed the Business Roundtable's 2019 statement on corporate purpose really tried to run their companies according to the altruistic principles laid out therein, they would find it an impossible task. Developing the set of objective and quantifiable metrics necessary to operationalize stakeholder capitalism will prove an intractable problem. Even if the requisite set of metrics could be designed, boundedly rational managers cannot reasonably be expected to balance the huge number of competing factors necessary to account for the varied interests of the firm's many constituencies.

Directors and executives who try to manage to ESG criteria face a daunting set of incentives to prefer shareholder interests over those of stakeholders. As the Etsy story illustrates, a firm using such criteria that operates in competitive product and capital markets likely would fail. Indeed, if the firm substitutes social responsibility for the profit motive, it may end up facing bankruptcy. More likely, of course, it would face the wrath of hedge fund activists. Put simply, investors simply will not cooperate with a regime of stakeholder capitalism. Only a monopoly could fend off the pressures that product and capital markets would bring to bear. Not surprisingly, it turns out that there is no business case for preferring stakeholder to shareholder capitalism.

Granted, executives and directors talk a lot about social responsibility and their commitment to ESG. But their incentive schedule suggests that such talk is more likely to be greenwashing than a true commitment. Indeed, the evidence suggests that when push comes to shove those incentives leads them to put profits ahead of ESG concerns. As with so much corporate puffery in this area, the Business Roundtable statement likely amounted to little more than greenwashing.

To the extent the signatory CEOs were motivated by concerns other than greenwashing, they likely hoped that embracing ESG would bring back the days of imperial CEOs. The basic problem with stakeholder capitalism is the lack of accountability. The effect of implementing stakeholder capitalism would be to remove CEOs from the impersonal discipline of the job and capital markets. CEOs who are responsible to everyone are responsible to no one. As the Bainbridge hypothetical illustrates, executives and directors whose fiduciary duty allows them to consider both stakeholder and shareholder interests will be tempted to side with whichever constituency's interests most closely align with management's self-interest.

The law declines to assume that directors and managers faced with such temptations are angels. Instead, the law recognizes that a workable legal regime "must be based on a certain realism about human beings and, therefore, on a theory of sin and a praxis for dealing with it."[1] Here, the sin in question is that of self-interest. While corporate social responsibility empowers honest directors to act in the best interests of all the corporation's constituents, it also empowers dishonest directors to pursue their own self-interest. There is a very real risk that directors and managers given discretion to consider interests other than shareholder wealth maximization will use stakeholder interests as a cloak for actions taken to advance their own selfish interests.

If there are entrepreneurs, managers, and shareholders who truly wish to embrace stakeholder capitalism despite the theoretical and empirical arguments against it, they now have an option. They can incorporate as a Benefit Corporation. The market can then decide whether a commitment to some stakeholder interest is a risk requiring investors to discount what they are willing to pay for shares or a reason to pay a premium for their shares. Accordingly, the case for allowing ordinary business corporations to embrace a corporate purpose other than shareholder value maximization has become even weaker than it was when scholars such as Berle and Dodd or Friedman were discussing the corporate purpose question.

The case for shareholder value maximization is not just a negative one. Pursuit of shareholder value maximization leads to more efficient resource allocation, creates new social wealth, and promotes economic and political liberty. To be sure, there will always be externalities. Just as pursuing profit is baked into the corporation's DNA, so is externalizing costs. There is no such thing as a free lunch. The theory and evidence recounted herein, however, suggests that the balance comes down strongly in favor of shareholder value maximization.

Notes

INTRODUCTION

1 Milton Friedman, *The Social Responsibility of Business Is to Increase Its Profits*, N.Y. TIMES, Sept. 13, 1970, § 6 (Magazine), at 32, 33.

2 Business Roundtable, *Our Commitment* (2019), https://opportunity.businessroundtable .org/ourcommitment/

3 *See* Lyman Johnson, *Law and Legal Theory in the History of Corporate Responsibility: Corporate Personhood*, 35 SEATTLE U.L. REV. 1135, 1136 n.2 (2012) ("There is a vast literature on law and corporate social responsibility."). Like Professor Johnson, I make no effort herein "to cite to all of it." *Id.*

4 Bronagh Ward et al., *Covid-19 & Inequality: A Test of Corporate Purpose* (Sept. 2020), www.kksadvisors.com/tcp-test-of-corporate-purpose-september2020.

5 Henry Hansmann & Reinier Kraakman, *The End of History for Corporate Law*, 89 GEO. L.J. 439 (2001).

6 FRANCIS FUKUYAMA, THE END OF HISTORY AND THE LAST MAN (1992).

7 Hansmann & Kraakman, *supra* note 5, at 439.

8 *See* Martin Petrin, *Beyond Shareholder Value: Exploring Justifications for a Broader Corporate Purpose* 4 (Nov. 1, 2020) (explaining that "leading scholars are discussing concepts such as the need for 'purposeful' corporations, and, generally, there seems to be a broad consensus that pure shareholder value thinking has become outdated"), https://papers.ssrn.com/sol3/papers.cfm?abstract_id=3722836; Christina Parajon Skinner, *Cancelling Capitalism?* 97 NOTRE DAME L. REV. 417, 418 (2021) (observing that "scholarly antipathy toward capitalism (and its instantiation in corporate profit-seeking) has become more fervent over the past eighteen months").

9 LYNN STOUT, THE SHAREHOLDER VALUE MYTH vi (2012).

10 JOEL BAKAN, THE CORPORATION: THE PATHOLOGICAL PURSUIT OF PROFIT AND POWER (2004).

11 Linda S. Mullenix, *Ending Class Actions as We Know Them: Rethinking the American Class Action*, 64 EMORY L.J. 399, 407 (2014).

12 *See, e.g.*, Veronica Root Martinez & Gina-Gail S. Fletcher, *Equality Metrics*, 130 YALE L.J. FORUM 869, 892 (2021) ("As a result of this pressure from institutional investors, ESG issues are now mainstream considerations for most firms, even as boards of directors and executives struggle with how to respond to such demands.").

13 Marco Rubio, *American Investment in the 21st Century* 22, www.rubio.senate.gov/public/_ cache/files/9f25139a-6039-465a-9cf1-feb5567aebb7/4526E9620A9A7DB74267ABEA58810 22F.5.15.2019.-final-project-report-american-investment.pdf (last visited June 7, 2021).

14 For a discussion of the intersection of populism and the corporate purpose debate, see Stephen M. Bainbridge, *Corporate Purpose in a Populist Era*, 98 Neb. L. Rev. 543 (2020).

15 *See* Richard A. Epstein, *Citizens United v. FEC: The Constitutional Right That Big Corporations Should Have but Do Not Want*, 34 Harv. J.L. & Pub. Pol'y 639, 660–61 (2011) (observing that the Tea Party "tends to be opposed to both parties and to large corporations that seek their favor"); Ilya Shapiro & Carl G. DeNigris, *Occupy Pennsylvania Avenue: How the Government's Unconstitutional Actions Hurt the 99 percent*, 60 Drake L. Rev. 1085, 1097 (2012) ("The understandable outrage [provoked by corporate bailouts during the Obama administration], voiced through the Tea Party and Occupy movements, has called into question not just the policy rationales behind such corporate welfare, but the legal authority supporting it."); R. Ryan Staine, *Crez II, Coming Soon to a Windy Texas Plain Near You?: Encouraging the Texas Renewable Energy Industry through Transmission Investment*, 93 Tex. L. Rev. 521, 547 (2014) ("The Tea Party and libertarian movements have emerged as powerful forces in the Republican Party, and those groups have expressed opposition to anything that could be seen as 'corporate welfare.'").

16 *Six Sects of Shareholder Value*, The Economist (Jan. 21, 2017), www.economist.com/business/2017/01/21/businesses-can-and-will-adapt-to-the-age-of-populism.

17 Thomas C. W. Lin, *Incorporating Social Activism*, 98 B.U. L. Rev. 1535, 1549 (2018).

18 *See* Gretchen Morgenson, *How Letting Bankers Off the Hook May Have Tipped the Election*, N.Y. Times (Nov. 11, 2016), www.nytimes.com/2016/11/13/business/how-letting-bankers-off-the-hook-may-have-tipped-the-election.html (last visited Feb. 3, 2018) (discussing "the populist, anti-establishment anger that swept Donald J. Trump into the White House").

19 Lin, *supra* note 17, at 1552.

20 *Id.*

21 Holger Fleischer, *Corporate Purpose: A Management Concept and Its Implications for Company Law* 2 (ECGI Working Paper Series in Law No. 561/2021, Jan. 2021), https://ssrn.com/abstract=3770656.

22 The Business Roundtable, Statement on Corporate Governance 3–4 (1997).

23 National Association of Corporate Directors, The Report of the NACD Blue Ribbon Commission Fit for the Future: An Urgent Imperative for Board Leadership 9 (2019).

24 Business Roundtable, *supra* note 2.

25 Daniel J. H. Greenwood, *Essay: Telling Stories of Shareholder Supremacy*, 2009 Mich. St. L. Rev. 1049, 1072 (2009).

26 Lawrence E. Mitchell, Corporate Irresponsibility: America's Newest Export 53 (2008).

27 *See id.* (observing that "limited liability has allowed the corporation to perfect its function"). For an overview of the historical, legal, and policy aspects of limited liability, see Stephen M. Bainbridge & M. Todd Henderson, Limited Liability: A Legal and Economic Analysis (2016).

28 *See* Henry G. Manne, *Our Two Corporation Systems: Law and Economics*, 53 Va. L. Rev. 259, 262 (1967).

29 *Id.*

30 Quoted in William P. Hackney & Tracey G. Benson, *Shareholder Liability for Inadequate Capital*, 43 U. Pitt. L. Rev. 837, 841 (1982).

31 The example is taken from Bainbridge & Henderson, *supra* note 27, at 47–51, on which the following discussion draws. In turn, that example was a modified version of one used in Michael P. Dooley, Fundamentals of Corporation Law 33–34 (1995), which in its turn drew on one from William A. Klein & John C. Coffee, Jr., Business Organization and Finance 228–229 (5th ed. 1992).

32 Charles Folson, *The Pollution of Streams, in* MASSACHUSETTS STATE BOARD OF HEALTH EIGHTH ANNUAL REPORT 61 (1877).

33 G. Mitu Gulati et. al., *Connected Contracts*, 47 UCLA L. REV. 887, 890 (2000) ("Reification, like the use of metaphor, can be useful. Indeed, it would be difficult to communicate effectively without it.").

34 Burwell v. Hobby Lobby Stores, Inc., 573 U.S. 682, 703 (2014).

35 *See* Marc A. Greendorfer, *Blurring Lines Between Churches and Secular Corporations: The Compelling Case of the Benefit Corporation's Right to the Free Exercise of Religion (with A Post-*Hobby Lobby *Epilogue)*, 39 DEL. J. CORP. L. 819, 834 (2015) ("In closely-held traditional for-profit corporations, such as Hobby Lobby Inc. or Conestoga Corp., the shareholders often choose some goal other than profit maximization and thus voluntarily act against their own financial interests since they have foregone profit maximization."); *see also* Benjamin Means, *A Contractual Approach to Shareholder Oppression Law*, 79 FORDHAM L. REV. 1161, 1177 (2010) (noting that "close corporation shareholders often have investment goals that are more complex than simple profit maximization").

36 *See generally* Ronald J. Gilson & Jeffrey N. Gordon, *Controlling Controlling Shareholders*, 152 U. PA. L. REV. 785 (2003).

37 Insofar as control is concerned, US corporate law is far more accurately described as a system of director primacy than one of shareholder primacy. As Delaware General Corporation Law § 141(a) commands, for example, "the business and affairs of every corporation" shall be managed not by the company's shareholders but rather "by or under the direction of a board of directors."

38 *See* Skinner, *supra* note 8, at 419 (stating that "in many scholarly quarters at least, 'purpose' has become synonymous with anti-profit").

39 Rebecca Henderson & George Serafeim, *Tackling Climate Change Requires Organizational Purpose*, 110 AM. ECON. ASS'N PAPERS & PROC. 177, 177–78 (2020).

40 E. Norman Veasey & Christine Di Guglielmo, *History Informs American Corporate Law: The Necessity of Maintaining a Delicate Balance in the Federal "Ecosystem,"* 1 VA. L. & BUS. REV. 201, 203 (2006).

41 *See, e.g.*, Central Transp. Co. v. Pullman's Palace Car Co., 139 U.S. 24, 59 (1891) ("A contract of a corporation, which is ultra vires, in the proper sense, that is to say, outside the object of its creation as defined in the law of its organization, and therefore beyond the powers conferred upon it by the legislature, is not voidable only, but wholly void, and of no legal effect."); McDermott v. Bear Film Co., 33 CAL. RPTR. 486, 489 (Cal. App. 1963) (defining *ultra vires* as "an action which is beyond the purpose or power of the corporation").

42 DEL. CODE ANN., tit. 8, § 101(b).

43 DEL. CODE ANN., tit. 8, § 102(a)(3).

44 *See* Dalia T. Mitchel, *From Dodge to eBay: The Elusive Corporate Purpose*, 13 VA. L. & BUS. REV. 155, 175 (2019) (explaining that beginning with the famous Berle–Dodd debate over corporate social responsibility in the 1930s, "the doctrine of fiduciary obligations (rather than ultra vires) [became] the site where corporate purpose was to be found").

45 Stephen M. Bainbridge, *Director Primacy in Corporate Takeovers: Preliminary Reflections*, 55 STAN. L. REV. 791, 794 (2002).

46 Friedman, *supra* note 1.

47 *Id.*

48 Leo E. Strine, Jr. & Nicholas Walter, *Conservative Collision Course?: The Tension between Conservative Corporate Law Theory and Citizens United*, 100 CORNELL L. REV. 335, 347 (2015).

49 *Id.*

50 Sanjai Bhagat & Glenn Hubbard, *Should the Modern Corporation Maximize Shareholder Value?* 4 (Mar. 3, 2020) (explaining that "managers and directors acting in shareholders' interest will want to preserve valuable relationships with stakeholders to the extent that the corporation's value can internalize the value of those relationships"), https://papers.ssrn .com/sol3/papers.cfm?abstract_id=3548293.

51 Leo E. Strine, Jr., *Our Continuing Struggle with the Idea That For-Profit Corporations Seek Profit*, 47 Wake Forest L. Rev. 135, 155 (2012). I note with approval but do not adopt a distinction drawn by Professor David Millon between what he calls "radical share-holder primacy" and "traditional shareholder primacy." The former "asserts that corporate management is the agent of the shareholders and as such owes them a duty to maximize the return on their investments" in the short term "even at the expense of possibly greater long-term value." The latter, "which emerged in the last years of the nineteenth century and was embodied in corporate law and widely accepted for much of the twentieth century," assumes "that a business corporation is organized in order to generate profit" but does not require that management maximize short term profit at the expense of long-term investments or "the interests of non-shareholder constituencies under circumstances management deems to be appropriate." David Millon, *Radical Shareholder Primacy*, 10 U. St. Thomas L.J. 1013, 1013–14 (2014).

52 R. Edward Freeman & David L. Reed, *Stockholders and Stakeholders: A New Perspective on Corporate Governance*, 25 Cal. Mgmt. Rev. 88, 89 (1983) (quoting the memorandum).

53 R. Edward Freeman, Strategic Management: A Stakeholder Approach 53 (1984).

54 *Id.*

55 *See* Bradford Cornell & Alan C. Shapiro, *Corporate Stakeholders, Corporate Valuation, and ESG*, The CLS Blue Sky Blog (Dec. 10, 2020), https://clsbluesky.law.columbia .edu/2020/12/10/corporate-stakeholders-corporate-valuation-and-esg/.

56 Eugene F. Fama, *Market Forces Already Address ESG Issues and the Issues Raised by Stakeholder Capitalism*, ProMarket.Org (Sept. 25, 2020), https://promarket .org/2020/09/25/market-forces-esg-issues-stakeholder-capitalism-contracts/.

57 *See generally* Lucian A. Bebchuk & Roberto Tallarita, *The Illusory Promise of Stakeholder Governance*, 106 Cornell L. Rev. 91, 116–19 (2020) (discussing the definition of stakeholder).

58 *See, e.g.*, Lisa M. Fairfax, *The Rhetoric of Corporate Law: The Impact of Stakeholder Rhetoric on Corporate Norms*, 31 J. Corp. L. 675, 680 (2006) (arguing that "stakeholder theory advocates that corporations achieve a better balance of all interests, while under-scoring the importance of corporations' willingness to subordinate or abandon their concerns for profit when appropriate").

59 D. Gordon Smith, *Response: The Dystopian Potential of Corporate Law*, 57 Emory L.J. 985, 989 (2008) (observing that "reformers ... have only two options for changing corporate decisionmaking: changing the decisionmaker or changing the decision rule").

60 For a very useful recent overview of the codetermination debate, see Grant M. Hayden & Matthew T. Bodie, Reconstructing the Corporation: From Shareholder Primacy to Shared Governance (2020). For a now admittedly somewhat dated argument against codetermination-based corporate governance, see Stephen M. Bainbridge, *Privately Ordered Participatory Management: An Organizational Failures Analysis*, 23 Del. J. Corp. L. 979 (1998).

61 *See* Cornell & Shapiro, *supra* note 55 (explaining that "many of the stakeholders being talked about today – groups like environmentalists and promoters of social and racial justice – are self-identified, with no business relationship with the company").

62 JEREMY MOON, CORPORATE SOCIAL RESPONSIBILITY 23 (2014).

63 For a "business ethnography" of corporate social responsibility and its practitioners, see John M. Conley & Cynthia A. Williams, *Engage, Embed, and Embellish: Theory Versus Practice in the Corporate Social Responsibility Movement*, 31 J. CORP. L. 1 (2005). In 1972, Henry Manne observed that:

> In the years up to the present, the list of items variously alleged to be the social responsibility of business has varied considerably. For instance, there have been periods when the predominant motif was business support of the arts. At another time, business concern with industrial architecture and urban planning seemed to predominate. Later the claim was widely aired that corporations were responsible for the financial health of private universities. Scholarship programs, endowed professorships, and research support laid heavy claim to corporate funds. More recently, training and special hiring programs for underprivileged minorities sparked the claim that business had broad social responsibilities. This has lately given way in part to issues of safety, the environment, and sexist hiring practices.

Henry G. Manne, *Shareholder Social Proposals Viewed by an Opponent*, 24 STAN. L. REV. 481, 481 (1972). As we shall see, the focus continues to cycle.

64 ALEX EDMANS, GROW THE PIE: HOW GREAT COMPANIES DELIVER BOTH PURPOSE AND PROFIT 3 (2020).

65 Skinner, *supra* note 8, at 422.

66 David Millon, *Personifying the Corporate Body*, 2 GRAVEN IMAGES 116, 127 (1995).

67 Robert B. Reich, *Secession of the Successful*, N.Y. TIMES, Jan. 20, 1991, § 6 (Magazine), at 16, 43 (explaining that most corporate philanthropy goes to the places and institutions that entertain, inspire, cure or educate wealthy Americans).

68 HENRY G. MANNE & HENRY CHRISTOPHER WALLICH, THE MODERN CORPORATION AND SOCIAL RESPONSIBILITY 1, 4–6 (1973).

69 Although corporate social responsibility is not limited to complying with the law, compliance is widely regarded as one of its essential aspects. As Leo Strine observed, the obligation of "legal fidelity" means that "one cannot act loyally as a corporate director by causing the corporation to violate the positive laws it is obliged to obey." Guttman v. Huang, 823 A.2d 492, 506 n.34 (Del. Ch. 2003).

70 ANN BUCHHOLTZ & ARCHIE CARROLL, BUSINESS AND SOCIETY: ETHICS, SUSTAINABILITY, AND STAKEHOLDER MANAGEMENT 34 (9th ed. 2015).

71 E. Christopher Johnson Jr., *Business Lawyers Are in A Unique Position to Help Their Clients Identify Supply-Chain Risks Involving Labor Trafficking and Child Labor*, 70 BUS. LAW. 1083, 1096 (2015).

72 Félix E. Mezzanotte, *The EU Policy on Sustainable Finance: A Discussion on the Design of ESG-Fit Suitability Requirements*, 40 REV. BANKING & FIN. L. 249, 277 (2020) (quoting a draft EU resolution).

73 Virginia Harper Ho, *Risk-Related Activism: The Business Case for Monitoring Nonfinancial Risk*, 41 J. CORP. L. 647, 650–51 (2016).

74 David F. Larcker et al., *Seven Myths of ESG* 1 (Stanford Closer Look Series, Nov. 3, 2021).

75 *See, e.g.*, Sonja Lyubomirsky et al., *The Benefits of Frequent Positive Affect: Does Happiness Lead to Success?* 131 PSYCHOL. BULL. 803 (2005) (arguing that employee happiness is positively correlated with a number of attributes that result in higher levels of productivity and, accordingly, business success). *But see* Stephen M. Bainbridge, *Privately Ordered Participatory Management: An Organizational Failures Analysis*, 23 DEL. J. CORP. L. 979, 997 (1998 ("Participating workers are not necessarily happy workers and happy workers are not necessarily productive workers.").

76 *See, e.g.*, Virginia Harper Ho, *"Enlightened Shareholder Value": Corporate Governance Beyond the Shareholder-Stakeholder Divide*, 36 J. CORP. L. 59, 82 (2010) (citing a

report arguing that "a focus on ESG matters 'may better align investors with the broader objectives of society,' but its fundamental rationale is solidly grounded in shareholder primacy – namely, that 'consideration of [ESG] issues is part of delivering superior risk-adjusted returns' to investors over the long run").

77 *See* Piyush Gupta, *The Evolution of ESG from CSR*, Lexology (Mar. 25, 2021), www .lexology.com/library/detail.aspx?g=80bbe258-a1df-4d4c-88f0-6b7a2d2cbd6a.

78 *Id.*

79 Moon, *supra* note 62, at 46. Moon observed that concern with corporate social responsibility began in Europe only in the last part of the twentieth century, but grew rapidly in the twenty-first century. *Id.* at 50–54. He identifies a number of commonalities and distinctions between European and American versions of corporate social responsibility. *See id.* at 54–54–55. For a global perspective on the legal and policy aspects of corporate social responsibility, see Michael Kerr et al., Corporate Social Responsibility (2009).

80 Holger Fleischer, *Corporate Purpose: A Management Concept and Its Implications for Company Law* 2 (ECGI Working Paper Series in Law No. 561/2021, Jan. 2021) (quoting Edward B. Rock, *For Whom Is the Corporation Managed in 2020? The Debate over Corporate Purpose*, 76 Bus. Law. 363 (2021)), https://ssrn.com/abstract=3770656.

81 One of my personal areas of scholarly interest has been the relationship between corporate purpose and Catholic social thought. *See, e.g.*, Stephen M. Bainbridge, *Christianity and Corporate Purpose, in* Christianity and Market Regulation: An Introduction 101 (2021).

82 Leo E. Strine, Jr., *The Dangers of Denial: The Need for a Clear-Eyed Understanding of the Power and Accountability Structure Established by the Delaware General Corporation Law*, 50 Wake Forest L. Rev. 761, 763 (2015).

83 *See* Andrew S. Gold, *A Decision Theory Approach to the Business Judgment Rule: Reflections on Disney, Good Faith, and Judicial Uncertainty*, 66 Md. L. Rev. 398, 438 (2007) (observing that "some theories suggest that a duty to the corporation should include consideration of the various constituencies that comprise the corporate entity"); Remus D. Valsan & Moin A. Yahya, *Shareholders, Creditors, and Directors' Fiduciary Duties: A Law and Finance Approach*, 2 Va. L. & Bus. Rev. 1, 17 (2007) (summarizing such arguments).

84 N. Am. Catholic Educ. Programming Found., Inc. v. Gheewalla, 930 A.2d 92, 101 (Del. 2007) (quoting Malone v. Brincat, 722 A.2d 5,9 (1998)) (emphasis in original).

85 *See* Diederich v. Yarnevich, 196 P.3d 411, 418 (Kan. App. 2008) ("Fiduciary duties owed by directors and officers do not extend to employees of the firm."); Cheryl Wade, *Lessons From Texaco For Corporate Executives*, 1997 WL 34982663, 2 ("Corporate officers and directors owe no fiduciary duties to their employees when making promotion and hiring decisions.").

86 *See* Andrew Zwecker, *The EU Takeover Directive: Eight Years Later, Implementation but Still No Harmonization Among Member States on Acceptable Takeover Defenses*, 21 Tul. J. Intl. & Comp. L. 233, 260 n.32 (2012) (explaining that "directors of Delaware corporations owe no fiduciary duties to other stakeholders in the company").

87 *See, e.g.*, FDIC v. Sea Pines Co., 692 F.2d 973, 976–77 (4th Cir.1982) (holding that "when the corporation becomes insolvent, the fiduciary duty of the directors shifts from the stockholders to the creditors"); Henderson v. Buchanan, 52 B.R. 743, 763 (Bankr.D.Nev.1985) (holding that when a corporation is insolvent the fiduciary of directors run to creditors); Production Resources Group, LLC v. NCT Group, Inc., 863 A.2d 772, 790–91 (Del.Ch.2004) ("When a firm has reached the point of insolvency, it is settled that under Delaware law, the firm's directors are said to owe fiduciary duties to the company's creditors.").

88 *See, e.g.,* Torch Liquidating Tr. ex rel. Bridge Associates L.L.C. v. Stockstill, 561 F.3d 377, 385 (5th Cir. 2009) ("If a corporation becomes insolvent, however, its creditors become the appropriate parties to bring a derivative suit on behalf of the corporation where those in control of it refuse to assert a viable claim belonging to it because the creditors are the beneficiaries of any increase in value.").

89 Readers familiar with the literature will recognize that this observation is a play on the title of the late Lynn Stout's article, Lynn A. Stout, *Bad and Not-So-Bad Arguments for Shareholder Primacy*, 75 S. CAL. L. REV. 1189 (2002). The array of disciplines that have been deployed in these debates is quite staggering. To cite but one example, a recent working paper blended Aristotle's theory of reciprocal justice and Chester Barnard's work on organization theory to advance a conception of corporate purpose founded on "ethical reciprocity." Malcolm S. Salter, *Rehabilitating Corporate Purpose* (Harvard Business School Working Paper 19–104 2019). Herein, I focus on legal and economic arguments.

90 Ecclesiastes 1:9–10 (NAB).

91 *See* C.A. Harwell Wells, *The Cycles of Corporate Social Responsibility: An Historical Retrospective for the Twenty-First Century*, 51 U. KAN. L. REV. 77, 78 (2002) (arguing that "each new round of debate on corporate social responsibility largely recapitulates the earlier debate in a slightly altered form"); *see also* HENRY G. MANNE & HENRY C. WALLICH, THE MODERN CORPORATION AND SOCIAL RESPONSIBILITY i (1972) (explaining that corporate social responsibility "has enjoyed periodic and substantial vogue in the business world" as a means to counteract public hostility towards business, with the focus of business "altruism" shifting over time with the "social and economic concerns of the broader public").

92 Although both are biased towards corporate social responsibility, I commend two histories of that movement to the reader who wishes a deeper dive into the historical debates: DOUGLAS M. EICHAR, THE RISE AND FALL OF CORPORATE SOCIAL RESPONSIBILITY (2015); MORRELL HEALD, THE SOCIAL RESPONSIBILITIES OF BUSINESS (rev. ed. 1988).

I   THE BATTLE OF RIVER ROUGE

1 Dodge v. Ford Motor Co., 170 N.W. 668, 670 (Mich. 1919).

2 RICHARD SNOW, I INVENTED THE MODERN AGE: THE RISE OF HENRY FORD 215 (2013).

3 *Id.* at 214.

4 For an excellent detailed history of the disputes between Ford and the Dodge brothers and legal analysis of the case, see M. Todd Henderson, *The Story of* Dodge v. Ford Motor Company: *Everything Old Is New Again, in* CORPORATE LAW STORIES 37 (J. Mark Ramseyer ed., 2009).

5 David B. Guenther, *Of Bodies Politic and Pecuniary: A Brief History of Corporate Purpose*, 9 MICH. BUS. & ENTREPRENEURIAL L. REV. 1, 23 (2019) ("The most common purposes thus appear to have involved public or quasi-public infrastructure.").

6 MORRELL HEALD, THE SOCIAL RESPONSIBILITIES OF BUSINESS 3–5 (rev. ed. 1988).

7 Citizens United v. Fed. Election Commn., 558 U.S. 310, 427 (2010) (Stevens, J., concurring in part).

8 Louis K. Liggett Co. v. Lee, 288 U.S. 517, 548 (1933).

9 *Id.* at 549.

10 *See* Lyman Johnson, *Law and Legal Theory in the History of Corporate Responsibility: Corporate Personhood*, 35 SEATTLE U.L. REV. 1135, 1145 (2012).

11 Trustees of Dartmouth Coll. v. Woodward, 17 U.S. 518, 637 (1819).

12 *Id.* at 638.

13 Steven A. Bank, *Entity Theory as Myth in the Origins of the Corporate Income Tax*, 43 WM. & MARY L. REV. 447, 493–94 (2001).

14 *See* Guenther, *supra* note 5, at 63 (explaining that by the 1850s "banking, insurance, and manufacturing corporations have lost all meaningful trace of the public purpose with which they were formerly seen to be endowed; their purpose is now only 'private advantage,' and any public benefit is 'incidental'").

15 *Id.*

16 Lawrence J. White, *The Rise and Fall of Dominant Firms in the U.S. Automobile Industry: A Twice Told Tale, in* MARKET DOMINANCE: HOW FIRMS GAIN, HOLD, OR LOSE IT AND THE IMPACT ON ECONOMIC PERFORMANCE 109, 113 (David I. Rosenbaum ed., 1988) (Table 7.2).

17 Daniel M. G. Raff & Lawrence H. Summers, *Did Henry Ford Pay Efficiency Wages?* 5 J. LAB. ECON. S57 (1987).

18 JOHN L. COTTON, EMPLOYEE INVOLVEMENT 4–5 (1993).

19 Adam B. King & Gary Alan Fine, *Ford on the Line: Business Leader Reputation and the Multiple-Audience Problem, in* 1 HENRY FORD: CRITICAL EVALUATIONS IN BUSINESS AND MANAGEMENT 84, 94 (John Cunningham Wood & Michael C. Wood eds., 2003).

20 Henderson, *supra* note 4, at 51.

21 Dalia Tusk Mitchell, *From* Dodge *to* eBay: *The Elusive Corporate Purpose*, 13 VA. L. & BUS. REV. 155, 166 (2019).

22 *Id.*

23 Mark J. Roe, Dodge v. Ford: *What Happened and Why?* 74 VAND. L. REV. 1755, 1758 (2021).

24 *Id.* at 1766.

25 Henderson, *supra* note 4, at 52.

26 People ex rel. Metro. Life Ins. Co. v. Hotchkiss, 120 N.Y.S. 649 (N.Y. App. Div. 3d Dept. 1909).

27 *Id.* at 651.

28 *Id.*

29 Henderson, *supra* note 4, at 60.

30 *Dodge*, 170 N.W. at 683.

31 *Id.* at 683–84.

32 Henderson, *supra* note 4, at 38.

33 *Dodge*, 170 N.W. at 680–81.

34 *See* Louis K. Liggett Co., 288 U.S. at 564 ("In 1921 the corporation laws of Michigan were revised, eliminating, among other things, the maximum limitation on capital stock.").

35 *Dodge*, 170 N.W. at 680.

36 *See id.* at 681.

37 *Id.* at 682.

38 *Id.* at 683.

39 *Id.* at 684.

40 *See, e.g.*, King & Fine, *supra* note 19, at 95 (arguing that Ford's communications to FMC's various constituencies contained subtle signals to shareholders that "profits were still be maximized").

41 *Dodge*, 170 N.W. at 684.

42 *Id.*

43 *Id.*

44 *Id.*

45 *Id.*
46 *Id.* at 682 (*quoting* Park v. Grant Locomotive Works, 3 A. 162, 165 (N.J. Ch. 1885), *aff'd*, 19 A. 621 (N.J. 1888)).
47 *Id.* (*quoting* Park v. Grant Locomotive Works, 3 A. 162, 165 (N.J. Ch. 1885), *aff'd*, 19 A. 621 (N.J. 1888)).
48 *Id.* at 683.
49 *Id.* at 684.
50 *Id.*
51 *See, e.g.*, Alaska Plastics, Inc. v. Coppock, 621 P.2d 270, 278 (Alaska 1980) ("Judges are not business experts, *Dodge v. Ford Motor Co.*, … a fact which has become expressed in the so-called 'business judgment rule.'").
52 Marcia M. McMurray, *An Historical Perspective on the Duty of Care, the Duty of Loyalty, and the Business Judgment Rule*, 40 VAND. L. REV. 605, 613 (1987) (citing cases).
53 Godbold v. Bank at Mobile, 11 Ala. 191, 200 (1847).
54 *See, e.g.*, Goebel v. Herancourt Brewing Co., 7 Ohio N.P. 230 (Ohio Super. 1893) ("The court will not interpose in matters which relate solely to the natural management of the concern, in the absence of fraud …."); *see generally* Ramesh K. S. Rao et al., *Fiduciary Duty A La Lyonnais: An Economic Perspective on Corporate Governance in a Financially-Distressed Firm*, 22 J. CORP. L. 53, 58 (1996) ("At least since the late nineteenth century, when the size and influence of American corporations began to increase astronomically, corporate directors were virtually immunized from liability by the business judgment rule unless their judgment was tainted by 'fraud, illegality, or conflict of interest'.").
55 Brehm v. Eisner, 746 A.2d 244, 264 (Del. 2000). The Delaware Supreme Court has noted but not adopted "a distinction between the business judgment rule, which insulates directors and management from personal liability for their business decisions, and the business judgment doctrine, which protects the decision itself from attack." Revlon, Inc. v. MacAndrews & Forbes Holdings, Inc., 506 A.2d 173, 180 n.10 (Del. 1986).
56 eBay Dom. Holdings, Inc. v. Newmark, 16 A.3d 1, 33 (Del. Ch. 2010).
57 Ford's machinations are ably summarized in Henderson, *supra* note 4, at 69–70.
58 *Id.* at 70.

2   FIREPLUG FUNDING FOR PRINCETON

1 MORRELL HEALD, THE SOCIAL RESPONSIBILITIES OF BUSINESS 204 (rev. ed. 1988).
2 *See* JAMES T. PATTERSON, GRAND EXPECTATIONS: THE UNITED STATES, 1945–1974 272 (2006) (arguing that Eisenhower "in no way threatened the welfare state begun in the New Deal years"); STEVEN WAGNER, EISENHOWER REPUBLICANISM: PURSUING THE MIDDLE WAY 4 (2006) (arguing that Eisenhower accepted "the continuation and, in some cases, the expansion of popular New Deal programs.").
3 HEALD, *supra* note 1, at 210.
4 *See id.* at 210–12.
5 *See id.* at 215–18.
6 *Id.* at 213.
7 HEALD, *supra* note 1, at 55.
8 Berle and Dodd are commonly credited with having anticipated much of the modern debate. For a provocative argument that the Berle–Dodd debate was addressed to different issues than "today's debate between management discretion and shareholder rights," see William W. Bratton & Michael L. Wachter, *Shareholder Primacy's Corporatist Origins: Adolf Berle and the Modern Corporation*, 34 J. CORP. L. 99, 102 (2008).

9 Amir N. Licht, *Varieties of Shareholderism: Three Views of the Corporate Purpose Cathedral* 24 (ECGI Law Working Paper No. 547, 2020).

10 *See, e.g.,* Adolf A. Berle, *For Whom Corporate Managers Are Trustees: A Note*, 45 HARV. L. REV. 1365, 1370 (1932) (contending that the "relatively unbridled scope of corporate management has, to date, brought forward in the main seizure of power without recognition of responsibility").

11 *See* Adolf A. Berle, *Corporate Powers as Powers in Trust*, 44 HARV. L. REV. 1049, 1074 (1931) ("Whenever a corporate power is exercised, … its use must also be judged in relation to the existing facts with a view toward discovering whether under all the circumstances the result fairly protects the interests of the shareholders.").

12 E. Merrick Dodd, Jr., *For Whom Are Corporate Managers Trustees?* 45 HARV. L. REV. 1145, 1149 (1932).

13 *Id.* at 1156–57.

14 *Id.* at 1157 n.30. For a strong critique of Dodd's argument, see Charles M. Elson & Nicholas J. Goossen, *E. Merrick Dodd and the Rise and Fall of Corporate Stakeholder Theory*, 72 BUS. LAW. 735, 735 (2017) (arguing that "Dodd's subordination of the equity holders through a time-based diminution of equity value is an unsupportable and inexplicable assault on fundamental property rights.").

15 Dodd, *supra* note 12, at 1155–56.

16 *Id.* at 1156.

17 *Id.* at 1155.

18 A. P. Smith Mfg. Co. v. Barlow, 98 A.2d 581, 582 (N.J. 1953).

19 HEALD, *supra* note 1, at 218.

20 Geoffrey Miller, *Narrative and Truth in Judicial Opinions: Corporate Charitable Giving Cases*, 2009 MICH. ST. L. REV. 831, 839 (2009).

21 *Smith Manufacturing*, 98 A.2d at 587.

22 *Id.*

23 *Id.*

24 *See, e.g.,* David G. Yosifon, *Corporate Aid of Governmental Authority: History and Analysis of an Obscure Power in Delaware Corporate Law*, 10 U. ST. THOMAS L.J. 1086, 1089 (2013) (discussing statutes requiring "corporations to specify in their articles of incorporation the purpose or purposes for which they were organized").

25 *See, e.g.,* Herbert v. Sullivan, 123 F.2d 477, 478 (1st Cir. 1941) (stating that "it has long been the rule in Massachusetts that an ultra vires contract is void").

26 *See* Katharina Pistor et. al., *The Evolution of Corporate Law: A Cross-Country Comparison*, 23 U. PA. J. INTL. ECON. L. 791, 818 (2002) ("Transactions ultra vires were null and void and directors could be held personally responsible.").

27 United Community Services v. Omaha Nat. Bank, 77 N.W.2d 576, 582 (Neb. 1956)

28 17 U.S. 518 (1819).

29 A. P. Smith Mfg. Co. v. Barlow, 98 A.2d 581, 587–88 (N.J. 1953).

30 *Id.* at 589.

31 *See, e.g.,* DEL. CODE ANN., tit. 8, § 122(9); MODEL BUS. CORP. ACT § 3.02(m).

32 *See, e.g.,* Memorial Hospital Ass'n v. Pacific Grape Products Co., 290 P.2d 481 (Cal.1955); Kahn v. Sullivan, 594 A.2d 48 (Del.1991); Theodora Holding Corp. v. Henderson, 257 A.2d 398 (Del.Ch.1969); Union Pac. R. Co. v. Trustees, Inc., 329 P.2d 398 (Utah 1958).

33 Einer Elhauge, *Sacrificing Corporate Profits in the Public Interest*, 80 N.Y.U. L. REV. 733, 767 (2005).

34 Leo E. Strine, Jr., *The Dangers of Denial: The Need for A Clear-Eyed Understanding of the Power and Accountability Structure Established by the Delaware General Corporation Law*, 50 WAKE FOREST L. REV. 761, 779 (2015). *See also* DAVID YOSIFON, CORPORATE

FRICTION: HOW CORPORATE LAW IMPEDES AMERICAN PROGRESS AND WHAT TO DO ABOUT IT 83 (2018) (concluding that the statutory "power to make charitable donations … represents no real exception or deviation from the fundamental rule of shareholder primacy").

35 *But see* Miller, *supra* note 20, at 840 (pointing out that "an 1867 decision by the New Jersey Supreme Court had ruled that the reserve power conferred in 1846 did not extend to fundamental changes, which still required the consent of the shareholders," and which might therefore have precluded retroactive application of the relevant statutes).

36 A. P. Smith Mfg. Co. v. Barlow, 98 A.2d 581, 590 (N.J. 1953).

37 *Id.* at 583–84.

38 *Id.* at 586.

39 Adam Winkler, *Corporate Law or the Law of Business?: Stakeholders and Corporate Governance at the End of History*, 67 L. & CONTEMP. PROBS. 109, 117 (Autumn 2004) (describing the opinion as being "laden with the fear of communism").

40 A. P. Smith Mfg. Co. v. Barlow, 98 A.2d 581, 590 (N.J. 1953).

41 *Id.* at 586.

42 *Id.* at 583.

43 E.C. Lashbrooke, Jr., *The Divergence of Corporate Finance and Law in Corporate Governance*, 46 S.C. L. REV. 449, 463 (1995).

44 HEALD, *supra* note 1, at 218.

45 A. P. Smith Mfg. Co. v. Barlow, 98 A.2d 581, 585 (N.J. 1953).

46 *Id.* at 583–84.

47 Marc A. Greendorfer, *Discrimination as a Business Policy: The Misuse and Abuse of Corporate Social Responsibility Programs*, 8 AM. U. BUS. L. REV. 307, 379 n.60 (2020).

48 *See, e.g.*, Joseph K. Leahy, *Intermediate Scrutiny for Corporate Political Contributions*, 44 FLA. ST. U.L. REV. 1119, 1224 n.426 (2017) ("Corporate philanthropy is widely assumed to increase public goodwill towards the corporation – i.e., the 'halo effect.'").

49 Nancy J. Knauer, *The Paradox of Corporate Giving*, 44 DEPAUL L. REV. 1, 19–20 (1994).

50 Jonathan D. Springer, *Corporate Constituency Statutes: Hollow Hopes and False Fears*, 1999 ANN. SURV. AM. L. 85, 88 (1999)

51 *See* David Rosenberg, *Delaware's "Expanding Duty of Loyalty" and Illegal Conduct: A Step towards Corporate Social Responsibility*, 52 SANTA CLARA L. REV. 81, 103 n.16 (2012) ("Corporate philanthropy or altruism is certainly protected from review in most cases by the business judgment rule.").

52 Miller, *supra* note 20, at 841.

53 *Id.*

3 WHY DIDN'T THE CUBS HAVE TO PLAY NIGHT BASEBALL?

1 Honorable Leo E. Strine, Jr., *The Dangers of Denial: The Need for A Clear-Eyed Understanding of the Power and Accountability Structure Established by the Delaware General Corporation Law*, 50 WAKE FOREST L. REV. 761, 776–77 (2015). *See, e.g.*, Dodge v. Ford Motor Co., 170 N.W. 668, 684 (Mich. 1919) ("The record, and especially the testimony of Mr. Ford, convinces that he has to some extent the attitude towards shareholders of one who has dispensed and distributed to them large gains and that they should be content to take what he chooses to give.").

2 eBay Dom. Holdings, Inc. v. Newmark, 16 A.3d 1, 34 (Del. Ch. 2010).

3 Strine, *supra* note 1, at 776.

4 STEVEN A. RIESS, SPORTS IN AMERICA FROM COLONIAL TIMES TO THE TWENTY-
FIRST CENTURY: AN ENCYCLOPEDIA 882 (2015).

5 CHARLIE BEVIS, BASEBALL UNDER THE LIGHTS: THE RISE OF THE NIGHT GAME 3
(2021).

6 *Id.* at 141.

7 Shlensky v. Wrigley, 237 N.E.2d 776 (Ill.App.1968).

8 Geoffrey Miller, *Narrative and Truth in Judicial Opinions: Corporate Charitable Giving
Cases,* 2009 MICH. ST. L. REV. 831, 842–43 (2009).

9 *Id.* at 843.

10 *Shlensky,* 237 N.E. 2d at 778.

11 Wheeler v. Pullman Iron & Steel Co., 32 N.E. 420, 423 (Ill. 1892).

12 Davis v. Louisville Gas & Electric Co., 142 A. 654, 659 (Del. Ch. 1928)

13 Helfman v. Am. Light & Traction Co., 187 A. 540, 550 (N.J. Ch. 1936).

14 *See, e.g.,* Andrew S. Gold, *The New Concept of Loyalty in Corporate Law,* 43 U. CAL.
DAVIS L. REV. 457, 528 (2009) (describing *Shlensky* as a "classic business judgment rule
case"); Emma M. Lloyd, *"Greening" the Supply Chain: Why Corporate Leaders Make It
Matter,* 27 J. LAND USE & ENVTL. L. 31, 41 (2011) ("An example of a court applying the
business judgment rule is in the case *Shlensky v. Wrigley.*").

15 As we saw in our discussion of *Dodge,* subsequent decisions have added additional pre-
conditions that must be satisfied in order for the business judgment rule to insulate the
actions of corporate directors and officers from judicial review. The most salient of these is
that the decision must be an informed one. *See, e.g.,* Smith v. Van Gorkom, 488 A.2d 858
(Del. 1985) (holding that plaintiff can rebut the business judgment rule by showing that
the directors were grossly negligent in failing to inform themselves of all material information reasonably available to them).

16 Shlensky v. Wrigley, 237 N.E.2d 776, 780 (Ill. App. 1st Dist. 1968).

17 *Id.*

18 *Id.* The court also found Shlensky's claim defective for failure to allege damages. *Id.* This
is mainly an issue of causation. To be sure, the Cubs' poor attendance probably contributed to the firm's losses. But was poor home attendance attributable to the lack of night
baseball or to the Cubs' performance? During the relevant time period, the Cubs were
pretty consistent losers. In any event, this portion of the court's opinion is dicta. Once the
court decided the business judgment rule was applicable, the inquiry could have (and
should have) ended.

19 Dodge v. Ford Motor Co., 170 N.W. 668, 684 (Mich. 1919).

20 Paramount Commun. Inc. v. Time Inc., 1989 WL 79880 at *19 (Del. Ch. July 14, 1989),
aff'd, 571 A.2d 1140 (Del. 1989). *See also* Hill v. State Farm Mut. Automobile Ins. Co., 83 Cal.
Rptr. 3d 651, 692 (Cal. App. 2d Dist. 2008) ("*Shlensky* interpreted *Dodge* to mean that 'there
must be fraud or a breach of that good faith which directors are bound to exercise toward the
stockholders in order to justify the courts entering into the internal affairs of corporations.'")

4 DEFENDING *DODGE*

1 Miriam A. Cherry & Judd F. Sneirson, *Beyond Profit: Rethinking Corporate Social
Responsibility and Greenwashing After the BP Oil Disaster,* 85 TUL. L. REV. 983, 1016
(2011).

2 ADAM WINKLER, WE THE CORPORATIONS: HOW AMERICAN BUSINESSES WON
THEIR CIVIL RIGHTS 248 (2018).

3 Lynn A. Stout, *Why We Should Stop Teaching* Dodge v. Ford, 3 Va. L. & Bus. Rev. 163 (2008).

4 Lynn Stout, The Shareholder Value Myth (2012).

5 Jonathan R. Macey, *Corporate Law As Myth*, 93 S. Cal. L. Rev. 923, 937 (2020).

6 Saule T. Omarova, *Bank Governance and Systemic Stability: The "Golden Share" Approach*, 68 Ala. L. Rev. 1029, 1070 (2017).

7 Marc A. Greendorfer, *Discrimination as a Business Policy: The Misuse and Abuse of Corporate Social Responsibility Programs*, 8 Am. U. Bus. L. Rev. 307, 322 n.60 (2020).

8 Portions of this Chapter were adapted from Stephen M. Bainbridge, *Making Sense of the Business Roundtable's Reversal on Corporate Purpose*, 46 J. Corp. L. 285 (2021).

9 Stout, *supra* note 3, at 165.

10 *See, e.g.*, Cherry & Sneirson, *supra* note 1, at 1021 (arguing that "the Dodge case speaks in dicta of shareholder profit as the central purpose of the corporation"); Eric H. Franklin, *A Rational Approach to Business Entity Choice*, 64 U. Kan. L. Rev. 573, 613 (2016) (asserting that "the [relevant] language in *Dodge* was merely dicta and had no bearing on the court's holding"); Jeffrey M. Lipshaw, *The False Dichotomy of Corporate Governance Platitudes*, 46 J. Corp. L. 345, 366 (2021) (noting "the dictum about corporate obligations in *Dodge*"); Judd F. Sneirson, *The Sustainable Corporation and Shareholder Profits*, 46 Wake Forest L. Rev. 541, 550 (2011).

11 Jonathan R. Macey, *A Close Read of an Excellent Commentary on* Dodge v. Ford, 3 Va. L. & Bus. Rev. 177, 180 (2008).

12 *Id.* at 183.

13 *Id.*

14 Dodge v. Ford Motor Co., 170 N.W. 668, 684 (Mich. 1919).

15 *Id. See, e.g.*, Leo E. Strine Jr., *Our Continuing Struggle with the Idea That For-Profit Corporations Seek Profit*, 47 Wake Forest L. Rev. 135, 146–48 (2012) (explaining that "the Michigan Supreme Court *held* that Ford could not justify his actions that way ... [because] he could not subordinate the stockholders' best interest" and describing the statement of that rule as a "*holding*"; emphasis supplied).

16 *Dodge*, 170 N.W. at 684.

17 *See* E. Merrick Dodd, Jr., *For Whom Are Corporate Managers Trustees?*, 45 Harv. L. Rev. 1145, 1158 (1932) (describing *Dodge* as the reflecting "orthodox legal attitude ... which is generally regarded as representing the law on the subject.").

18 Steinway v. Steinway & Sons, 40 N.Y.S. 718, 720 (N.Y. Sup. Ct. 1896).

19 *Compare Dodge*, 170 N.W. at 684 ("The difference between an incidental humanitarian expenditure of corporate funds for the benefit of the employés, like the building of a hospital for their use and the employment of agencies for the betterment of their condition, and a general purpose and plan to benefit mankind at the expense of others, is obvious.") *with Steinway*, 40 N.Y.S. at 720 ("I am not prepared to hold that the very moderate expenditures or contributions of the company toward church, school, library and baths were outside of its incidental powers.").

20 *Steinway*, 40 N.Y.S. at 721. *See also* People ex rel. Metro. Life Ins. Co. v. Hotchkiss, 120 N.Y.S. 649, 651 (App. Div. 1909) (finding that an insurance corporation's decision to finance hospital grounds that would benefit their employees was permissible as "the enlightened spirit of the age ... has thrown upon the employer other duties, which involve ... [the] well-being of the employé" and although this decision "formerly might have been questioned as not fairly within the powers or duties of the corporation" it has become essential to acquire "competent and effective service" and is "merely transacting the business of the corporation.").

21 Armstrong Cork Co. v. H.A. Mendrum Co., 285 F. 58, 58–59 (W.D.N.Y. 1922).

22 McCrory v. Chambers, 48 Ill. App. 445, 453 (Ill. App. Ct. 1892).

23 *Id. See also* Brinson Ry. Co. v. Exch. Bank of Springfield, 85 S.E. 634, 635 (1915) (holding it was beyond the powers of a railway company to donate company funds to assist in the erection of a public school or promoting of the town the in which the school is located even though the railway's "transportation business might thereby be increased" as a result).

24 60 A. 941 (N.J. Ch. 1905).

25 *Id.* at 945.

26 *Id.* The court even alluded to the possibility that this "starvation" could be entirely plausible if the expansion strategy and retention of dividends continued for only one or two more years. *See id.* at 944 ("An entirely different conclusion might be proper … one or two years from the present time.").

27 *See id.* at 945 ("I cannot, as a single equity judge sitting here, say that these gentlemen … were not doing an act that was absolutely necessary to the preservation of the successful business of the corporation.").

28 *Id.*

29 *Id.* at 948.

30 David B. Guenther, *Of Bodies Politic and Pecuniary: A Brief History of Corporate Purpose*, 9 MICH. BUS. & ENTREPRENEURIAL L. REV. 1, 64–65 (2019).

31 *Id.* at 68.

32 (1883) 23 Ch D 654.

33 *Id.* at 673.

34 *Id.*

35 Robert T. Miller, *How Would Directors Make Business Decisions Under a Stakeholder Model?*, 77 BUS. LAW. 773, 775 n.4 (2022) (citation omitted).

36 (1912) 16 CLR 50.

37 *Id.* at 70.

38 Annot., *Right of Business Corporation to Use Its Funds or Property for Humanitarian Purposes*, 3 A. L. R. 443 (1919).

39 *Using Corporate Funds for Humanitarian Purposes*, 52 CHI. LEGAL NEWS 300 (1920).

40 Donald R. Richberg, *Developing Ethics and Resistant Law*, 32 YALE L.J. 109, 117–118 (1922–1923).

41 Other contemporaneous commentary quoting the relevant passages from Dodge with either approval or, at least, without surprise, includes H.L. Wilgus, *Corporations, Shareholders' Right to Have a Dividend Declared and Paid Out of Surplus*, 17 MICH. L. REV. 502, 503 (1919); Editorial, *Minority Stockholders – Compelling Directors to Declare Dividends – Right of a Corporation Organized for Business Purposes to Devote Any of its Assets to Eleemosynary Purposes*, 5 VA. L. REG. 558, 565 (1919).

42 Josh Blackman, *Much Ado About Dictum; or, How to Evade Precedent Without Really Trying: The Distinction between Holding and Dictum* 26 (December 19, 2008), https://ssrn .com/abstract=1318389.

43 David Klein & Neal Devins, *Dicta, Schmicta: Theory versus Practice in Lower Court Decision Making*, 54 WM. & MARY L. REV. 2021, 2035 (2013).

44 *Id.* at 2036.

45 *Id.* at 2041.

46 Patricia M. Wald, *The Rhetoric of Results and the Results of Rhetoric: Judicial Writings*, 62 U. CHI. L. REV. 1371, 1411 (1995). *See also* Michael C. Dorf, *Dicta and Article III*, 142 U. PA. L. REV. 1997, 2003 (1994) ("[N]o universal agreement exists as to how to measure the scope of judicial holdings. Consequently, neither is there agreement as to how to distinguish between holdings and dicta.");

47 Stout, *supra* note 3, at 166.
48 In re Ryan, 80 B.R. 264, 267 (D. Mass. 1987), aff'd, 851 F.2d 502 (1st Cir. 1988).
49 *Id.*
50 Del Norte, Inc. v. Provencher, 703 A.2d 890, 893 (N.H. 1997). The California Court of Appeal has held that it was unaware of any authority "that makes the mere age of an opinion relevant in determining its precedential value." Mech. Contractors Assn. v. Greater Bay Area Assn., 78 CAL. RPTR. 2d 225, 233 (Cal. App. 1st Dist. 1998).
51 South Carolina v. Gathers, 490 U.S. 805, 824 (1989) (Scalia, J., dissenting).
52 *Id. See also* Daniel M. Tracer, *Stare Decisis in Antitrust: Continuity, Economics, and the Common Law Statute*, 12 DEPAUL BUS. & COM. L.J. 1, 38 (2013) ("In fact, older cases that have been continually affirmed are thought to have greater precedential value.").
53 Stout, *supra* note 3, at 168.
54 *Dodge*, 170 N.W. at 684.
55 *See* Stout, *supra* note 3, at 169–72.
56 671 N.W.2d 125 (Mich. App. 2003).
57 83 Cal.Rptr.3d 651 (Cal. App. 2 Dist. 2008).
58 *Churella*, 671 N.W.2d at 132.
59 Thompson v. Walker, 234 N.W. 144, 147 (Mich. 1931); Wagner Electric Corp. v. Hydraulic Brake Co., 257 N.W. 884, 887 (Mich. 1934).
60 Wojcik v. McNish, 2006 WL 2061499, at *5 (Mich. App. July 25, 2006).
61 Smith v. Smith, 2020 WL 2308683, at *8 (E.D. Mich. May 8, 2020).
62 Murphy v. Inman, 161454, 2022 WL 1020127, at *7 (Mich. Apr. 5, 2022).
63 Gilbert v. Norfolk & W. Ry. Co., 171 S.E. 814, 815 (W. Va. 1933) (citing *Dodge* for "the general rule that a private business corporation is carried on primarily for the profit of its stockholders").
64 Long v. Norwood Hills Corp., 380 S.W.2d 451, 476 (Mo. Ct. App. 1964).
65 Levin v. Mississippi River Corp., 59 F.R.D. 353, 365 (S.D.N.Y. 1973), *aff'd sub nom.* Wesson v. Mississippi River Corp., 486 F.2d 1398 (2d Cir. 1973).
66 Dirks v. SEC, 463 U.S. 646, 674 (1983) (Blackmun, J., dissenting).
67 In re Rigden, 795 F.2d 727, 737 (9th Cir. 1986) (Hall, J., concurring in part and dissenting in part).
68 Roxanne Thorelli, *Providing Clarity for Standard of Conduct for Directors Within Benefit Corporations: Requiring Priority of A Specific Public Benefit*, 101 MINN. L. REV. 1749, 1761–62 (2017). *See also* William W. Bratton, *Confronting the Ethical Case Against the Ethical Case for Constituency Rights*, 50 WASH. & LEE L. REV. 1449, 1456 (1993) ("Both *Dodge v. Ford Motor Co.*, the leading precedent for shareholder primacy, and *A.P. Smith Manufacturing Co. v. Barlow*, a leading precedent for a management privilege to make charitable contributions, are good law."); David Braun, *Turbulent Times in Corporate Board Rooms: The Emerging Changes in Corporate Governance*, 1993 DET. C.L. REV. 1663, 1685 (1993) ("The current state of the law regarding corporate governance remains represented by the seventy-four year old doctrine in *Dodge v. Ford Motor Co.*"); William H. Clark, Jr. & Elizabeth K. Babson, *How Benefit Corporations Are Redefining the Purpose of Business Corporations*, 38 WM. MITCHELL L. REV. 817, 825–26 (2012) (*Dodge* remains good law"); David B. Guenther, *The Strange Case of the Missing Doctrine and the "Odd Exercise" of Ebay: Why Exactly Must Corporations Maximize Profits to Shareholders?*, 12 VA. L. & BUS. REV. 427, 432 (2018) ("*Dodge v. Ford* remains good law …").
69 Former Delaware Chief Justice Leo Strine helpfully collected a list of such claims in a long string cite in Leo E. Strine, Jr., *The Dangers of Denial: The Need for a Clear-Eyed Understanding of the Power and Accountability Structure Established by the Delaware General Corporation Law*, 50 WAKE FOREST L. REV. 761, 763 n.7 (2015).

70 *Dodge*, 170 N.W. at 684 (emphasis supplied).

71 Eric C. Chaffee, *A Theory of the Business Trust*, 88 U. Cin. L. Rev. 797, 833 (2019); Einer Elhauge, *Sacrificing Corporate Profits in the Public Interest*, 80 N.Y.U. L. Rev. 733, 773 (2005).

72 For a particularly detailed examination of Delaware law, see David Yosifon, Corporate Friction: How Corporate Law Impedes American Progress and What to Do about It 60–95 (2018). Professor Yosifon concludes that "Delaware's law requires shareholder primacy ...." *Id.* at 93.

73 Katz v. Oak Industries Inc., 508 A.2d 873, 879 (Del. Ch. 1986).

74 *Id.* at 878.

75 *Id.* at 879.

76 *Id.*

77 As to Chancellor Allen's status in the field, see Lee C. Buchheit & G. Mitu Gulati, *Exit Consents in Sovereign Bond Exchanges*, 48 UCLA L. Rev. 59, 74 n.58 (2000) ("Chancellor William Allen ... was one of the most respected judges in the area of corporate law ...."); John C. Coffee, Jr., *Court Has a New Idea on Directors' Duty*, Nat'l L.J., Mar. 2, 1992, at 18 ("Chancellor Allen is probably the country's most influential and respected judge on corporate law matters ...."). As for whether anyone seriously argues that directors should violate the law in pursuit of shareholder value maximization, I have argued that directors should not be liable to shareholders in breach of fiduciary duty litigation for violating *malum prohibitum* laws, but have not argued that they should go unpunished by the criminal or other relevant civil laws for doing so. *See, e.g.*, Stephen M. Bainbridge et. al., *The Convergence of Good Faith and Oversight*, 55 UCLA L. Rev. 559, 592 (2008).

78 Stout, *supra* note 3, at 170.

79 TW Services, Inc. v. SWT Acq. Corp., 1989 WL 20290, at *7 (Del. Ch. Mar. 2, 1989) (Allen, J.) (stating that directors "owe a duty to shareholders as a class to manage the corporation within the law, with due care and in a way intended to maximize the long run interests of shareholders").

80 Malone v. Brincat, 722 A.2d 5, 9 (Del. 1998).

81 Unocal Corp. v. Mesa Petroleum Co., 493 A.2d 946, 955 (Del. 1985). For an overview of takeover defenses and the law governing them, see Stephen M. Bainbridge, Mergers and Acquisitions 353–445 (4th ed. 2021).

82 Yosifon, *supra* note 71, at 66 (calling that omission remarkable).

83 506 A.2d 173 (Del. 1986).

84 *Id.* at 182.

85 *See generally* Stephen M. Bainbridge, *The Geography of* Revlon-*Land*, 81 Fordham L. Rev. 3277, 3314 (2013) (describing *Revlon*-land's borders).

86 *Revlon*, 506 A.2d at 182.

87 *Id.*

88 Stout, *supra* note 3, at 172. Again, Leo Strine helpfully collected a list of commentators making similar claims in a long string cite in Strine, *supra* note 68, at 766 n.20.

89 Matteo Gatti, *Upsetting Deals and Reform Loop: Can Companies and M&A Law in Europe Adapt to the Market for Corporate Control?* 25 Colum. J. Eur. L. 1, 74 n.381 (2019).

90 Robert T. Miller, *Smith v. Van Gorkom and the Kobayashi Maru: The Place of the Trans Union Case in the Development of Delaware Corporate Law*, 9 Wm. & Mary Bus. L. Rev. 65, 73 (2017).

91 Stout, *supra* note 4, at 30. Professor Lipshaw likewise dismissed *Revlon* as an "exception that proves the ordinary rule." Lipshaw, *supra* note 10, at 368.

92 STOUT, *supra* note 4, at 31. Professor Elhauge makes the same error, arguing that directors' "profit-maximization duty applies only to … sales of corporate control" and "does not apply otherwise." *See* Elhauge, *supra* note 70, at 766.

93 *See* Amy Y. Yeung & Charles B. Vincent, *Delaware's "No-Go" Treatment of No-Talk Provisions: Deal-Protection Devices after* Omnicare, 33 DEL. J. CORP. L. 311, 325 (2008) ("Enhanced scrutiny under Revlon applies generally in situations where 'a fundamental change of corporate control occurs or is contemplated,' particularly where the target corporation: (1) undertakes a transaction causing a change in corporate control; (2) initiates an active bidding process seeking to sell the corporation; or (3) makes the break-up of the corporate entity inevitable.").

94 David G. Yosifon, *The Law of Corporate Purpose*, 10 BERKELEY BUS. L.J. 181, 199 (2013).

95 *Id.* at 204.

96 *Id.*

97 YOSIFON, supra note 71, at 61.

98 STOUT, *supra* note 4, at 28–29.

99 Stout, *supra* note 3, at 170 (emphasis supplied).

100 *Revlon*, 506 A.2d at 176 (emphasis supplied).

101 Yosifon, *supra* note 93, at 199.

102 *See* Elhauge, *supra* note 70, at 764.

103 *See id.* at 849–50 (arguing that "this language apparently just reflects the incomplete waning of the prior incompletely theorized agreement, for … Delaware case law in fact does not make shareholder interests controlling and thus allows consideration of nonshareholder interests other than just when that happens to maximize shareholder value"); *see also* Strine, *supra* note 68, at 766 n.20 ("Professor Elhauge gives little weight to this key statement, and Professor Stout does not quote it in her influential book on this subject.").

104 16 A.3d 1 (Del. Ch. 2010).

105 *Id.* at 34.

106 Yosifon, *supra* note 93, at 200.

107 *See, e.g.,* Elisabeth de Fontenay, *Individual Autonomy in Corporate Law*, 8 HARV. BUS. L. REV. 183, 211 (2018) (noting that "Delaware courts have recently suggested that managers of for-profit corporations are bound to maximize shareholder wealth"); Janine S. Hiller & Scott J. Shackelford, *The Firm and Common Pool Resource Theory: Understanding the Rise of Benefit Corporations*, 55 AM. BUS. L.J. 5, 16 (2018) (stating that *eBay* "is in a line of cases that can give a director pause before taking nonshareholder interests into consideration in corporate decision making, and it highlights the application of shareholder wealth maximization not just to publicly held corporations but also under certain circumstances to closely held corporations"); Kristin A. Neubauer, *Benefit Corporations: Providing A New Shield for Corporations with Ideals Beyond Profits*, 11 J. BUS. & TECH. L. 109, 123–24 (2016) ("As Chandler's analysis clearly articulates, while a company's decision to embark on charitable endeavors is admirable under traditional corporate law, if that charitable endeavor threatens the traditional fiduciary obligations of directors, then the charitable endeavor will not be sustained as a viable defense in Delaware courts").

108 *See, e.g.,* Lyman Johnson, *Pluralism in Corporate Form: Corporate Law and Benefit Corps.*, 25 REGENT U. L. REV. 269, 274–75 (2013) (stating "the 2010 *eBay* decision is touted by some … as mandating shareholder primacy. Yet, the opinion … did nothing to alter craigslist's business focus strategy"); Robert A. Katz & Antony Page, *Sustainable Business*, 62 EMORY L.J. 851, 868 (2013) ("The *eBay* case may even permit a company's

directors to pursue a philanthropic purpose, as long as it is not the company's exclusive purpose"); Jena Martin, *Business and Human Rights: What's the Board Got to Do with It?* 2013 U. ILL. L. REV. 959, 970 n.53 (2013) (claiming "that a determined corporation could still maintain a strategy that values stakeholders (perhaps even above shareholders) in Delaware, so long as the corporation were to frame it within a shareholder-benefit framework").

109 *See, e.g.,* Paul Weitzel & Zachariah J. Rodgers, *Broad Shareholder Value and the Inevitable Role of Conscience,* 12 N.Y.U. J.L. & BUS. 35, 79 (2015) (stating Chancellor Chandler's comments in eBay are "just strongly worded dicta"); David A. Wishnick, *Corporate Purposes in A Free Enterprise System: A Comment on Ebay v. Newmark,* 121 YALE L.J. 2405, 2417 (2012) ("Future interpreters should read [*eBay's*] 'mandatory' language as dicta because the opinion offers two grounds for rescission of the poison pill that do not require inquiry into the definition of 'proper corporate purposes'").

110 Strine, *supra* note 68, at 775–76. Delaware Vice Chancellor Travis Laster, in an extended and favorable treatment of eBay, observed that "directors owe duties to the corporation for the ultimate benefit of the residual claimants." J. Travis Laster, Revlon *Is a Standard of Review: Why It's True and What It Means,* 19 FORDHAM J. CORP. & FIN. L. 5, 28 (2013).

111 Strine, *supra* note 68, at 763.

112 *Id.* at 765.

113 *Id.* at 766–67.

114 *Id.* at 767.

115 *Id.* at 763–64 nn. 7 & 9.

116 *Id.* at 763 (emphasis supplied).

117 Statute of International Court of Justice, art. 38, para. 1(d).

118 The Paquete Habana, 175 U.S. 677, 700 (1900).

119 *Id.*

120 *Quoted in* Buckner F. Melton, Jr., *The Supreme Court and the Federalist: A Citation List and Analysis, 1789–1996,* 85 KY. L.J. 243 (1997).

121 LORI FISLER DAMROSCH & SEAN D. MURPHY, INTERNATIONAL LAW: CASES AND MATERIALS 239 (7th ed 2019).

122 D. Gordon Smith, *The Shareholder Primacy Norm,* 23 J. CORP. L. 277, 320 (1998) ("In short, *Dodge v. Ford Motor Co.* is best viewed as a minority oppression case."). *See also* Geoffrey Miller, *Narrative and Truth in Judicial Opinions: Corporate Charitable Giving Cases,* 2009 MICH. ST. L. REV. 831, 835 (contending that that *Dodge* is about not shareholder value maximization but rather protection of minority shareholders); Dalia T. Mitchel, *From* Dodge *to* eBay: *The Elusive Corporate Purpose,* 13 VA. L. & BUS. REV. 155, 169–75 (2019) (same).

123 Stout, *supra* note 3, at 4.

124 Elhauge, *supra* note 70, at 774 ("That is, the otherwise aberrational court decision to interfere with the exercise of managerial discretion about dividend levels seems best explained on the view that the case really involved a conflict of interest raising duty of loyalty concerns.").

125 *Dodge,* 170 N.W. at 671 (stating that "the board of directors has been dominated and controlled absolutely by Henry Ford, the president of the company, who owns and for several years has owned 58 per cent. of the entire capital stock of the company").

126 Current Decisions, *Corporations – Distribution of Dividends – Arbitrary Withholding on the Part of Directors,* 28 YALE L. J. 710, 711 (1918–1919) (describing the dividend portion of *Dodge* as addressing "protection of minority holders against the arbitrary acts of a numerically small majority").

127 Amir N. Licht, *The Maximands of Corporate Governance: A Theory of Values and Cognitive Style*, 29 DEL. J. CORP. L. 649, 689 (2004).

128 *See, e.g., Right of Business Corporation to Use Its Funds or Property for Humanitarian Purposes*, 3 A. L. R. 443 (1919) ("the fundamental purpose of a business corporation …") (emphasis added); 52 Chi. Legal News 298, 300 (1920) ("the fundamental purpose of a business corporation …") (emphasis added); 50 Wash. L. Rep 17, 25 (1922) ("When a corporation has a surplus …").

129 *See* eBay Dom. Holdings, Inc. v. Newmark, 16 A.3d 1, 31 (Del. Ch. 2010) (quoting Kurz v. Holbrook, 989 A.2d 140, 183 (Del.Ch.2010), *rev'd on other grounds*, 992 A.2d 377 (Del.2010)).

130 Stout, *supra* note 3, at 169.

131 MOD. BUS. CORP. ACT § 2.02(b)(2)(i).

132 DEL. CODE ANN., tit. 8, § 102(3).

133 Yosifon, *supra* note 93, at 185 (stating that most articles of incorporation state that the business' purpose to pursue "any lawful" activity).

134 Strine, *supra* note 68, at 783.

135 Having said that, however, it must be acknowledged that default rules often prove sticky and thus difficult to opt out of. *See* Russell B. Korobkin & Thomas S. Ulen, *Law and Behavioral Science: Removing the Rationality Assumption from Law and Economics*, 88 CAL. L. REV. 1051, 1112 (2000) (observing that "contracting parties are likely to see default terms as part of the status quo and, consequently, prefer them to alternative terms, all other things equal").

136 *See* AMERICAN LAW INSTITUTE, PRINCIPLES OF CORP. GOVERNANCE § 2.01 illus. 1 (1994) (indicating that a board decision to perform on an unenforceable contract would be consistent with the board's duties).

137 *See id.* § 2.01 illus. 3 (offering a version of that hypothetical).

138 Stout, *supra* note 3, at 170–71.

139 Lipshaw, *supra* note 10, at 365.

140 David Millon, *Two Models of Corporate Social Responsibility*, 46 WAKE FOREST L. REV. 523, 527 (2011).

141 Elhauge, *supra* note 70, at 770.

142 *See* Strine, *supra* note 68, at 782–83 (stating that "the problem" with the claim that "the business judgment rule is cloaking a system of law that is focused on giving directors the ability to act for any reason they deem appropriate" "is that it does not happen to be true").

143 *See* William T. Allen et al., *Function over Form: A Reassessment of Standards of Review in Delaware Corporation Law*, 56 BUS. LAW. 1287, 1297 (2000) (describing the business judgment rule as "an expression of a policy of non-review of a board of directors' decision when a judge has already performed the crucial task of determining that certain conditions exist"); Bernard S. Sharfman, *Being Informed Does Matter: Fine Tuning Gross Negligence Twenty Plus Years After Van Gorkom*, 62 BUS. LAW. 135, 145 (2006) (arguing that "the BJR is better described as a 'standard of non-review'").

144 Stephen M. Bainbridge, *The Business Judgment Rule as Abstention Doctrine*, 57 VAND. L. REV. 83 (2004). No less an authority than former Delaware Chief Justice Norman Veasey has confirmed that that articulation of the rule is "consistent" with Delaware law. See E. Norman Veasey & Christine T. Di Guglielmo, *What Happened in Delaware Corporate Law and Governance from 1992–2004? A Retrospective on Some Key Developments*, 153 U. PA. L. REV. 1399, 1421–28 (2005) (["Professor Bainbridge's] approach is consistent with the Delaware doctrine that the [business judgment] rule is a presumption that courts will not interfere with, or second-guess, decision making by directors."). *See also* Boland

v. Boland, 5 A.3d 106, 122 (Md. Spec. App. 2010) (holding that "the business judgment rule serves as one of abstention"), *rev'd on other grounds*, 31 A.3d 529 (Md. 2011); Houle v. Low, 556 N.E.2d 51, 59 (Mass. 1990) ("Massachusetts has always recognized the need for courts to abstain from interfering in business judgments."); Gut v. MacDonough, 2007 WL 2410131, at *12 (Mass. Super. Aug. 14, 2007) ("The business judgment rule allows courts to presume that the board of directors acted in the best interests of the corporation and, therefore, to largely abstain from evaluating the validity of the board's decisions.").

145   *See, e.g.*, Quackenbush v. Allstate Ins. Co., 517 U.S. 706, 713 (1996) (explaining that abstention-based stay orders raise "an important issue separate from the merits" of the case).

146   *See, e.g.*, In re Jt. E. and S. Dist. Asbestos Litig., 78 F.3d 764, 775 (2d Cir. 1996) (discussing *Burford* abstention, under "which a federal district court may properly decline to decide difficult questions of state law").

147   This is so because the business judgment rule does not preclude judicial review of violations of the duty of loyalty. *See, e.g.*, Bayer v. Beran, 49 N.Y.S.2d 2, 6 (N.Y. Sup. Ct. 1944) ("The 'business judgment rule' … yields to the rule of undivided loyalty.").

148   *See* In re Fleming Packaging Corp., 351 B.R. 626, 634 (Bankr. C.D. Ill. 2006) (stating that "the rule serves to preclude judicial review of the substantive merits of the decision"); eBay Domestic Holdings, Inc. v. Newmark, 16 A.3d 1, 33 (Del. Ch. 2010) ("When director decisions are reviewed under the business judgment rule, this Court will not question rational judgments about how promoting non-stock-holder interests – be it through making a charitable contribution, paying employees higher salaries and benefits, or more general norms like promoting a particular corporate culture – ultimately promote stockholder value.").

149   Stephen M. Bainbridge, The New Corporate Governance in Theory and Practice (2008).

150   Kenneth J. Arrow, The Limits of Organization 68–69 (1974).

151   *Id.* at 68–69.

152   *See, e.g.*, Mod. Bus. Corp. Act § 8.01(b).

153   Arrow, *supra* note 148, at 78.

154   *See, e.g.*, Kamin v. American Express Co., 383 N.Y.S.2d 807, 811 (N.Y. Sup. 1976) (stating that absent "fraud, dishonesty, or nonfeasance," the court would not substitute its judgment for that of the directors), *aff'd*, 387 N.Y.S.2d 993 (N.Y. A.D. 1976).

155   *See, e.g.*, Joy v. North, 692 F.2d 880, 885 (2d Cir. 1982) ("While it is often stated that corporate directors and officers will be liable for negligence in carrying out their corporate duties, all seem agreed that such a statement is misleading …. Whatever the terminology, the fact is that liability is rarely imposed upon corporate directors or officers simply for bad judgment and this reluctance to impose liability for unsuccessful business decisions has been doctrinally labeled the business judgment rule."); Brehm v. Eisner, 746 A.2d 244, 262–64 (Del. 2000) (rejecting plaintiff's contention that the business judgment rule includes an element of "substantive due care" and holding that the business judgment rule requires only "process due care").

156   Macey, *supra* note 11, at 180–81.

157   *Id.*

158   Yosifon, *supra* note 93, at 223.

159   Mass. Gen. Laws ch. 156D, § 8.30(a).

160   *See* Nathan E. Standley, *Lessons Learned from the Capitulation of the Constituency Statute*, 4 Elon L. Rev. 209, 212 (2012) (explaining that "corporate constituency statutes were rushed through state legislatures as part of antitakeover legislation packages").

161 *See* Michael E. DeBow & Dwight R. Lee, *Shareholders, Nonshareholders and Corporate Law: Communitarianism and Resource Allocation*, 18 DEL. J. CORP. L. 393, 400 (1993) (arguing that the "statutes' primary beneficiaries appear to have been incumbent managers"); Robert T. Miller, *How Would Directors Make Business Decisions under a Stakeholder Model?* 677 Bus. Law. 773, 782 n.19 (2022) ("Management strongly favored these laws, not because of any solicitude for other corporate constituencies, but rather because such statutes allowed management to rebuff takeover bids, no matter how favorable to the company's shareholders, by arguing that the offers would have negative effects on some non-shareholder constituency or other."); Ryan J. York, *Visages of Janus: The Heavy Burden of Other Constituency Anti-Takeover Statutes on Shareholders and the Efficient Market for Corporate Control*, 38 WILLAMETTE L. REV. 187, 207 (2002) ("Instead of protecting nonshareholder constituencies, these statutes act as a subterfuge for management, allowing them to extract gains rightfully belonging to the corporation's shareholders.").

162 *See* Stephen M. Bainbridge, *Interpreting Nonshareholder Constituency Statutes*, 19 PEPP. L. REV. 971, 1015 (1992) (explaining that "the nonshareholder constituency statutes reject the *Revlon* gloss" on director fiduciary duties in takeover settings); *see, e.g.*, Shoen v. AMERCO, 885 F. Supp. 1332, 1341 n.22 (D. Nev. 1994) ("The text of [the Nevada constituency statute] makes clear that the statute is an anti-takeover provision, designed to give directors greater discretion to resist hostile tender offers by allowing them to consider factors other than the shareholders' immediate financial gain."); Dixon v. Ladish Co., Inc., 785 F. Supp. 2d 746, 752 (E.D. Wis. 2011) (arguing that the Wisconsin constituency statute precludes *Revlon* from being part of Wisconsin law), *aff'd sub nom.* Dixon v. ATI Ladish LLC, 667 F.3d 891 (7th Cir. 2012); Crandon Capital Partners v. Shelk, 181 P.3d 773, 783 n.10 (Or. App. 2008) ("Other states have rejected the heightened scrutiny standard of *Unocal* by [adopting a constituency] statute.").

163 *See* Lee-Ford Tritt & Ryan Scott Teschner, *Re-Imagining the Business Trust as a Sustainable Business Form*, 97 WASH. U. L. REV. 1, 55 n.107 (2019) (noting "the permissive language in all state constituency statutes"); *see, e.g.*, Hill v. State Farm Mut. Automobile Ins. Co., 83 Cal. Rptr. 3d 651, 686 (Cal. App. 2d Dist. 2008) (explaining that the Illinois statute "permits, but does not require, a director to consider the interests of the listed constituencies").

164 Tritt & Teschner, *supra* note 161, at 55 n.107.

165 In re I.E. Liquidation, Inc., 06–62179, 2009 WL 2707223, at *4 (Bankr. N.D. Ohio Aug. 25, 2009). *See also* In re Amcast Indus. Corp., 365 B.R. 91 (Bankr. S.D. Ohio 2007); Custom Associates, L.P. v. VSM Logistics, LLC, 154 N.E.3d 178, 182 (Ohio App. 11th Dist. 2020).

166 Lawrence E. Mitchell, *A Theoretical and Practical Framework for Enforcing Corporate Constituency Statutes*, 70 TEX. L. REV. 579, 631 (1992) ("Curiously, the centerpiece of constituent recognition, the constituency statute, stops short of fulfilling its ultimate goal.").

167 *See* Committee on Corporate Laws, *Other Constituencies Statutes: Potential for Confusion*, 45 BUS. LAW. 2253, 2265 (1990).

168 First Union Corp. v. SunTrust Banks, Inc., 2001 WL 1885686, at *5 (N.C. Super. Aug. 10, 2001).

169 *See* Committee on Corporate Laws, *supra* note 165, at 2266.

170 Macey, *supra* note 11, at 179.

171 *See* Jitendra Aswani et. al, *The Cost (and Unbenefit) of Conscious Capitalism* 36 (table 1) (September 16, 2021).

172 Data on file with author.
173 Standley, *supra* note 158, at 223.
174 Anthony Bisconti, *The Double Bottom Line: Can Constituency Statutes Protect Socially Responsible Corporations Stuck in Revlon Land?*, 42 Loy. L.A. L. Rev. 765, 784 (2009).
175 *See* Committee on Corporate Laws, *supra* note 165, at 2253.
176 Yosifon, *supra* note 71, at 71.
177 *See* Julian Velasco, *Shareholder Ownership and Primacy*, 2010 U. Ill. L. Rev. 897, 945.
178 Julian Velasco, *The Fundamental Rights of the Shareholder*, 40 U. Cal. Davis L. Rev. 407, 464 (2006).
179 Stout, *supra* note 3, at 176.
180 Greendorfer, *supra* note 7, at 342.

5   TO MAKE STAKEHOLDER CAPITALISM THE RULE, YOU WOULD HAVE TO CHANGE MOST OF CORPORATE LAW

1 *See* J. Haskell Murray, *Adopting Stakeholder Advisory Boards*, 54 Am. Bus. L.J. 61, 75 (2017) (observing that "with shareholders as the only constituent holding an accountability whip, it is easy to see why directorial focus typically rests on shareholders").
2 Paramount Commun. Inc. v. Time Inc., 1989 WL 79880, at *30 (Del. Ch. July 14, 1989), *aff'd sub nom.* In re Time Inc. Shareholder Litig., 565 A.2d 281 (Del. 1989).
3 *See* Strougo v. Bassini, 282 F.3d 162, 173 (2d Cir. 2002) ("Maryland courts have clearly established the proposition that directors and officers owe fiduciary duties to both the corporation and the shareholders."); Cargill, Inc. v. JWH Spec. Circumstance LLC, 959 A.2d 1096, 1116 n.75 (Del. Ch. 2008) (opining that "in the corporate context, both officers and directors of a corporation owe fiduciary duties to the company and its shareholders"); Adelman v. Conotti Corp., 213 S.E.2d 774, 779 (Va. 1975) (holding that both the officers and the directors of a corporation owe fiduciary duties to the corporation and its shareholders). I have argued elsewhere that "the corporation is not a thing to which duties can be owed, except as a useful legal fiction." Stephen M. Bainbridge, *Much Ado about Little? Directors' Fiduciary Duties in the Vicinity of Insolvency*, 1 J. Bus. & Tech. L. 335, 353 (2007).
4 *See, e.g.,* Shenker v. Laureate Educ., Inc., 983 A.2d 408, 424 (Md. 2009) (holding that "a shareholder may bring a direct action, either individually or as a representative of a class, against alleged corporate wrongdoers when the shareholder suffers the harm directly or a duty is owed directly to the shareholder").
5 *See* Eric J. Gouvin, *Resolving the Subsidiary Director's Dilemma*, 47 Hastings L.J. 287, 303–04 (1996).
6 As to the extent to which executive pay induces higher firm performance, *compare* Lucian Bebchuk & Jesse Fried, Pay Without Performance: The Unfulfilled Promise of Executive Compensation 6 (2004) (contending that "managers have used their influence [over corporate boards of directors] to obtain higher compensation through arrangements that have substantially decoupled pay from performance") *with* Marlo A. Bakris, *Executive Compensation Disclosure: The SEC's Newest Weapon in Its Arsenal against Executive Compensation Abuses*, 71 U. Det. Mercy L. Rev. 105, 153 (1993) (citing studies suggesting "monetary rewards and stock ownership are, as a rule, the most effective incentives and are therefore significant elements of executive pay packages").

7 Lucian A. Bebchuk & Roberto Tallarita, *The Perils and Questionable Promise of ESG-Based Compensation* 15–17 (Mar. 1, 2022), https://papers.ssrn.com/sol3/papers.cfm?abstract_id=4048003.
8 The data in this paragraph is taken from Lucian A. Bebchuk & Roberto Tallarita, *The Illusory Promise of Stakeholder Governance*, 106 Cornell L. Rev. 91, 151 (2020).
9 James F. Cotter et. al., *The First Year of Say-on-Pay under Dodd-Frank: An Empirical Analysis and Look Forward*, 81 Geo. Wash. L. Rev. 967, 970 (2013).
10 John C. Coffee, Jr. & Darius Palia, *The Wolf at the Door: The Impact of Hedge Fund Activism on Corporate Governance*, 41 J. Corp. L. 545, 557–58 (2016).
11 *Id.*
12 Douglas Sarro, *Proxy Advisors as Issue Spotters*, 15 Brook. J. Corp. Fin. & Com. L. 371, 388 (2021).
13 *See id.* at 389–94 (reviewing 11 studies).
14 *Id.* at 394.
15 Nadya Malenko & Yao Shen, *The Role of Proxy Advisory Firms: Evidence from a Regression-Discontinuity Design*, 29 Rev. Fin. Stud. 3394, 3399 (2016).
16 ISS, United States FAQ: Compensation Practices 9 (2021) ("ISS' quantitative pay-for-performance screen uses four measures of alignment between executive pay and company performance: three relative measures where a company's CEO pay magnitude and the degree of pay-for- performance alignment are evaluated in reference to a group of comparable companies, and one absolute measure, where alignment is evaluated independently of other companies' performance.").
17 ISS, Proxy Voting Guidelines for 2021: Benchmark Policy Recommendations 41 (2020).
18 *Id.*
19 Bebchuk & Tallarita, *supra* note 8, at 152–53.
20 *See, e.g.*, Del. Code Ann., tit. 8, § 220.
21 *See, e.g.*, Del. Code Ann., tit. 8, § 170.
22 *See, e.g.*, Rondeau v. Mosinee Paper Corp., 422 U.S. 49 (1975) (holding that target company shareholders have standing to sue under Exchange Act § 13(d)).
23 Rohe v. Reliance Training Network, Inc., 2000 WL 1038190, at *11 (Del. Ch. July 21, 2000).

6   WHAT ABOUT THE BENEFIT CORPORATION?

1 *See About B Lab*, www.bcorporation.net/en-us/movement/about-b-lab/.
2 *See, e.g.*, Renatto Garcia, *Re-Engineering Georgia's Corporate DNA: A Benefit Analysis and Practicality Assessment for Benefit Corporation Legislation in Georgia*, 6 J. Marshall L.J. 627, 660 (2013) (stating that "constituency statutes are not adequate substitutes as they lack certain provisions which form the basis for B-Corps"); Alexandra Leavy, *Necessity Is the Mother of Invention: A Renewed Call to Engage the SEC on Social Disclosure*, 2014 Colum. Bus. L. Rev. 463, 494 (2014) ("Many constituency statutes are not as broad as the range of B-Corp statutes and do not allow consideration of environmental concerns."); Anna R. Kimbrell, *Benefit Corporation Legislation: An Opportunity for Kansas to Welcome Social Enterprises*, 62 U. Kan. L. Rev. 549, 559–60 (2013) ("B Lab encourages companies seeking B Corp Certification to incorporate in a state with a constituency statute; however, the extent of the protection to dual mission corporate directors is unclear.").

3 *See* Corporate Laws Committee, *Benefit Corporation White Paper*, 68 Bus. Law. 1083, 1087
   (2013) ("Generally speaking, and though each state's version of the benefit corporation statute
   is different, these provisions (1) require that a benefit corporation consider general public
   welfare before acting, (2) permit that more specific interests be considered as well, and (3)
   require that the firm's compliance be measured against a standard imposed by an independent third party.").
4 *See generally* Frederick Alexander, Benefit Corporation Law and Governance:
   Pursuing Profit With Purpose (Berrett-Koehler 2018).
5 J. William Callison, *Putting New Sheets on a Procrustean Bed: How Benefit Corporations
   Address Fiduciary Duties, the Dangers Created, and Suggestions for Change*, 2 Am. U. Bus.
   L. Rev. 85, 109 (2012).
6 *See, e.g.*, Cal. Corp. Code § 14600(c) ("The provisions of the General Corporation
   Law … shall apply to benefit corporations, except where those provisions are in conflict with
   or inconsistent with the provisions of this part."); Del. Code Ann. tit. 8, § 361 (2019) (stating
   that a PBC shall be subject "in all respects to the provisions of this chapter [i.e., the Delaware
   General Corporation Law] except to the extent this subchapter [the Delaware PBC statute]
   imposes additional or different requirements, in which case such requirements shall apply").
7 Callison, *supra* note 5, at 109.
8 *See, e.g.*, Del. Code Ann., tit. 8, § 354(b) ("A director of a public benefit corporation shall
   not, by virtue of the public benefit provisions or § 362(a) of this title, have any duty to any
   person on account of any interest of such person in the public benefit or public benefits
   identified in the certificate of incorporation or on account of any interest materially affected
   by the corporation's conduct ….").
9 *See, e.g.*, Del. Code Ann., tit. 8, § 367; *see generally* Dana Brakman Reiser, Benefit
   Corporations – A Sustainable Form of Organization? 46 Wake Forest L. Rev. 591, 613
   (2011) ("The statutes uniformly exclude other potential parties from engaging in enforcement
   through litigation. Beneficiaries and the public will not have standing to challenge actions by
   benefit corporation directors.").

7   POSSIBLE MERITS OF THE BUSINESS ROUNDTABLE'S EMBRACE OF STAKEHOLDER CAPITALISM

1 Business Roundtable, *Statement on Corporate Purpose* (Aug. 19, 2019), https://s3.amazonaws
   .com/Business Royundtable.org/Business Roundtable-StatementonthePurposeofaCorporatio
   nJuly2021.pdf.
2 Malcolm S. Salter, *Rehabilitating Corporate Purpose* 12–15 (Harvard Business School
   Working Paper 19–104 2019).
3 Martin Lipton, *The Friedman Essay and the True Purpose of the Business Corporation*,
   Harv. L. School. Forum on Corp. Gov. (Sept. 17, 2020), https://corpgov.law.harvard
   .edu/2020/09/17/the-friedman-essay-and-the-true-purpose-of-the-business-corporation/.
4 Gerald F. Davis, *Corporate Purpose Needs Democracy*, 58 J. Mgmt. Stud. 902, 905 (2021).
5 Martin Petrin, *Beyond Shareholder Value: Exploring Justifications for a Broader Corporate
   Purpose* 13 (November 1, 2020), https://ssrn.com/abstract=3722836.
6 *Id.* at 14.
7 *See* Robert H. Bork Jr., *Court Movies Don't Mimic Life; Culture: Couldn't the Demands of
   Lively Entertainment Still Accommodate a More Balanced View of the System?*, L.A. Times,
   April 5. 2000, at B9 (arguing that such films create "a whole new mythology around avenging
   angels of the trial bar").

8 Greenwashing is the use of public statements, conduct, and "advertising and promotional materials … to convey a false impression that a company is more environmentally responsible than it really is, and so to induce consumers to purchase its products." Massachusetts v. Exxon Mobil Corp., 462 F. Supp. 3d 31, 37 (D. Mass. 2020).

9 Robert S. Kaplan & Karthik Ramanna, *Accounting for Climate Change*, Harv. Bus. Rev., Nov.–Dec. 2021), https://hbr.org/2021/11/accounting-for-climate-change.

10 Yashoda Bhagwat et al., *Corporate Sociopolitical Activism and Firm Value*, 84 J. Marketing, no. 5, 2020, at 1.

11 Federica Balluchi et al., *CSR and Greenwashing: A Matter of Perception in the Search of Legitimacy* 1 (Dec. 15, 2020), https://papers.ssrn.com/sol3/papers.cfm?abstract_id=3721199.

12 Aneesh Raghunandan & Shivaram Rajgopal, *Do ESG Funds Make Stakeholder-Friendly Investments?*, Harv. L. Sch. Forum on Corp. Gov. (May 15, 2021), https://corpgov .law.harvard.edu/2021/05/15/do-esg-funds-make-stakeholder-friendly-investments/.

13 *Id.*

14 *Id.*

15 Margaret M. Blair & Lynn A. Stout, *A Team Production Theory of Corporate Law*, 85 Va. L. Rev. 247, 299 (1999)

16 *See* Grant Christensen, *Indigenous Perspectives on Corporate Governance*, 23 U. Pa. J. Bus. L. 902, 948 (2021).

17 Jonathan R. Macey, *Corporate Social Responsibility: A Law & Economics Perspective*, 17 Chap. L. Rev. 331, 333 (2014) (observing that such "benefits will vary depending on the nature of the nonshareholder constituency at issue. They may take the form of higher interest rates for bondholders, higher wages or greater job security for workers, or higher taxes for local communities.").

18 Macey, *supra* note 17, at 346–48 (discussing available contracting mechanisms).

19 *See* Katz v. Oak Indus. Inc., 508 A.2d 873, 879 (Del. Ch. 1986) ("Arrangements among a corporation, the underwriters of its debt, trustees under its indentures and sometimes ultimate investors are typically thoroughly negotiated and massively documented.").

20 *See, e.g.*, Wolfgang Streeck, *The Sociology of Labor Markets and Trade Unions*, in The Handbook of Economic Sociology 254, 266–68 (Neil J. Smelser & Richard Swedberg eds., 2d ed. 2005) (explaining that unions relied "on seniority rights and promotion ladders").

21 ALI, Principles of Corp. Governance § 2.01 (1994).

22 In re Massey Energy Co., 2011 WL 2176479, at *20 (Del. Ch. May 31, 2011).

23 *See* Larry E. Ribstein, *Accountability and Responsibility in Corporate Governance*, 81 Notre Dame L. Rev. 1431, 1437 (2006). On the one hand, Ribstein argued that regulators can "channel business behavior or organizational form by making certain types of behavior or organizational forms more costly than others. A prime example is laws that tax some forms or behaviors differently than others." *Id.* On the other hand, Ribstein acknowledged that corporations can impact regulation through lobbying. *Id.*

24 Sanjai Bhagat & Glenn Hubbard, *Should the Modern Corporation Maximize Shareholder Value?* 6 (Mar. 3, 2020); Ribstein, *supra* note 23, at 1444.

25 558 U.S. 310 (2010).

26 Leo E. Strine, Jr. & Nicholas Walter, *Conservative Collision Course?: The Tension between Conservative Corporate Law Theory and Citizens United*, 100 Cornell L. Rev. 335, 340 (2015). The following discussion is adapted from my response to Strine & Walter. *See* Stephen M. Bainbridge, Corporate Social Responsibility in the Night-Watchman State, 115 Colum. L. Rev. Sidebar 39 (2015).

27 Strine & Walter, *supra* note 26, at 387.

28 *Id.* at 345.
29 *The Criminalization of American Business*, THE ECONOMIST, Aug. 30, 2014, at 9.
30 Thomas Z. Horton, *Lenity Before* Kisor: *Due Process, Agency Deference, and the Interpretation of Ambiguous Penal Regulations*, 54 COLUM. J.L. & SOC. PROBS. 629, 632 (2021).
31 Keith B. Belton, Ph.D. & John D. Graham, *Trump's Deregulation Record: Is It Working?*, 71 ADMIN. L. REV. 803, 842 (2019) ("We are not aware of any published count of the total number of federal regulations on the books, but it has to be at least in the hundreds of thousands.").
32 LexisNexis Risk Solutions, *Global True Cost of Compliance 2020* (https://risk.lexisnexis .com/insights-resources/research/true-cost-of-financial-crime-compliance-study-global-report.
33 Laura Alix, *Rising Compliance Costs Are Hurting Customers, Banks Say*, AM. BANKER (Apr. 12, 2018).
34 CLYDE WAYNE CREWS JR., TEN THOUSAND COMMANDMENTS: AN ANNUAL SNAPSHOT OF THE FEDERAL REGULATORY STATE 17 (2018).
35 *See What's Wrong with Corporate Social Responsibility?: The Arguments against CSR*, CORPORATE WATCH, www.corporatewatch.org/content/whats-wrong-corporate-social-responsibility-arguments-against-csr (on file with the Columbia Law Review) (last visited Feb. 19, 2015) ("Because companies will only lobby for the type of regulation that makes them more competitive, any regulation they support will be counterweighted by lobbying from competitors who would lose out if regulation is brought in."). A friend who wishes to remain anonymous commented that:
    I think there's a further reason why Citizens United may not result in the high levels of political expenditure that S&W seem to assume. Big institutional shareholders – especially pension funds and some mutual funds – have powerful incentives to demand short-term share price maximization from corporate management. So this means that any discretionary expenditure that reduces net income in a given quarter is potentially problematic. That includes current expenses like R&D, advertising, etc. that have the potential to yield net gains over the long term. Political expenditures would fall into that category too. So there's a built-in limit, at least at companies that are managed to maximize quarterly earnings, on these kinds of expenditures. This also goes to S&W's criticism of Kennedy's naïve belief that shareholders can constrain political spending. Retail investors can't, but institutions can and probably do. Anyway, the amounts involved are usually so small for the large corporations that they don't even appear on the income statement.
36 Thomas W. Joo, *Corporate Governance and the Constitutionality of Campaign Finance Reform*, 1 ELECTION L.J. 361, 362 (2002)
37 Michael A. Behrens, Citizens United, *Tax Policy, and Corporate Governance*, 12 FLA. TAX REV. 589, 607 (2012).
38 *See* Bhagat & Hubbard, *supra* note 24 at 6 ("In a competitive labor market, the employee can resign and seek alternative employment,"), https://papers.ssrn.com/sol3/papers .cfm?abstract_id=3548293. For a more elaborate version of this argument, see Stephen M. Bainbridge, *Corporate Decisionmaking and the Moral Rights of Employees: Participatory Management and Natural Law*, 43 VILLANOVA L. REV. 741, 817–18 (1998).
39 *See* Tom C.W. Lin, *Incorporating Social Activism*, 98 B.U. L. REV. 1535, 1546 (2018) ("Many in society and within corporations now expect businesses and executives, particularly those at large public companies, to engage with the critical social issues of today.").
40 *See* Lin, *supra* note 39, at 1546 ("Corporations are now frequently expected to engage in social issues through public statements, sponsorships, partnerships, and policies supporting a position or a cause.").

41 David F. Larcker et al., *The Double-Edged Sword of CEO Activism* 1 (Stanford Closer Look Series, 2018), https://ssrn.com/abstract=3283297.

42 Edward B. Rock, *For Whom Is the Corporation Managed in 2020? The Debate over Corporate Purpose*, 76 Bus. Law. 363, 368 (2021).

43 Larry Fink, *A Fundamental Reshaping of Finance*, www.blackrock.com/hk/en/larry-fink-ceo-letter (last visited June 7, 2021).

44 Larry Fink, *The Power of Capitalism*, www.blackrock.com/corporate/investor-relations/larry-fink-ceo-letter (last visited Jan. 26, 2022).

45 E. Merrick Dodd, Jr., *For Whom Are Corporate Managers Trustees?* 45 Harv. L. Rev. 1145, 1151 (1932) (suggesting that "the day may not be far distant when public opinion will demand a much greater degree of protection to the worker").

46 Milton Friedman, *The Social Responsibility of Business Is to Increase Its Profits*, N.Y. Times, Sept. 13, 1970 (Magazine) at 32. *See, e.g.*, Keith Davis & Robert Blomstrom, Business, Society, and Environment: Power and Social Responses 95 (2d ed. 1971) (arguing that "(1) Industrial society faces serious human and social problems brought on largely by the rise of the large corporation, and (2) managers must conduct the affairs of the corporation in ways to solve or at least ameliorate those problems.").

47 Trustees of Dartmouth College v. Woodward, 17 U.S. 518, 636 (1819).

48 *See, e.g.*, Stefan J. Padfield, *Rehabilitating Concession Theory*, 66 Okla. L. Rev. 327, 329 (2014) (explaining that concession theory "views the corporation as fundamentally a creature of the state and thus presumptively subject to broad state regulation"); *see also* Stefan J. Padfield, *Corporate Social Responsibility & Concession Theory*, 6 Wm. & Mary Bus. L. Rev. 1, 34 (2015) ("Corporate personality theory, specifically concession theory, can be a meaningful source of leverage in advancing mandatory CSR"); Michael E. DeBow & Dwight R. Lee, *Shareholders, Nonshareholders and Corporate Law: Communitarianism and Resource Allocation*, 18 Del. J. Corp. L. 393, 397 (1993) ("Concession theorists argue that corporations exist at the sufferance of the government, which retains a legitimate role in conditioning its grant of a corporate charter (viewed as the concession of the government) on the receipt of some quid pro quo.").

49 Citizens United v. Fed. Election Commn., 558 U.S. 310, 432 (2010) (Stevens, J., concurring in part) (observing that "many legal scholars have long since rejected the concession theory of the corporation"); Ronit Donyets-Kedar, *Challenging Corporate Personhood Theory: Reclaiming the Public*, 11 Law & Ethics Hum. Rts. 61, 65 (2017) ("Scholars today are in agreement that the grant theory has in fact withered away."); J. Haskell Murray, *An Early Report on Benefit Reports*, 118 W. Va. L. Rev. 25, 38 (2015) ("Concession theory was most popular between the 17th and 19th centuries ....").

50 Bradford Cornell & Alan C. Shapiro, *Corporate Stakeholders, Corporate Valuation, and ESG*, The CLS Blue Sky Blog (Dec. 10, 2020), https://clsbluesky.law.columbia.edu/2020/12/10/corporate-stakeholders-corporate-valuation-and-esg/.

51 I commend David Yosifon's treatment of this issue to the reader's attention. David Yosifon, Corporate Friction: How Corporate Law Impedes American Progress and What to Do about It 96–120 (2018).

52 *Id.*

53 Ribstein, *supra* note 23, at 1463.

54 Karthik Ramanna, *Friedman at 50: Is It Still the Social Responsibility of Business to Increase Profits?* 62(3) Cal. Mgmt. Rev. 28, 29 (2020).

55 Rock, *supra* note 42, at 381 ("For example, Brealey, Myers, and Allen assume that, on the whole, managers manage the firm in the interests of shareholders and do so by investing in the highest net present value projects.").

56 Robert T. Miller, *How Would Directors Make Business Decisions under a Stakeholder Model?*, 18–19 (Feb. 18, 2022), https://papers.ssrn.com/sol3/papers.cfm?abstract_id=4032539.

57 Dodd, *supra* note 45 at 1158.

58 Margaret M. Blair & Lynn Stout, *A Team Production Theory of Corporate Law*, 85 Va. L. Rev. 247, 325 (1999) (emphasis in original).

59 Eugene F. Fama, *Contract Costs, Stakeholder Capitalism, and ESG* 5 (*Chicago Booth Paper* No. 20–46, 2020), http://ssrn.com/abstract=3722179 ("Since firms are not privy to the total ESG exposures of their consumers and investors, they are typically in the dark on how to move them toward max welfare, and max wealth is the appropriate decision rule.").

60 Ramanna, *supra* note 54, at 29 ("It is in the corporate DNA to engineer the rules in ways that increase their own profit.").

61 *See* Thomas Ferguson et al., *Industrial Structure and Party Competition in an Age of Hunger Games: Donald Trump and the 2016 Presidential Election* (Inst. for New Econ. Thinking, Working Paper No. 66, 2018).

62 Richard C. Schragger, *The Political Economy of City Power*, 44 Fordham Urb. L.J. 91, 95 (2017) ("Neither the nation-state nor the transnational corporation seem able to address the political alienation and economic instability felt by many citizens in the U.S. and elsewhere. This felt instability has given rise to both left-and right-wing populism, often tainted by xenophobia and nationalism. In the United States, Donald Trump's presidential victory is illustrative of the latter.").

63 Martha Minow, *Reforming School Reform*, 68 Fordham L. Rev. 257, 270 (1999) ("Education has dimensions of a public good, with crucial externalities affecting the entire population.").

64 *See* Paul H. Brietzke, *Democratization and Administrative Law*, 52 Okla. L. Rev. 1, 34 (1999).

65 *See* Bhagat & Hubbard, *supra* note 24 at 3.

66 *Id.*

67 Petrin, *supra* note 5, at 9.

68 Camden Hutchison, *Progressive Era Conceptions of the Corporation and the Failure of the Federal Chartering Movement*, 2017 Colum. Bus. L. Rev. 1017, 1035 (2017) (noting that "a common concern" among late nineteenth century populists "was protecting the public from concentrated economic power").).

69 Stephen B. Presser, *Thwarting the Killing of the Corporation: Limited Liability, Democracy, and Economics*, 87 Nw. U. L. Rev. 148, 155–56 (1992).

70 Martha T. McCluskey, *The Substantive Politics of Formal Corporate Power*, 53 Buff. L. Rev. 1453, 1479 (2006).

71 Lyle H. Lanier, *A Critique of the Philosophy of Progress*, in Twelve Southerners: I'll Take My Stand 122, 141 (La. State Univ. Press, reprt. 2006).

72 Frank Lawrence Owsley, *The Pillars of Agrarianism*, in The Southern Agrarians and the New Deal Essays After I'll Take My Stand 199, 202 (Emily S. Bingham & Thomas A. Underwood eds., 2001).

73 Peter Kolozi, Conservatives Against Capitalism: From the Industrial Revolution to Globalization 93 (2017).

74 Henry Clay Evans, Jr., *Liberty under the Old Deal*, in Who Owns America? A New Declaration of Independence 295 (Herbert Agar & Allen Tate eds., 1936) (discussing conditions of work in large corporations during the Depression).

75 Citizens United v. Fed. Election Comm'n., 558 U.S. 310 (2010).

76 Greg Coleridge, *The System Isn't Broken, It's Fixed: Ending Big Money and Corporations in Our Elections*, 44 U. Tol. L. Rev. 541, 557 (2013) (alteration in original).

77 *See* Ann Southworth, *Elements of the Support Structure for Campaign Finance Litigation in the Roberts Court*, 43 LAW & SOC. INQUIRY 319, 347 (2018) ("Advocates for business interests, such as the Chamber of Commerce, tend to be uncomfortable with the issue agendas of some of the social conservative and Tea-Party-affiliated groups, and vice versa.").

78 Sarah Smarsh, *Liberal Blind Spots Are Hiding the Truth about 'Trump Country,'* N.Y. TIMES, July 19, 2018, www.nytimes.com/2018/07/19/opinion/trump-corporations-white-working-class.html.

79 See Petrin, *supra* note 5, at 8.

80 *See id.* at 9 ("The existence of corporate power suggests that there should be responsibility for consequences that flow from the exercise of such power.").

81 *See* Jessica Love, Is Maximizing Shareholder Value a Thing of the Past?, KELLOGGINSIGHT .COM (Sept. 19, 2019), https://insight.kellogg.northwestern.edu/article/shareholder-value-purpose-corporation ("Young people, who are becoming these firms' new employees and customers, are paying attention to the environment and how companies are sourcing certain materials."); *see also* Sarah Landrum, *Millennials Driving Brands to Practice Socially Responsible Marketing*, FORBES (Mar. 17, 2017), www.forbes.com/sites/sarahlandrum/2017/03/17/millennials-driving-brands-to-practice-socially-responsible-marketing/#16beba3d4990 ("Millennials prefer to do business with corporations and brands with pro-social messages, sustainable manufacturing methods and ethical business standards."); *Why Millennials Choose CSR*, MORNINGFUTURE (Aug. 16, 2017), www .morningfuture.com/en/article/2017/08/16/millennials-csr-companies-responsible/60/ ("92.1% of those surveyed think that working for an environmentally and socially responsible company is important …. More than 50% of respondents are willing to give up 20% of their salary to work for a company that makes corporate social responsibility (CSR) efforts.").

82 Michal Barzuza et al., *The Millennial Corporation* (September 6, 2021), https://ssrn.com/abstract=3918443 or http://dx.doi.org/10.2139/ssrn.3918443.

83 *See* Monica Langley, *Salesforce's Marc Benioff Has Kicked Off New Era of Corporate Social Activism*, WALL ST. J. (May 2, 2016), www.wsj.com/articles/salesforces-marc-benioff-has-kicked-off-new-era-of-corporate-social-activism-1462201172 ("To attract promising young employees in many parts of America and to woo today's customers, the argument goes, companies must project a corporate ethos that goes beyond profit."); Richard Levick, *The New "Rules" of Corporate Social Activism*, FORBES (Dec. 18, 2019), www.forbes.com/sites/richardlevick/2019/12/18/the-new-rules-of-corporate-social-activism/#4265316651a9 ("Eight in ten consumers say they want their brands to have a social purpose; most Millennials expect it as a point-of-entry before they even consider a brand.").

84 Ribstein, *supra* note 23, at 1453.

85 As to Nike, see Jonathan Berr, *Nike Stock Price Reaches All-Time High after Colin Kaepernick Ad*, CBS NEWS (September 14, 2018), www.cbsnews.com/news/nike-stock-price-reaches-all-time-high-despite-colin-kaepernick-ad-boycott/ (concluding that the Kaepernick campaign "is resonating with the company's core customer base"). As to Walmart, see Levick, *supra* note 83 (arguing that "Walmart 'productized' its good citizenship").

86 TOM C.W. LIN, THE CAPITALIST AND THE ACTIVIST: CORPORATE SOCIAL RESPONSIBILITY AND THE NEW BUSINESS OF CHANGE 23–26 (2022).

87 EVAN OSBORNE, THE RISE OF THE ANTI-CORPORATE MOVEMENT: CORPORATIONS AND THE PEOPLE WHO HATE THEM 209 (2009).

88 Ribstein, *supra* note 23, at 1453.

89 Farhad Manjoo, *How Battling Brands Online Has Gained Urgency, and Impact*, N.Y. TIMES, June 22, 2017, at B7.

8   WAS THERE A BUSINESS CASE FOR THE BUSINESS ROUNDTABLE'S EMBRACE OF STAKEHOLDER CAPITALISM?

1 Katja Rost & Thomas Ehrmann, *Reporting Biases in Empirical Management Research: The Example of Win-Win Corporate Social Responsibility*, 56 Bus. & Soc. 840 ("The research field expects to find a positive association between corporate social performance (CSP) and corporate financial performance (CFP), and findings meet that expectation.").
2 Henry G. Manne & Henry Christopher Wallich, The Modern Corporation and Social Responsibility 1, 13 (1973).
3 *Id.* at 31.
4 Liliana Nicoleta Simionescu & Dalina Dumitrescu, *Empirical Study towards Corporate Social Responsibility Practices and Company Financial Performance*, 10 Sustainability 3141 (2018).
5 *See, e.g.*, Chris Doucouliagos, *Worker Participation and Productivity in Labor-Managed and Participatory Capitalist Firms: A Meta-Analysis*, 49 Ind. & Lab. Rel. Rev. 58, 63 (1995) (discussing problems with studies of worker participation).
6 Sanjai Bhagat & Robert Glenn Hubbard, *Should the Modern Corporation Maximize Shareholder Value?* 11 (March 3, 2020), https://ssrn.com/abstract=3548293.
7 *Id.*
8 Faisal Mahmood et al., *Corporate Social Responsibility and Firms' Financial Performance: A New Insight* (May 21, 2020), https://ssrn.com/abstract=3607558.
9 Robert T. Miller, *How Would Directors Make Business Decisions under a Stakeholder Model?* 2–3 n.7 (Feb. 18, 2022), https://papers.ssrn.com/sol3/papers.cfm?abstract_id=4032539.
10 Hao Liang & Luc Renneboog, *Corporate Social Responsibility and Sustainable Finance: A Review of the Literature* 14 (ECGI Finance Working Paper No. 701 2020), http://ssrn.com/abstract_id=3698631.
11 Davidson Heath et al., *Does Socially Responsible Investing Change Firm Behavior?* (ECGI Finance Working Paper No. 762 2021), https://ssrn.com/abstract=3837706.
12 David F. Larcker et al., *Seven Myths of ESG* 1 (Stanford Closer Look Series, Nov. 3, 2021).
13 *Id.* at 2. Some studies have looked at the effect of ESG activism such as investor engagement with management or the use of shareholder proposals. Activist campaigns have had success in improving the target companies' ratings on various ESG measures, but no increase in most measures of firm performance. Liang & Renneboog, *supra* 10, at 19–20.
14 Aneesh Raghunandan, & Shivaram Rajgopal, *Do ESG Funds Make Stakeholder-Friendly Investments?* (May 3, 2021), https://ssrn.com/abstract=3826357.
15 Amit Batish et al., *Sharing The Pain: How did Boards Adjust CEO Pay in Response to Covid-19?* (Stanford Closer Look Series, Sept. 1, 2020).
16 *Id.* at 5.
17 Lauren Cohen et al., *The ESG-Innovation Disconnect: Evidence from Green Patenting* (European Corporate Governance Institute – Finance Working Paper No. 744/2021, October 25, 2020).

9   WHY DID THE BUSINESS ROUNDTABLE CEOs SHIFT THEIR POSITION?

1 Stephen M. Bainbridge, *Director Primacy: The Means and Ends of Corporate Governance*, 97 Nw. U.L. Rev. 547, 575–76 (2003) (discussing those studies).
2 Business Roundtable, Principles of Corporate Governance 6 (2016).

3 NATIONAL ASSOCIATION OF CORPORATE DIRECTORS, THE REPORT OF THE NACD BLUE RIBBON COMMISSION FIT FOR THE FUTURE: AN URGENT IMPERATIVE FOR BOARD LEADERSHIP 9 (2019).

4 NATIONAL ASSOCIATION OF CORPORATE DIRECTORS, PUBLIC COMPANY GOVERNANCE SURVEY 5 (2019).

5 DILIGENT INSTITUTE, STAKEHOLDERS TAKE CENTER STAGE: DIRECTOR VIEWS ON PRIORITIES AND SOCIETY 4 (2019).

6 RANI DOYLE & STEPHEN KLEMASH, ERNST AND YOUNG GLOB. LTD., HOW LONG-TERM VALUE IS BEING REDEFINED AND COMMUNICATED 1–3 (2019); Martin Lipton et al., *Thoughts for Boards of Directors in 2020*, HARVARD LAW SCHOOL FORUM ON CORPORATE GOVERNANCE (Dec. 10, 2019), https://corpgov.law.harvard.edu/2019/12/10/thoughts-for-boards-of-directors-in-2020. Additionally, certain countries in the global corporate landscape have explicitly adopted this all-inclusive stakeholder-oriented view: notably the United Kingdom and South Africa. FINANCIAL REPORTING COUNCIL, THE UK CORPORATE GOVERNANCE CODE 4 (2018) (stating the first principle of a successful board leadership "is to promote the long-term sustainable success of the company, generating value for shareholders and contributing to wider society"); INSTITUTE OF DIRECTORS IN SOUTHERN AFRICA NPC, KING IV REPORT ON CORPORATE GOVERNANCE FOR SOUTH AFRICA 4–5 (2016).

7 Jeffrey M. Lipshaw, *The False Dichotomy of Corporate Governance Platitudes*, 46 J. CORP. L. 345, 377 (2021).

8 *Id.* at 383.

9 This schema is loosely based on a typology proposed by W.C. Bunting, *Against Corporate Activism: Examining the Use of Corporate Speech to Promote Corporate Social Responsibility* 6 (July 26, 2021), https://ssrn.com/abstract=3893628. For a defense of CEO social activism, see Don Mayer, *The Law and Ethics of CEO Social Activism*, 23 J. L. BUS. & ETHICS 21 (2017).

10 Jayne W. Barnard, *Corporate Philanthropy, Executives' Pet Charities and the Agency Problem*, 41 N.Y.L. SCH. L. REV. 1147, 1160−64 (1997).

11 Paul Constant, *The Scam of Reputation-Washing: How Corporations Successfully Cover Up Their Big-Money Messes with Small-Dollar Philanthropic Giving*, BUS. INSIDER (Oct. 2, 2019), www.businessinsider.com/corporations-successfully-cover-up-messes-with-philanthropic-giving-2019-10.

12 Bunting, *supra* note 9, at 15.

13 Jeffrey Sonnenfeld, *CEOs Lead America's New Great Awakening*, WALL ST. J., Apr. 15, 2021, www.wsj.com/articles/ceos-lead-americas-new-great-awakening-11618505076.

14 *Id.* at 43–44.

15 David F. Larcker et al., *The Double-Edged Sword of CEO Activism* 2 (*Stanford Closer Look Series*, 2018), https://ssrn.com/abstract=3283297.

16 Daniel Gross, *Jamie Dimon Steps in It*, SLATE (May 17, 2017), www.slate.com/articles/business/moneybox/2017/05/jamie_dimon_steps_in_it.html. *See also* R.R. Reno, *The Spirit of Democratic Capitalism*, FIRST THINGS, Oct. 2017, at 63, 65 ("Today, large-scale global companies scramble to position themselves as agents of social change.").

17 Robert T. Miller, *How Would Directors Make Business Decisions under a Stakeholder Model?* 20 (Feb. 18, 2022), https://papers.ssrn.com/sol3/papers.cfm?abstract_id=4032539.

18 Monica Langley, *Salesforce's Marc Benioff Has Kicked Off New Era of Corporate Social Activism*, WALL ST.J., May 2, 2016, www.wsj.com/articles/salesforces-marc-benioff-has-kicked-off-new-era-of-corporate-social-activism-1462201172.

19 Joshua Hochberg, *The Political Preferences of Activist CEOs*, 20(2) Pi Sigma Alpha Undergraduate J. Pol. 7 (2020).

20 Alma Cohen et al., *The Politics of CEOs*, 11 J. Leg. Anal. 1, 38–39 (2019).

21 Hochberg, *supra* note 19.

22 KKS Advisors & Test of Corporate Purpose, COVID-19 and Inequality: A Test of Corporate Purpose 6 (Sept. 2020). TCP offers car rental company Hertz Global Holdings as an especially egregious example. At the height of the pandemic, Hertz paid out over $16 million in retention bonuses to top executives while laying off thousands of employees. Hertz subsequently entered Chapter 11, shedding many more jobs. *Id.*

23 Lucian A. Bebchuk & Roberto Tallarita, *The Illusory Promise of Stakeholder Governance*, 106 Cornell L. Rev. 91, 156 (2020).

24 Lucian A. Bebchuk et al., *Stakeholder Capitalism in the Time of COVID* (February 9, 2022), https://ssrn.com/abstract=4026803 or http://dx.doi.org/10.2139/ssrn.4026803

25 *Id.* at 55.

26 *Id.*

27 Aneesh Raghunandan & Shiva Rajgopal, *Is There Real Virtue behind the Business Roundtable's Signaling?*, Wall St. J. (Dec. 2, 2019), www.wsj.com/articles/is-there-real-virtue-behind-the-business-roundtables-signaling-11575330172.

28 Aneesh Raghunandan & Shivara Rajgopal, *Do the Socially Responsible Walk the Talk?* 37 (May 24, 2020), https://ssrn.com/abstract=3609056.

29 Monica Langley, *Salesforce's Marc Benioff Has Kicked Off New Era of Corporate Social Activism*, Wall St. J. (May 2, 2016), www.wsj.com/articles/salesforces-marc-benioff-has-kicked-off-new-era-of-corporate-social-activism-1462201172.

30 Karthik Ramanna, *Friedman at 50: Is It Still the Social Responsibility of Business to Increase Profits?* 62(3) Cal. Mgmt. Rev. 28, 30 (2020).

31 Patrick Thomas et al., *New COVID-19 Layoffs Make Job Reductions Permanent*, Wall St. J., Aug. 28, 2020, www.wsj.com/articles/new-covid-19-layoffs-make-job-reductions-permanent-11598654257.

32 John D. Stoll, *How's the CEO 'Stakeholder Pledge' Working Out? Depends Who You Ask*, Wall St. J. (Aug. 28, 2020), www.wsj.com/articles/hows-the-ceo-stakeholder-pledge-working-out-depends-who-you-ask-11598632678.

33 Mayer, *supra* note 9, at 28 ("In short, offending employees and other stakeholders is, at times, an inevitable feature of doing business, especially in a globalized economy.").

34 *See* Tom C.W. Lin, *Incorporating Social Activism*, 98 B.U. L. Rev. 1535, 1586 (2018).

35 Editorial, *The Price of Woke Politics*, Wall St. J., May 20, 2021, at A16.

36 *CEO Activism in America Is Risky Business*, The Econ., Apr. 17, 2021, www.economist.com/business/2021/04/14/ceo-activism-in-america-is-risky-business.

37 Rita Panahi, Jordan Peterson on Corporate Virtue Signaling, HearldSun.com (Mar. 14, 2018), www.heraldsun.com.au/blogs/rita-panahi/jordan-peterson-on-corporate-virtue-signalling/news-story/ffa37e3615980f5f0641d4dcb6864c6b.

38 Daniel Arkin, *Uproar over Mike Pence's Memoir Highlights Growing Conflicts in Publishing, Experts Say*, NBCNews.com (Apr. 28, 2021), www.nbcnews.com/news/all/uproar-over-mike-pence-s-memoir-highlights-growing-conflicts-publishing-n1265701.

39 Archie B. Carroll, Business & Society: Managing Corporate Social Performance 41–42 (1981). *See also* David J. Vogel, *Is There a Market for Virtue?* 47 Cal. Mgmt. Rev. 19 (2005) ("Self-regulation can also reduce the likelihood of more government regulation or place a firm in a better competitive position if and when new regulations emerge").

40 *Id.* at 107–08.

41 David Benoit, *Move Over, Shareholders: Top CEOs Say Companies Have Obligations to Society*, Wall St. J. (Aug. 19, 2019), www.wsj.com/articles/business-roundtable-steps-back-from-milton-friedman-theory-11566205200.

42 Jessica Love, *Is Maximizing Shareholder Value a Thing of the Past?* KelloggInsight .com (Sep.19, 2019), https://insight.kellogg.northwestern.edu/article/shareholder-value-purpose-corporation ("Some of the CEOs' posturing here is to say, 'You don't have to change many of the laws. We are responsible people. We will do it ourselves.'").

43 Tunku Varadarajan, *Can This Man Put Wokeism Out of Business?*, Wall St. J., June 26, 2021, at A15.

44 *See* David Chan Smith, *How Milton Friedman Read His Adam Smith: The Liberal Suspicion of Business and the Critique of Corporate Social Responsibility* 21 (Aug. 15, 2020) ("The corporate leaders that Dodd and others cited in support of their ideas about social responsibility also led very large enterprises with monopolistic histories, including Irving Olds (U.S. Steel), Gerard Swope (General Electric), and Frank Abrams (Standard Oil of New Jersey)."), https://ssrn.com/abstract=3674604.

45 *Id.*

46 *Id.* at 32.

47 *Id.* at 25.

48 Mark J. Roe, *Corporate Purpose and Corporate Competition*, 99 Wash. U. L. Rev. 223 (2021).

49 *See* Jeffrey N. Gordon, *The Rise of Independent Directors in the United States, 1950–2005: Of Shareholder Value and Stock Market Prices*, 59 Stan. L. Rev. 1465, 1511 (2007) (describing the 1950s and 1960s as "the high-water mark of managerialism in U.S. corporate governance").

50 *See* David Skeel, Icarus in the Boardroom: The Fundamental Flaws in Corporate America and Where They Came From 108 (2005) ("The most prominent CEOs were more likely to be corporate bureaucrats than entrepreneurial geniuses.").

51 *See* Brian R. Cheffins, *The Corporate Governance Movement, Banks, and the Financial Crisis*, 16 Theoretical Inquiries L. 1, 15 (2015) (suggesting that "talented executives realized that investors responded favorably to companies with bold, charismatic CEOs").

52 Jay B. Kesten, *Managerial Entrenchment and Shareholder Wealth Revisited: Theory and Evidence from a Recessionary Financial Market*, 2010 B.Y.U. L. Rev. 1609, 1622 (2010) ("In his now famous manifesto, *Takeover Bids in the Target's Boardroom*, Martin Lipton asserted that the stakes were no less than the very fabric of the American economy.").

53 E. Norman Veasey, *Corporate Governance and Ethics in a Post Enron/WorldCom Environment*, 72 U. Cin. L. Rev. 731, 734 (2003) ("The board is boss. The CEO works for the board.").

54 *See* Peter B. Heller, *Involvement Overboard: An Evaluation of How and Why Corporate Boards Have Become Increasingly Active and the Problems the Activity Presents*, 41 Colum. J.L. & Soc. Probs. 53, 66 (2007) ("Frequently, boards are taking a more active role in questioning management's proposals."); Patricia G. Butler, *Board Committees and Avoiding Director Liability under Sarbanes-Oxley*, 51 Prac. Law. 27 (December 2005) ("With the increased responsibility arising from the Sarbanes-Oxley Act, corporate directors have to take an active role in compliance and supervision.").

55 *See* James D. Cox & Randall S. Thomas, *Corporate Darwinism: Disciplining Managers in a World with Weak Shareholder Litigation*, 95 N.C. L. Rev. 19, 62 (2016) ("Hedge funds are constantly on the lookout for undervalued target firms.").

56 *See generally* Marcel Kahan & Edward Rock, *Embattled CEOs*, 88 Tex. L. Rev. 987, 989 (2010) ("The CEOs of publicly held corporations in the United States are losing power.").

57 Lucian A. Bebchuk & Roberto Tallarita, *The Illusory Promise of Stakeholder Governance*, 106 Cornell L. Rev. 91, 165 (2020).

58 Robert G. Eccles, *Is Stakeholder Capitalism Real Or Not?: The Natural Experiment Of COVID-19*, Forbes.com (Feb. 25, 2022), www.forbes.com/sites/bobeccles/2022/02/25/is-stakeholder-capitalism-real-or-not-the-natural-experiment-of-covid-19/.

59 Martin L. Lipton et al., *The New Paradigm: A Roadmap For an Implicit Corporate Governance Partnership between Corporations and Investors to Achieve Sustainable Long-Term Investment and Growth* 1 (Sept. 2, 2016), www.wlrk.com/webdocs/wlrknew/AttorneyPubs/WLRK.25960.16.pdf. Admittedly, this is not a new position on Lipton's part. In 1991, for example, he argued that corporate law "places stockholder wishes [and] stockholder profit … on an undeserved pedestal." Martin Lipton & Steven A. Rosenblum, *A New System of Corporate Governance: The Quinquennial Election of Directors*, 58 U. Chi. L. Rev. 187, 253 (1991).

60 Martin Lipton et al., *Wachtell Lipton Discusses Stakeholder Governance and the Fiduciary Duties of Directors*, The CLS Blue Sky Blog (Sept. 3, 2019), https://clsbluesky.law.columbia.edu/2019/09/03/wachtell-lipton-discusses-stakeholder-governance-and-the-fiduciary-duties-of-directors/.

61 *See Battling for Corporate America*, Economist, Mar. 11, 2006, at 69 ("Martin Lipton, a veteran Wall Street lawyer, [complained] that 'we have gone from the imperial CEO to the imperial stockholder.'").

62 Bebchuk & Tallarita, *supra* note 24, at 50.

63 Michael Novak, The Fire of Invention: Civil Society and the Future of the Corporation 26 (1997).

64 *Id.*

65 *See id.* at 116.

66 *See id.*

67 Gerald F. Davis, *Corporate Purpose Needs Democracy*, 58 J. Mgmt. Stud. 902, 908 (2021) (citation omitted).

68 *See* Bebchuk & Tallarita, *supra* note 57, at 148 (noting that "more than 60% of the average CEO pay in large corporations is directly linked to shareholder value and provides strong incentives to enhance it").

69 Lucian A. Bebchuk & Roberto Tallarita, The Perils and Questionable Promise of ESG-Based Compensation (Mar. 1, 2022), https://papers.ssrn.com/sol3/papers.cfm?abstract_id=4048003.

70 *Id.* at 31.

71 David I. Walker, *The Economic (In) Significance of Executive Pay ESG Incentives* (February 14, 2022), https://ssrn.com/abstract=4034877.

72 Edward E. Lawler III, Pay and Organizational Effectiveness: A Psychological View 62 (1971) (stating that "pay can be and usually is important enough to motivate most kinds of job behavior"); Herbert H. Meyer, *The Pay-for-Performance Dilemma*, 4 Organizational Dynamics 39 (1975) (explaining that for a majority of people pay is a powerful incentive). Having said that, however, "monetary compensation probably serves less as a direct incentive than as a status counter for top CEOs." Stephen M. Bainbridge, *Executive Compensation; Who Decides?*, 83 Tex. L. Rev. 1615, 1633 (2005).

73 Jay C. Hartzell et al., *Is a Higher Calling Enough? Incentive Compensation in the Church*, 28 J. Lab. Econ. 509 (2010).

74 Bebchuk & Tallarita, *supra* note 57, at 153.

75 *Id.* at 98.

76 Aneesh Raghunandan & Shiva Rajgopal, *Is There Real Virtue behind the Business Roundtable's Signaling?* WALL ST. J., Dec. 2, 2019, www.wsj.com/articles/is-there-real-virtue-behind-the-business-roundtables-signaling-11575330172.

77 *Id.* Professors Raghunandan and Rajgopal provide more detailed evidence in a May 2020 paper. *See* Aneesh Raghunandan & Shivara Rajgopal, *Do the Socially Responsible Walk the Talk?* 37 (May 24, 2020), https://ssrn.com/abstract=3609056 ("We find that Business Roundtable signatories exhibit worse records with respect to labor and the environment than their peers.... Finally, we find no evidence that firms' fundamental records with respect to "E" and "S" predict their inclusion in key mutual funds that purport to be ESG-oriented.").

78 Jeffrey Useem, *Beware of Corporate Promises*, THE ATLANTIC, Aug. 6, 2020, www.theatlantic.com/ideas/archive/2020/08/companies-stand-solidarity-are-licensing-themselves-discriminate/614947/.

79 Nell Minow, *Six Reasons We Don't Trust the New "Stakeholder" Promise from the Business Roundtable*, HARV. L. SCH. FORUM ON CORP. GOV., Sept. 2, 2019, https://corpgov.law.harvard.edu/2019/09/02/six-reasons-we-dont-trust-the-new-stakeholder-promise-from-the-business-roundtable/.

80 Bebchuk & Tallarita, *supra* note 57, at 98.

81 *Id.*

82 *Id.* at 135.

83 Jeffrey M. Lipshaw, *The False Dichotomy of Corporate Governance Platitudes*, 46 J. CORP. L. 345, 351 (2021).

84 *Id.* at 353.

85 *Id.* at 351 n.25.

86 Eccles, *supra* note 58.

10 WHY THE BUSINESS ROUNDTABLE CEOs SHOULD HAVE STAYED THE COURSE

1 Beaston v. Farmers' Bank of Delaware, 37 U.S. 102, 113 (1838).

2 MODEL BUS. CORP. ACT § 3.02 (2016).

3 *See* Herbert Hovenkamp, *The Classical Corporation in American Legal Thought*, 76 GEO. L.J. 1593, 1641 (1988) (noting that the corporation by the end of the nineteenth Century was "a creation of the law yet so much a 'person' that it even had constitutional rights").

4 Penn-Yale Corp. v. C.I.R., 7 B.T.A. 1228, 1229 (B.T.A. 1927).

5 *See* Toni M. Massaro, *Foreign Nationals, Electoral Spending, and the First Amendment*, 34 HARV. J.L. & PUB. POLICY 663, 673 (2011) (arguing that the Supreme Court's *Citizens United* decision rested on a premise "that a corporation is a 'real entity,' distinct from its owners and the sovereign that gives it life"); *see, e.g.*, Carliss N. Chatman, *The Corporate Personhood Two-Step*, 18 NEV. L.J. 811, 855 (2018) ("The corporation is a real entity, and, like a natural person, it is not born with all rights."); Don Mayer, *Community, Business Ethics, and Global Capitalism*, 38 AM. BUS. L.J. 215, 222–23 (2001) (stating that "the corporation is a 'real entity,' but it is difficult to locate its moral center"); Michael B. Metzger & Dan B. Dalton, *Seeing the Elephant: An Organizational Perspective on Corporate Moral Agency*, 33 AM. BUS. L.J. 489, 554–55 (1996) (suggesting that most models of the firm popular within organizational theory support the view that the corporation is a real entity).

6 Milton Friedman, The Social Responsibility of Business is to Increase its Profits, N.Y. TIMES, Sept. 13, 1970, § 6 (mag.) at 32.

7 Melvin A. Eisenberg, *The Conception that the Corporation is a Nexus of Contracts, and the Dual Nature of the Firm*, 24 J. CORP. L. 819, 825 (1999).

8 Friedman, *supra* note 6 ("In a free-enterprise, private-property system, a corporate executive is an employe [sic] of the owners of the business."). This view continues to appear in the literature. Professor Julian Velasco, for example, has offered a vigorous defense – on both normative and doctrinal grounds – of shareholder ownership of the corporation. *See* Julian Velasco, *Shareholder Ownership and Primacy*, 2010 U. ILL. L. REV. 897, 928–39 (setting out "affirmative case for shareholder ownership"). In turn, he contends that because "shareholders own the corporation, the end and means of corporate governance must be shareholder primacy." *Id.* at 948.

9 *See* WILLIAM A. KLEIN & JOHN C. COFFEE, JR., BUSINESS ORGANIZATION AND FINANCE: LEGAL AND ECONOMIC PRINCIPLES 117–18 (9th ed. 2004) (critiquing reification of the corporation); Mitu Gulati et al., *Connected Contracts*, 47 UCLA L. REV. 887, 891 (2000) (arguing that "it is dangerous to ignore the reality that firms transact only through individuals").

10 The actual quote reportedly was "corporations have neither bodies to be punished, nor souls to be condemned, they therefore do as they like." ANDREW L. FRIEDMAN & SAMANTHA MILES, STAKEHOLDERS THEORY AND PRACTICE 20 (2006).

11 *See, e.g.*, Frank H. Easterbrook & Daniel R. Fischel, *The Corporate Contract*, 89 COLUM. L. REV. 1416, 1418 (1989) ("The corporation is a complex set of explicit and implicit contracts, and corporate law enables the participants to select the optimal arrangement for the many different sets of risks and opportunities that are available in a large economy."); *see generally* Stephen M. Bainbridge, *The Board of Directors as Nexus of Contracts*, 88 IOWA L. REV. 1, 9 (2002) ("The dominant model of the corporation in legal scholarship is the so-called nexus of contracts theory."). In that article, I argued that it is conceptually more accurate to say that the corporation has a nexus of contracts – i.e., the board of directors – but that is a nuance that need not concern us here. *See id.* at 17–24.

12 William T. Allen, *Contracts and Communities in Corporation Law*, 50 WASH. & LEE L. REV. 1395, 1401 (1993). *See also Id.* at 1400 (noting that the nexus of contracts model is now the "dominant legal academic view"); Central States, S.E. and S.W. Areas Pension Fund v. Sherwin-Williams Co., 71 F.3d 1338, 1341 (7th Cir. 1995) ("A corporation is just a nexus of contracts, subject to rearrangement in many ways."); New Orleans Opera Ass'n, Inc. v. S. Regl. Opera Endowment Fund, 993 So. 2d 791, 798 (La. App. 4th Cir. 2008) ("A corporation is in law a contractual creature, a nexus of contracts."; internal quotation marks omitted), writ denied, 996 So. 2d 1114 (La. 2008); E. Norman Veasey, *An Economic Rationale for Judicial Decisionmaking in Corporate Law*, 53 BUS. LAW. 681 (1998) ("Although the contract analogy is imperfect, it comes reasonably close to a working hypothesis.").

13 *See* Margaret M. Blair, Corporate Law and the Team Production Problem, in RESEARCH HANDBOOK ON THE ECONOMICS OF CORPORATE LAW 33, 34 (Claire A. Hill & Brett H. McDonnell eds., 2012) (explaining that contractarianism "dominated corporate law and economics scholarship in the 1980s and 1990s, and continues to be influential today"); Matthew T. Bodie, Employees and the Boundaries of the Corporation, in RESEARCH HANDBOOK ON THE ECONOMICS OF CORPORATE LAW 85, 85 (Claire A. Hill & Brett H. McDonnell eds., 2012) (arguing that the "nexus of contracts" approach "remains foundational in the field"); GRANT M. HAYDEN & MATTHEW T. BODIE, RECONSTRUCTING THE CORPORATION: FROM SHAREHOLDER PRIMACY TO SHARED GOVERNANCE 50–67 (2020) (offering multiple criticisms of contractarianism).

14 W. Clay Jackson Enterprises, Inc. v. Greyhound Leasing and Financial Corp., 463 F. Supp. 666, 670 (D. P.R. 1979).

15 Manson v. Curtis, 119 N.E. 559, 562 (N.Y. 1918).

16 *See* Stephen M. Bainbridge, *Director Primacy: The Means and Ends of Corporate Governance*, 97 Nw. U. L. Rev. 547, 565 (2003) (arguing contractarian model allows one to throw "Friedman's concept of ownership out the window, along with its associated economic and ethical baggage"); Eugene F. Fama, *Agency Problems and the Theory of the Firm*, 88 J. Pol. Econ. 288, 289 (1980) (explaining corporations do not have "owners in any meaningful sense").

17 Del Code Ann., tit. 8, § 281 ("Any remaining assets shall be distributed to the stockholders of the dissolved corporation.").

18 Del Code Ann., tit. 8, § 170.

19 *See* Citizens United v. Fed. Election Commn., 558 U.S. 310, 475 (2010) (Stevens, J., concurring in part) ("When corporations use general treasury funds to praise or attack a particular candidate for office, it is the shareholders, as the residual claimants, who are effectively footing the bill."); Eliasen v. Itel Corp., 82 F.3d 731, 733 (7th Cir. 1996) ("Ordinarily, when a corporation is sold, the proceeds above what is needed to pay off creditors, including bondholders – including therefore debenture holders – go to the shareholders, as the residual claimants to the corporation's assets."). Note that "ownership of the residual claim is not the same as ownership of the firm itself. Ownership of the residual claim, for example, does not entitle the shareholders to trespass on corporation property." Bainbridge, *supra* note 16, at 565.

20 *See, e.g.,* Frank H. Easterbrook & Daniel R. Fischel, The Economic Structure of Corporate Law 36–37 (1991); *see generally* Brian R. Cheffins, *Stop Blaming Milton Friedman!*, 98 Wash. U. L. Rev. 1607, 1638 (2021) ("A further point advocates of shareholder primacy have made to justify a strong managerial focus on shareholder returns is that everyone associated with a corporation should be doing well if the shareholders are."); Kelli A. Alces, *Balance and Team Production*, 38 Seattle U.L. Rev. 187, 194 (2015) ("Maximizing the value of the residual claim, they argue, will maximize the value of the corporation, and that rising tide of corporate profits will raise all ships, from shareholders to directors.").

21 John Micklethwait & Adrian Wooldridge, The Company: A Short History of a Revolutionary Idea xv (2005).

22 *Id.* at 190.

23 Lynn A. Stout, *Bad and Not-So-Bad Arguments for Shareholder Primacy*, 75 S. Cal. L. Rev. 1189, 1193–94 (2002). Note that "ownership of the residual claim is not the same as ownership of the firm itself. Ownership of the residual claim, for example, does not entitle the shareholders to trespass on corporation property." Bainbridge, *supra* note 16, at 565.

24 Margaret M. Blair & Lynn A. Stout, *Specific Investment: Explaining Anomalies in Corporate Law*, 31 J. Corp. L. 719, 728 (2006).

25 Stout, *supra* note 23, at 1194–95. *See also* Amir N. Licht, *The Maximands of Corporate Governance: A Theory of Values and Cognitive Style*, 29 Del. J. Corp. L. 649, 652 (2004) (arguing that "the corporate enterprise comprises several constituencies whose interests are both interdependent and indeterminate").

26 Jonathan R. Macey, *A Close Read of an Excellent Commentary on* Dodge v. Ford, 3 Va. L. & Bus. Rev. 177, 186 (2008).

27 Micklethwait & Wooldridge, *supra* note 21, at 189–90.

28 Portions of this section were adapted from the first and ninth chapters of my book, Stephen M. Bainbridge, Corporation Law and Economics (2002).

29 For an argument that Berle gets too much credit, see Stephen M. Bainbridge, *The Politics of Corporate Governance*, 18 Harv. J.L. & Pub. Policy 671, 683 n.54 (1995).

30 Adolf A. Berle, Jr. and Gardiner C. Means, The Modern Corporation and Private Property (1932). A number of scholars have discussed the role that the separation of ownership and control played in the Berle–Dodd debate. *See, e.g.*, William W. Bratton & Michael L. Wachter, *Shareholder Primacy's Corporatist Origins: Adolf Berle and the Modern Corporation*, 34 J. Corp. L. 99, 124–33 (2008); Christopher M. Bruner, *The Enduring Ambivalence of Corporate Law*, 59 Ala. L. Rev. 1385, 1392–94 (2008); Ronald Chen & Jon Hanson, *The Illusion of Law: The Legitimating Schemas of Modern Policy and Corporate Law*, 103 Mich. L. Rev. 1, 35 (2004).

31 Directors are not agents of the shareholders in a legal sense. *See* Restatement (Third) of Agency § 1.01 cmt. f(2) at 29 (2006) (stating "directors are neither the shareholders' nor the corporation's agents"). Nevertheless, their relationship creates a classic example of what economists refer to as the principal–agent problem. *See* Andrei Shleifer & Robert W. Vishny, *A Survey of Corporate Governance*, 52 J. Fin. 737, 740 (1997) (arguing principal–agent problem inherent in relationship between directors and shareholders is central problem of corporate governance).

32 Eric W. Orts, *Shirking and Sharking: A Legal Theory of the Firm*, 16 Yale L. & Policy Rev. 265, 276 (1998).

33 *See* Lyman P.Q. Johnson & David Millon, *Recalling Why Corporate Officers Are Fiduciaries*, 46 Wm. & Mary L. Rev. 1597, 1623 (2005) ("Drawing on the insights of financial economists who conceive the business firm as a nexus of contracts, many corporate law scholars recast the core accountability concern in corporate governance into a principal–agent 'agency costs' issue.").

34 *See* Leo E. Strine, Jr., *Why Excessive Risk-Taking Is Not Unexpected*, N.Y. Times Dealbook (Oct. 5, 2009, 1:30 pm), http://dealbook.nytimes.com//2009/10/05/dealbook-dialogue-leo-strine/ ("Ideally, we want a system where corporate boards are highly accountable and responsive to their stockholders for the generation of sustainable profits."); *see also* William T. Allen et al., *The Great Takeover Debate: A Meditation on Bridging the Conceptual Divide*, 69 U. Chi. L. Rev. 1067, 1100 (2002) (explaining "the system we advocate should make corporate directors more accountable to the stockholders").

35 Richard J. Shinder, *The Business Roundtable's Recipe for Confusion*, Wall St. J., Sept. 17, 2019, www.wsj.com/articles/the-business-roundtables-recipe-for-confusion-11568760132. *See* Larry E. Ribstein, *Accountability and Responsibility in Corporate Governance*, 81 Notre Dame L. Rev. 1431, 1464 (2006) (arguing that "shareholder wealth maximization provides a familiar metric by which the success or failure of these decisions can be tested").

36 I believe Australian lawyer and blogger Peter Tunjic was the first person to refer to this as "the Bainbridge Hypothetical." Peter Tunjic, *Revisiting the Bainbridge Hypothetical: Corporate Purpose in Australia*, On Directorship (May 12, 2017), https://ondirectorship.com/ondirectorship/4ttslzs85gw4cwe78khn92kp295s2w [https://perma.cc/332Q-7FDK].

37 Micklethwait & Wooldridge, *supra* note 21, at 189–90.

38 Milton Friedman, *The Social Responsibility of Business Is to Increase Its Profits*, N.Y. Times, Sept. 13, 1970, § 6 (Magazine), at 32.

39 Michael C. Jensen, *Value Maximization, Stakeholder Theory, and the Corporate Objective Function*, J. App. Corp. Fin., Fall 2001, at 8, 16.

40 Eugene F. Fama, *Market Forces Already Address ESG Issues and the Issues Raised by Stakeholder Capitalism*, ProMarket.Org (Sept. 25, 2020), https://promarket.org/2020/09/25/market-forces-esg-issues-stakeholder-capitalism-contracts/. For an excellent argument that legal rules promoting corporate social responsibility have limited effect because "the existence of powerful product markets, capital markets, and managerial

labor markets restricts the options" available to corporate decision makers, see D. Gordon Smith, *Response: The Dystopian Potential of Corporate Law*, 57 EMORY L.J. 985, 989 (2008). Conversely, however, some commentators argue "that there are numerous market mechanisms that reduce the apparent divergence between managing for shareholders and managing for society." Larry E. Ribstein, *Accountability and Responsibility in Corporate Governance*, 81 NOTRE DAME L. REV. 1431, 1459 (2006). Larry Ribstein developed this argument at length, examining market forces he claimed incentivized even firms committed to shareholder value maximization to take measures to protect the long-term interests of stakeholders. He individually examined the way market forces would impact creditors, employees, consumers, suppliers, and local communities. *Id.* at 1442–60. He acknowledged that market forces are imperfect, but suggested that those imperfections "may not be sufficient to justify the significant risk of opportunism to shareholders entailed in making managers accountable to stakeholders." *Id.* at 1460.

41 Fama, *supra* note 40.

42 Jensen, *supra* note 39, at 10–11.

43 David Fleming, *False Consistency*, LEANLOGIC.COM, https://leanlogic.online/glossary/false-consistency/.

44 Thomas W. Dunfee, *Corporate Governance in A Market with Morality*, 62 L. & CONTEMP. PROBS. 129, 138 (Summer 1999). This is why Michael Jensen's concept of enlightened value maximization (a.k.a., enlightened stakeholder theory) does not work. According to Jensen, although enlightened value maximization focuses management's "attention on meeting the demands of all important corporate constituencies," it "specifies long-term value maximization as the firm's objective." Jensen, *supra* note 39, at 9. In zero sum cases, however, it is not possible to do both.

45 Lucian A. Bebchuk & Roberto Tallarita, *The Illusory Promise of Stakeholder Governance*, 106 CORNELL L. REV. 91, 120 (2020).

46 *Id. See also* James O'Toole & David Vogel, Two and a Half Cheers for Conscious Capitalism, CAL. MGMT. REV., May 2011, at 60, 67 ("Without doubt, there are some – even many – business decisions that benefit multiple stakeholders .... Nonetheless, it strains credulity to believe that all business decisions fall into this category. At publicly traded corporations, in particular, meeting investor expectations is critical, and mangers have no choice but to put the interests of shareholders first.").

47 Robert T. Miller, *How Would Directors Make Business Decisions Under A Stakeholder Model?*, 77 BUS. LAW. 773, 777 (2022).

48 *Id. See also* Lee A. Tavis, *Modern Contract Theory and the Purpose of the Firm, in* RETHINKING THE PURPOSE OF BUSINESS: INTERDISCIPLINARY ESSAYS FROM THE CATHOLIC SOCIAL TRADITION 215, 221 (S. A. Cortright and Michael J. Naughton eds., 2002) (arguing that stakeholder theory does not provide "the kind of systemic, prescriptive, prioritizing guidance that is so crisply present in shareholder wealth-maximization theory").

49 Lucian A. Bebchuk & Roberto Tallarita, *The Perils and Questionable Promise of ESG-Based Compensation* 17 (Mar. 1, 2022), https://papers.ssrn.com/sol3/papers.cfm?abstract_id=4048003.

50 Larry E. Ribstein, *Accountability and Responsibility in Corporate Governance*, 81 NOTRE DAME L. REV. 1431, 1464 (2006).

51 Fama, *supra* note 40.

52 Bebchuk & Tallarita, *supra* note 49, at 18–20.

53 *Id.* at 25.

54 *Id.* at 26.

55 Professor Jeff Lipshaw has argued that "[t]he Bainbridge Hypothetical is the corporate equivalent of the famous ethical trolley problem and its variants, the basic one involving an uncontrolled trolley rolling down the tracks toward a junction and the protagonist having to decide whether to pull a switch that would cause only one and not six people to die ...." Jeffrey M. Lipshaw, *The False Dichotomy of Corporate Governance Platitudes*, 46 J. CORP. L. 345, 349 (2021). I defended the Bainbridge Hypothetical as a useful thought experiment elsewhere. *See* Stephen M. Bainbridge, *Making Sense of the Business Roundtable's Reversal on Corporate Purpose*, 46 J. CORP. L. 285, 301–310 (2021).

56 *See* ROBERT C. CLARK, CORPORATE LAW 20 (1986); Andrew Keay, *Stakeholder Theory in Corporate Law: Has It Got What It Takes?*, 9 RICH. J. GLOBAL L. & BUS. 249, 270 (2010). ("The point has been made that stakeholder theory has failed to provide any normative foundations for its justification. In particular, it fails to provide a normative base on which to ascertain who can be a stakeholder and what weight ought to be given to each stakeholder. Consequently, there is no basis for a manager, in running the corporation, to prefer stakeholderism to other moral approaches."). Professor Miller observes "that, in providing that the board should consider the interests of each of various constituencies, the stakeholder model says no more than that, in distributing value among certain possible recipients, the board should consider giving at least some value to each of the various possible recipients; it says nothing about how much any particular recipient should receive in any particular circumstances or when one recipient ought to receive less in order that another may receive more." Miller, *supra* note 47, at 784.

57 John P. Frank, *The Legal Ethics of Louis D. Brandeis*, 17 STAN. L. REV. 683, 708 (1965).

58 1 GEOFFREY C. HAZARD, JR. & W. WILLIAM HODES, THE LAW OF LAWYERING § 2.2:103, at 513 (2d ed. 1990 & Supp. 1993).

59 *See* David Hess, *Social Reporting: A Reflexive Law Approach to Corporate Social Responsiveness*, 25 J. CORP. L. 41, 60 (1999) (arguing when "management [becomes] accountable to everyone, they may become accountable to no one").

60 Hester Peirce, *We Are Not the Securities and Environment Commission – At Least Not Yet*, SEC.GOV (Mar. 21, 2022), www.sec.gov/news/statement/peirce-climate-disclosure-20220321.

61 Ryan Flugum & Matthew E. Souther, *Is Stakeholder Value an Excuse for Underperfoming Managers?*, THE CLS BLUE SKY BLOG (Nov. 25, 2020), https://clsbluesky.law.columbia.edu/2020/11/25/is-stakeholder-value-an-excuse-for-underperfoming-managers/.

62 *Id.*

63 Bainbridge, *supra* note 16, at 604.

64 Jitendra Aswani et al., *The Cost (and Unbenefit) of Conscious Capitalism* (Sep. 16, 2021), https://papers.ssrn.com/sol3/papers.cfm?abstract_id=3926335.

65 E. Merrick Dodd, Jr., *For Whom Are Corporate Managers Trustees?*, 45 HARV. L. REV. 1145, 1157 (1932).

66 Jeffrey J. Hass, *Directional Fiduciary Duties in A Tracking Stock Equity Structure: The Need for A Duty of Fairness*, 94 MICH. L. REV. 2089, 2177 n.140 (1996).

67 City Capital Assoc. v. Interco Inc., 551 A.2d 787, 796 (Del. Ch.) (emphasis deleted), *appeal dismissed*, 556 A.2d 1070 (Del. 1988).

68 Bebchuk & Tallarita, *supra* note 49, at 32.

69 A. A. Berle, Jr., *For Whom Corporate Managers Are Trustees: A Note*, 45 HARV. L. REV. 1365, 1367 (1932).

70 Eugene F. Fama, *Contract Costs, Stakeholder Capitalism, and ESG* 2 (*Chicago Booth Paper No. 20–46*, 2020), http://ssrn.com/abstract=3722179.

71 Bebchuk & Tallarita, *supra* note 49, at 35–36.

72 Sanjai Bhagat & Robert Glenn Hubbard, *Should the Modern Corporation Maximize Shareholder Value?* 6 (March 3, 2020), https://ssrn.com/abstract=3548293

73 *See generally* Thomas P. Lyon & John W. Maxwell, *Greenwash: Corporate Environmental Disclosure under Threat of Audit,* 20 J. ECON. & MGMT. STRATEGY 3 (2011).

74 Victor Brudney, *Contract and Fiduciary Duty in Corporate Law,* 38 B.C. L. REV. 595, 645 (1997).

75 Amir N. Licht, *Varieties of Shareholderism: Three Views of the Corporate Purpose Cathedral* 29 (*ECGI Law Working Paper No. 547/2020,* October 2020).

76 RALPH K. WINTER, GOVERNMENT AND THE CORPORATION 51 (1978).

77 *Id.* Judge Winter also critiqued proposals to give affected constituencies a vote on corporate actions, concluding that such a system would be unworkable. *See id.* at 52–53.

78 For a provocative recent argument in favor of a codetermination-like system in the U.S., see GRANT M. HAYDEN & MATHHEW T. BODIE, RECONSTRUCTING THE CORPORATION: FROM SHAREHOLDER PRIMACY TO SHARED GOVERNANCE (2020). Although my critical assessments of codetermination admittedly are now somewhat dated, I have drawn on them in portions of this section. *See* Stephen M. Bainbridge, *Privately Ordered Participatory Management: An Organizational Failures Analysis,* 23 DEL. J. CORP. L. 979 (1998); Stephen M. Bainbridge, *Corporate Decisionmaking and the Moral Rights of Employees: Participatory Management and Natural Law,* 43 VILL. L. REV. 741 (1998); Stephen M. Bainbridge, *Participatory Management Within A Theory of the Firm,* 21 J. CORP. L. 657 (1996).

79 Jens Dammann & Horst Eidenmüller, *Codetermination: A Poor Fit for U.S. Corporations,* 2020 COLUM. BUS. L. REV. 870.

80 *See generally* Bainbridge, *supra* note 77, at 784–828.

81 Dammann & Eidenmüller, *supra* note 79, at 876.

82 *Id.* at 100.

83 *Id.* at 910.

84 Michael P. Dooley, *European Proposals for Worker Information and Codetermination: An American Comment, in* HARMONIZATION OF THE LAWS IN THE EUROPEAN COMMUNITIES: PRODUCTS LIABILITY, CONFLICT OF LAWS, AND CORPORATION LAW 126, 129 (Peter E. Herzog ed. 1983).

85 Bainbridge, *Privately Ordered, supra* note 77, at 1066–67 (summarizing the studies).

86 *Id.* at 1066.

87 MARK J. ROE, STRONG MANAGERS, WEAK OWNERS: THE POLITICAL ROOTS OF AMERICAN CORPORATE FINANCE 44 (1994).

88 *Id.* at 214.

89 *Id.*

90 Mirella Damianki, *Shareholder Rights and Stakeholder Rights in Corporate Governance, in* A HANDBOOK OF CORPORATE GOVERNANCE AND SOCIAL RESPONSIBILITY 171, 178 (Güler Aras & David Crowther eds., 2020).

91 Mary O'Sullivan, *Variety and Change in the Role of Employees in Corporate Governance,* 22 COMP. LAB. L. & POLICY J. 179, 190 (2000).

92 *Board Level Representation,* WORKER-PARTICIPATION.EU (2021), www.worker-participation.eu/National-Industrial-Relations/Countries/Germany/Board-level-Representation.

93 Simon Jäger et al., *What Does Codetermination Do?* (NBER Working Paper 289921, Oct. 2021).

94 *Id.*

95 *Id.* at 22.

96 See, e.g., Martin Gelter, *The Dark Side of Shareholder Influence: Managerial Autonomy and Stakeholder Orientation in Comparative Corporate Governance*, 50 HARV. INTL. L.J. 129, 134 (2009) (discussing "legal strategies responding to shareholder influence, focusing on employees, who are the most important stakeholder group"); Brett H. McDonnell, *Shareholder Bylaws, Shareholder Nominations, and Poison Pills*, 3 BERKELEY BUS. L.J. 205, 248 (2005) ("The most important stakeholder group other than shareholders and managers is employees, with creditors also of some importance.").

97 See, e.g., Issachar Rosen-Zvi, *You Are Too Soft!: What Can Corporate Social Responsibility Do for Climate Change?*, 12 MINN. J.L. SCI. & TECH. 527, 542 (2011) ("The high visibility of climate change in both public discourse and the media, and the enormous social and political attention it receives, has resulted in the emergence of climate change as 'one of the most important and urgent corporate responsibility issues.'").

98 K.J. Martijn Cremers et al., *Commitment and Entrenchment in Corporate Governance*, 110 NW. U.L. REV. 727, 782 (2016).

99 See, e.g., R. Edward Freeman & John McVea, *A Stakeholder Approach to Strategic Management*, in THE BLACKWELL HANDBOOK OF STRATEGIC MANAGEMENT 189 (Michael A. Hitt et al. 2001) (explaining that for advocates of stakeholder capitalism "the very idea of maximizing a single-objective function as a useful way of thinking about management strategy. Rather, [they posit,] stakeholder management is a never ending task of balancing and integrating multiple relationships and multiple objectives.").

100 See, e.g., Marleen A. O'Connor, *The Human Capital Era: Reconceptualizing Corporate Law to Facilitate Labor-Management Cooperation*, 78 CORNELL L. REV. 899, 954 (1993).

101 Margaret M. Blair & Lynn A. Stout, *Director Accountability and the Mediating Role of the Corporate Board*, 79 WASH. U.L.Q. 403 (2001); Margaret M. Blair & Lynn A. Stout, *A Team Production Theory of Corporate Law*, 85 VA. L. REV. 247 (1999); Margaret M. Blair & Lynn A. Stout, *Team Production in Business Organizations: An Introduction*, 24 J. CORP. L. 743 (1999). Portions of this section were adapted from my article Stephen M. Bainbridge, *Director Primacy: The Means and Ends of Corporate Governance*, 97 NW. U.L. REV. 547 (2003).

102 Blair & Stout, *A Team Production Theory*, *supra* note 101, at 290 (emphasis in original).

103 *Id.* at 280 (emphasis removed). The mediating hierarch model resembles Lynne Dallas' theory of the relational board, which "assist[s] the corporation in forging relationships with various stakeholders and others in its social environment." Lynne L. Dallas, *The Relational Board: Three Theories of Corporate Boards of Directors*, 22 J. CORP. L. 1, 3 (1996). It also resembles Larry Mitchell's proposal to "to recast the board of directors as a mediating body among the different corporate constituent groups." Lawrence E. Mitchell, *A Critical Look at Corporate Governance*, 45 VAND. L. REV. 1263, 1272 (1992).

104 Blair & Stout, *A Team Production Theory*, *supra* note 101, at 286.

105 *Id.* at 288.

106 John C. Coates IV, *Measuring the Domain of Mediating Hierarchy: How Contestable are U.S. Public Corporations?*, 24 J. CORP. L. 837 (1999).

107 Blair & Stout, *A Team Production Theory*, *supra* note 101, at 281.

108 The following tracks the taxonomy suggested by Johnson et al., who map "directors responsibilities into three broadly defined roles ... labeled control, service, and resource dependence." Jonathan L. Johnson et al., *Boards of Directors: A Review and Research Agenda*, 22 J. MGMT. 409, 411 (1996).

109 See OLIVER E. WILLIAMSON, THE MECHANISMS OF GOVERNANCE 176–77 (1996) (discussing the organizational concerns of transaction cost economics).

110 *Id.* at 175.
111 Michael Novak, The Fire of Invention: Civil Society and the Future of the Corporation 85 (1997).
112 Novak, *supra* note 111, at 115.
113 Milton Friedman, *The Social Responsibility of Business is to Increase its Profits*, N.Y. Times, Sept. 13, 1970 (Magazine) at 32.
114 Milton Friedman & Rose D. Friedman, Capitalism and Freedom 133–34 (2002).
115 Nell Minow, *Six Reasons We Don't Trust the New "Stakeholder" Promise from the Business Roundtable*, Harv. L. School. Forum on Corp. Gov., Sept. 2, 2019, https://corpgov.law.harvard.edu/2019/09/02/six-reasons-we-dont-trust-the-new-stakeholder-promise-from-the-business-roundtable/.
116 Bradford Cornell & Alan C. Shapiro, *Corporate Stakeholders, Corporate Valuation, and ESG*, CLS Blue Sky Blog (Dec. 10, 2020), https://clsbluesky.law.columbia.edu/2020/12/10/corporate-stakeholders-corporate-valuation-and-esg/.
117 Miller, *supra* note 47, at 799.
118 Bryan Gruley & Rick Clough, *Remember When Trump Said He Saved 1,100 Jobs at a Carrier Plant? Well, Globalization Doesn't Give a Damn*, Bloomberg (Mar. 29, 2017, 4:00 AM), www.bloomberg.com/news/features/2017-03-29/remember-when-trump-said-he-saved-1-100-jobs-at-a-carrier-plant.
119 David Chan Smith, *How Milton Friedman Read His Adam Smith: The Neoliberal Suspicion of Business and the Critique of Corporate Social Responsibility* 24–25 (August 15, 2020), https://ssrn.com/abstract=3674604.
120 *Id.* at 27.
121 William Power, *Does Sustainable Investing Really Help the Environment?*, Wall St. J., Nov. 8, 2021, at R1.
122 David Chan Smith, *How Milton Friedman Read His Adam Smith: The Neoliberal Suspicion of Business and the Critique of Corporate Social Responsibility* (August 15, 2020), https://ssrn.com/abstract=3674604.
123 3 Friedrich Hayek, Law, Legislation and Liberty: A New Statement of the Liberal Principles of Justice and Political Economy 82 (1982).
124 R. H. Coase, *The Problem of Social Cost*, 3 J. L. & Econ. 1 (1960).
125 For a contrary argument that transaction costs are sufficiently low to permit bargaining between the corporation and its various constituencies, see Robert T. Miller, The Coasean Dissolution of Corporate Social Responsibility, 17 Chapman L. Rev. 381 (2014).
126 In some situations, alternatives to the majoritarian default – such as penalty and muddy defaults – may be appropriate. *See* Ian Ayres & Robert Gertner, *Majoritarian vs. Minoritarian Defaults*, 51 Stan. L. Rev. 1591 (1999). For a defense of majoritarian defaults, see Stephen M. Bainbridge, *Contractarianism in the Business Associations Classroom: Kovacik v. Reed and the Allocation of Capital Losses in Service Partnerships*, 34 Ga. L. Rev. 631, 651–59 (2000).
127 Andrew S. Gold, Dynamic Fiduciary Duties, 34 Cardozo L. Rev. 491, 520 (2012) ("Corporate law primarily uses majoritarian defaults, rather than defaults tailored to the preferences of the specific parties."). Although corporate law includes many seemingly mandatory rules, at its core Delaware corporate law "allows immense freedom for businesses to adopt the most appropriate terms for the organization, finance, and governance of their enterprise" "provided the statutory parameters and judicially imposed principles of fiduciary duty are honored." Manti Holdings, LLC v. Authentix Acq. Co., Inc., 261

A.3d 1199, 1217 (Del. 2021). Many mandatory corporate law rules are trivial, moreover, in the sense that they are subject to evasion through choice of form or jurisdiction, or are rules almost everyone would reach in the event of actual bargaining. Bernard S. Black, *Is Corporate Law Trivial?: A Political and Economic Analysis*, 84 Nw. U. L. Rev. 542 (1990).

128 *See* Robert P. Bartlett, III, *Shareholder Wealth Maximization As Means to an End*, 38 Seattle U.L. Rev. 255, 296 (2015) ("Viewing the shareholder wealth maximization as a default rule for directors is common among corporate legal scholars subscribing to a contractarian view of corporate law."); *see also* Justin Blount & Patricia Nunley, *Social Enterprise, Corporate Objectives, and the Corporate Governance Narrative*, 52 Am. Bus. L.J. 201, 223 (2015) (arguing that "the corporate objective of shareholder wealth maximization [is] a majoritarian default to an incomplete contract").

129 Fama, *supra* note 40.

130 *See* Bainbridge, *supra* note 11, at 8 ("In the director primacy model, the corporation is a vehicle by which the board of directors hires various factors of production.").

131 Lucian A. Bebchuk & Roberto Tallarita, *The Illusory Promise of Stakeholder Governance*, 106 Cornell L. Rev. 91, 141 (2020) ("Under current compensation practices, 99% of S&P 500 companies give directors substantial equity compensation, mainly in the form of restricted or deferred stock.").

132 Charles M. Elson, *Director Compensation and the Management-Captured Board – The History of a Symptom and a Cure*, 50 SMU L. Rev. 127, 166 (1996).

133 *Outside Directors: The Fading Appeal of the Boardroom*, The Economist, Feb. 20, 2001, at 67, 69.

134 Jonathan R. Macey, *Corporate Social Responsibility: A Law & Economics Perspective*, 17 Chap. L. Rev. 331, 331–32 (2014).

135 Charles M. Elson & Nicholas J. Goossen, *E. Merrick Dodd and the Rise and Fall of Corporate Stakeholder Theory*, 72 Bus. Law. 735, 740 (2017).

136 Gerald F. Davis, *Corporate Purpose Needs Democracy*, 58 J. Mgmt. Stud. 902, 911 (2021).

137 Henry G. Manne & Henry Christopher Wallich, The Modern Corporation and Social Responsibility 1, 14 (1973).

138 Elson & Goossen, supra note 135, at 740.

139 Stephen M. Bainbridge, Corporation Law and Economics 423–24 (2002). Professor Robert Miller considered whether Kaldor-Hicks efficiency could be used as a way of providing a determinate metric for stakeholder capitalism, but concluded that it cannot. Miller, *supra* note 47, at 787.

140 Miller, *supra* note 47, at 778.

141 *Id.* at 778-79 Miller argues that the same is true of constituencies whose claims are defined by law rather than contract. *Id.* at 779-80.

142 *Id.*

143 D. Gordon Smith, *Response: The Dystopian Potential of Corporate Law*, 57 Emory L.J. 985, 1008 (2008).

144 William Power, *Does Sustainable Investing Really Help the Environment?*, Wall St. J., Nov. 8, 2021, at R1.

145 *See, e.g.*, Peter Eavis & Clifford Krauss, *What's Really Behind Corporate Promises on Climate Change?*, N.Y. Times, Feb. 22, 2021.

146 Tao Li et al., *Contradictory Voting by ESG Funds* (Jan. 5, 2021), https://ssrn.com/abstract=3760753.

147 Giovanni Strampelli, *Can BlackRock Save the Planet? The Institutional Investors' role in Stakeholder Capitalism* (October 24, 2020), https://papers.ssrn.com/sol3/papers .cfm?abstract_id=3718255. *See generally* Lucian Bebchuk & Scott Hirst, *Index Funds and the Future of Corporate Governance: Theory, Evidence, and Policy*, 119 COLUM. L. REV. 2029, 2077 (2019) (arguing that "although the Big Three stress the importance of steward-ship, their stewardship budgets are economically insignificant relative to the fees that they charge").

148 Caleb Griffin's analysis of the Big Three's ownership and voting control over Fortune 250 companies found that they have the power to determine the outcome of up to 49 per-cent of environmental proposals, Vanguard and BlackRock combined (the "Big Two") have sufficient voting control to determine the outcome of up to 35 percent of such pro-posals, and Vanguard alone has sufficient voting control to determine the outcome of up to 15.8 percent of such proposals. Caleb N. Griffin, Environmental and Social Voting at the Big Three, The CLS Blue Sky Blog (June 16, 2020), https://clsbluesky.law.columbia .edu/2020/06/16/environmental-and-social-voting-at-the-big-three/.

149 Aaron Yoon & George Serafeim, *Which Corporate ESG News Does the Market React To?*, *Harvard Law School Forum on Corporate Governance* (May 17, 2021), https:// corpgov.law.harvard.edu/2021/05/17/which-corporate-esg-news-does-the-market-react-to/.

150 Tao Li et al., *supra* note 146.

151 Matt Phillips, *Exxon's Board Defeat Signals the Rise of Social-Good Activists*, N.Y. TIMES (June 9, 2021), www.nytimes.com/2021/06/09/business/exxon-mobil-engine-no1-activist .html.

152 David Nicklaus, *Exxon Board Fight*, ST. LOUIS DISPATCH (June 6, 2021), www.stltoday .com/business/subscriber/article_53207bb5-a365-5642-b347-39ff623c030a.html.

153 Malcolm S. Salter, *Rehabilitating Corporate Purpose* 24 (*Harv. Bus. Such. Working Paper* 19–104, 2019).

154 Maria Goranova & Lori Verstegen Ryan, *The Corporate Objective and Contemporary Shareholders: Is It Time for "Strategic" Corporate Governance?*, THE CLS BLUE SKY BLOG (June 8, 2021), https://clsbluesky.law.columbia.edu/2021/06/08/the-corporate-objective-and-contemporary-shareholders-is-it-time-for-strategic-corporate-governance/.

155 *See* JENNIFER J. DEAL & ALEC LEVENSON, WHAT MILLENNIALS WANT FROM WORK: HOW TO MAXIMIZE ENGAGEMENT IN TODAY'S WORKFORCE 182–183 (2016); JEFF FROMM & CHRISTIE GARTON, MARKETING TO MILLENNIALS: REACH THE LARGEST AND MOST INFLUENTIAL GENERATION OF CONSUMERS EVER 35 (2013).

156 Heather Haddon, *Starbucks to Prioritize Cafes, Not Stock Price*, WALL ST. J., Apr.5, 2022, at A1, A4.

157 Spencer Jakab, *Why Starbucks Went Cold Turkey on Buybacks*, WALL ST. J., Apr.5, 2022, at B12.

158 Emilie Aguirre, *Beyond Profit*, 54 U. CAL. DAVIS L. REV. 2077, 2079 (2021).

159 Etsy, Inc. Registration Statement on Form S-1, at p. 92.

160 Brian R. Cheffins & John Armour, *The Past, Present, and Future of Shareholder Activism by Hedge Funds*, 37 J. CORP. L. 51 (2011).

161 *See generally* Mihaela Butu, SHAREHOLDER ACTIVISM BY HEDGE FUNDS: MOTIVATIONS AND MARKET'S PERCEPTIONS OF HEDGE FUND INTERVENTIONS (2013) (exploring techniques activist hedge funds use in attempts to increase shareholder value, including proxy contests).

162 Hadiye Aslan, *A Review of Hedge Fund Activism: Impact on Shareholders vs. Stakeholders* 19 (Feb. 18, 2021), https://ssrn.com/abstract=3785292.

163 Alon Brav et al., *Hedge Fund Activism, Corporate Governance, and Firm Performance*, 63 J. FIN. 1729 (2008).

164 Lucian Bebchuk et al., *The Long-Term Effects of Hedge Fund Activism*, 115 COLUM. L. REV. 1085 (2015).

165 ALEX EDMANS, GROW THE PIE: HOW GREAT COMPANIES DELIVER BOTH PURPOSE AND PROFIT 141–32 (2020) (summarizing the research). *But see* Yvan Allaire & Francois Dauphin, *The Game of "Activist" Hedge Funds: Cui Bono?*, 13 INT'L J. DISCLOSURE & GOVERNANCE 279 (2016) (reporting that gains from hedge fund activism come primarily from changes in the target's financial rather than strategic policies, such as buying back shares, increasing dividends, or having the company sold).

166 Leo E. Strine, Jr., *Making It Easier for Directors to "Do the Right Thing"?*, 4 HARV. BUS. L. REV. 235, 237 (2014). *See generally* Marcel Kahan & Edward B. Rock, *Hedge Funds in Corporate Governance and Control*, 155 U. PA. L. REV. 1021 (2007) (discussing the possibility that hedge funds owning corporate shares and voting rights may maximize short-term profits at the expense of the corporation's long-term vitality).

167 Marcel Kahan & Edward Rock, *Embattled CEOs*, 88 TEX. L. REV. 987, 998–1000 (2010).

168 Kimball Chapman et al., *Investor Relations, Activism, and Engagement*, THE CLS BLUE SKY BLOG (May 17, 2021), https://clsbluesky.law.columbia.edu/2021/05/17/investor-relations-engagement-and-shareholder-activism.

169 DELOITTE LLP, CFO SIGNALS: WHAT NORTH AMERICA'S TOP FINANCE EXECUTIVES ARE THINKING – AND DOING 21–24 (2015). *See also* Melissa Sawyer et al., *Review and Analysis of 2018 U.S. Shareholder Activism*, HARV. L. SCH. FORUM ON CORP. GOV. (Apr. 5, 2019), https://corpgov.law.harvard.edu/2019/04/05/review-and-analysis-of-2018-u-s-shareholder-activism (discussing findings on actions taken by directors in response to shareholder activism).

170 Thomas W. Briggs, *Corporate Governance and the New Hedge Fund Activism: An Empirical Analysis*, 32 J. CORP. L. 681, 713 (2007). *See also* Lisa M. Fairfax, *Making the Corporation Safe for Shareholder Democracy*, 69 OHIO ST. L.J. 53, 105 (2008) (observing that "hedge funds are not the kinds of shareholders who are likely to advance stakeholder issues"); Larry Smith, *Activist Investors, Restructurings, and Criminal Investigations*, 31 OF COUNSEL 16 (2012) (arguing that hedge funds "push companies to 'maximize' shareholder value").

171 *See* Bebchuk & Tallarita, *supra* note 131, at 153 ("Shareholder discontent with performance may put pressure on the board to replace the CEO or may lead to hedge fund intervention or even a proxy fight.").

172 *Id.* at 153. *See generally* D. Gordon Smith, *Response: The Dystopian Potential of Corporate Law*, 57 EMORY L.J. 985, 996 (2008) (arguing that "powerful capital and takeover markets provide strong incentives for corporate managers to maximize profits").

173 Thornton McEnery, *Etsy Pivots From Crunchy Hipster To Gordon Gekko In One Afternoon*, DEALBREAKER.COM (May 2, 2017), https://dealbreaker.com/2017/05/etsy-pivoting-like-a-mofo. *See generally* Jill E. Fisch & Steven Davidoff Solomon, *The "Value" of a Public Benefit Corporation, in* Research Handbook on Corporate Purpose and Personhood (Elizabeth Pollman & Robert B. Thompson, eds., 2021).

174 McEnery, *supra* note 173.

175 Davis, *supra* note 136, at 909.

176 Michael Greene, *Del. Judge Urges Companies Not to Cave in to Activists*, BLOOMBERG LAW: CORPORATE GOVERNANCE REPORT (Apr. 4, 2016).

177 Aguirre, *supra* note 158, at 2080 ("The story of a company losing its multiple objectives after scaling up is a common one, whether the company chooses to scale through an IPO like Etsy, or through another avenue such as an acquisition.").

178 Leo E. Strine, Jr., *Who Bleeds When the Wolves Bite?: A Flesh-and-Blood Perspective on Hedge Fund Activism and Our Strange Corporate Governance System*, 126 YALE L.J. 1870, 1938 (2017).

179 John C. Coffee, Jr. & Darius Palia, *The Wolf at the Door: The Impact of Hedge Fund Activism on Corporate Governance*, 41 J. CORP. L. 545, 576 (2016).

180 Strine, *supra* note 178, at 1873.

181 Nell Minow, *Six Reasons We Don't Trust the New "Stakeholder" Promise from the Business Roundtable*, HARV. L. SCHOOL. FORUM. CORP. GOV., Sept. 2, 2019, https://corpgov .law.harvard.edu/2019/09/02/six-reasons-we-dont-trust-the-new-stakeholder-promise-from-the-business-roundtable/.

182 Zohar Goshen & Doron Levit, *Common Ownership and the Decline of the American Worker* 4 (Columbia Law and Economics Working Paper No. 653; European Corporate Governance Institute Law Working Paper No. 584/2021).

183 *Id.* at 19.

184 *See* Martin Petrin & Barnali Choudhury, *Corporate Purpose and Short-Termism* 19 (2020), https://ssrn.com/abstract=3538156 (arguing that "the market's typical primary demand of an investee company is that it generates a consistently positive rate of periodic EPS growth, preferably coupled with a corresponding rise in its declared rate of dividend").

185 MICHAEL NOVAK, BUSINESS AS CALLING: WORK AND THE EXAMINED LIFE 13 (1996).

186 Elson & Goossen, *supra* note 135, at 740.

187 Michael E. DeBow & Dwight R. Lee, *Shareholders, Nonshareholders and Corporate Law: Communitarianism and Resource Allocation*, 18 DEL. J. CORP. L. 393, 416 (1993)

188 *Id.* at 420–21.

189 Christina Parajon Skinner, *Cancelling Capitalism?*, 97 NOTRE DAME L. REV. 417, 429 (2021)

190 *Id.*

191 ALEX EDMANS, GROW THE PIE: HOW GREAT COMPANIES DELIVER BOTH PURPOSE AND PROFIT 58–59 (2020).

192 Skinner, *supra* note 189, at 432.

193 MICKLETHWAIT & WOOLDRIDGE, *supra* note 21, at 77.

194 *Id.*

195 MICHAEL NOVAK, TOWARD A THEOLOGY OF THE CORPORATION 44–45 (2d ed. 1990).

196 Skinner, *supra* note 189, at 429.

197 NOVAK, *supra* note 195, at 45.

198 *Id.*

CONCLUSION

1   MICHAEL NOVAK, TOWARD A THEOLOGY OF THE CORPORATION 77 (2d ed. 1990).

Index

For EU product safety concerns, contact us at Calle de José Abascal, 56–1°,
28003 Madrid, Spain or eugpsr@cambridge.org.

www.ingramcontent.com/pod-product-compliance
Ingram Content Group UK Ltd.
Pitfield, Milton Keynes, MK11 3LW, UK
UKHW020353140625

459647UK00020B/2443

* 9 7 8 1 0 0 9 0 1 2 1 5 7 *